THE COMMANDER

THE COMMANDER

by

VLADIMIR V. KARPOV

English translation by
Yuri S. Shirokov and Nicholas Louis

BRASSEY'S DEFENCE PUBLISHERS
(a member of the Pergamon Group)
LONDON · OXFORD · WASHINGTON · NEW YORK
BEIJING · FRANKFURT · SÃO PAULO · SYDNEY · TOKYO · TORONTO

U.K. (Editorial)	Brassey's Defence Publishers, 24 Gray's Inn Road, London WC1X 8HR
(Orders)	Brassey's Defence Publishers, Headington Hill Hall, Oxford OX3 0BW, England
U.S.A. (Editorial)	Pergamon-Brassey's International Defense Publishers, 8000 Westpark Drive, Fourth Floor, McLean, Virginia 22102, U.S.A.
(Orders)	Pergamon Press, Maxwell House, Fairview Park, Elmsford, New York 10523, U.S.A.
PEOPLE'S REPUBLIC OF CHINA	Pergamon Press, Room 4037, Qianmen Hotel, Beijing, People's Republic of China
FEDERAL REPUBLIC OF GERMANY	Pergamon Press, Hammerweg 6, D-6242 Kronberg, Federal Republic of Germany
BRAZIL	Pergamon Editora, Rua Eça de Queiras, 346, CEP 04011, Paraiso, São Paulo, Brazil
AUSTRALIA	Pergamon-Brassey's Defence Publishers, P.O. Box 544, Potts Point, N.S.W. 2011, Australia
JAPAN	Pergamon Press, 8th Floor, Matsuoka Central Building, 1–7–1 Nishishinjuku, Shinjuku-ku, Tokyo 160, Japan
CANADA	Pergamon Press Canada, Suite No. 271, 253 College Street, Toronto, Ontario, Canada M5T 1R5

Copyright English Edition © 1987 Brassey's Defence Publishers Ltd.

First edition 1987

British Library Cataloguing in Publication Data
Karpov, Vladimir V.
The Commander
1, World War, 1933–1945
I. Title
940.53   D743

ISBN 0-08-036261-3

Printed in Great Britain by A. Wheaton & Co. Ltd., Exeter

Publisher's Introduction

Brassey's has decided to publish this book, at the time of the anniversary of the Russian Revolution, as part of our policy of publishing works on defence matters from across a wide range of countries and ideologies. In 1987 alone, for example, we have published books, on Field Marshal Sir John Dill and General George Marshal, NATO, Marshal Tukhachevskii, the Turkish Generals, the Soviet Marshals in World War Two, the fighting between the Germans and Russians in 1944, the Russian bases today on the Kola Peninsula, nuclear deterrence and British defence policy.

We publish *The Commander*, not because it is a work of historical scholarship or military theory, but because it presents the reader with a colourful and exciting account of life in the Soviet Union during the Second World War and because it tells the story of a remarkable Soviet fighting man, General Petrov, who fought with distinction in many campaigns.

The views expressed in the Epilogue will not find much sympathy in the West. They do, however, illuminate most clearly what many Soviet citizens think about the military policies of the United States and the NATO Alliance.

Understanding, we believe, is the key to stable and peaceful international relations.

Contents

PREFACE   ix

The Battle of Odessa   1

July 1941   1
The Years 1939–1940 in Retrospect   3
July 1941   4
The Years 1896–1924 in Retrospect   7
July 1941   11
The Year 1945 in Retrospect   15
August 1941   19
The General Situation in the Autumn of 1941   28
August 1941   30
Late August 1941   35
September 1941   40
October 1941   43
A New Appointment   45
The Evacuation Plan   48
October 15, 1941   52

The Battle of Sevastopol   59

The Crimea, October 17–24, 1941   59
Reminiscences of Prewar Years   65
The Retreat to Sevastopol, October 1941   67
The First Assault on Sevastopol, November 1941   68
Another Assault, December 1941   73
Bracing Up for a New Fight   80
A Sudden Blow   81
The Third Assault on Sevastopol   85
The Last Days   93

The Battle of the Caucasus   101

A New Appointment   101
Operation Edelweiss   103
Preliminary Considerations   107

The 44th Army   110
Order 227   112
Beyond the Front Line   116
A Fight to the Death   119
The Tuapse Operation   124
Operation Mountains and Operation Sea   129
Marshal Zhukov   133
A Front Commander   135
The Gothenkopf Line   137
A Meeting with Stalin   139
The Battle of Novorossiisk   140
Some Implications   147
A Strike Across the Straits   148

The Last Battles   159

Expectation   159
Commander of the 2nd Byelorussian Front   162
Before the Strike   163
More About Myself   168
Commander of the 4th Ukrainian Front   176
Across the Eastern Carpathians   179
A New Directive of the High Command   187
The Vistula–Oder Operation   191
The Battle of Moravska Ostrava   197
What Happened?   201

The Battle of Berlin   205

The Rescue of Prague   217

The Rescue of the Dresden Art Gallery   227

The Homecoming   231

The Ashkhabad Earthquake   235

The Epilogue   237

Preface

As I take my pen to write this story, I seem to experience the same excitement I felt in my youth when looking at my hero. Few of those who knew him still live. The generation of World War II veterans is bidding farewell to life. The laws of nature are inexorable, and we must face them with the same courage as we faced death in war. But it pains me to think that those who will follow us may never learn about this remarkable man. That is why I am committing my memories to writing.

In the "roaring forties", when survival and death often meant a choice between disgrace and honour, there were many brave hearts which could be taken as a model by anybody today. He was my idol—not a hero of a book or a film, but a man of flesh and blood whom I saw every day.

Today he is no longer with us, and my own life is in its declining years. I am over sixty, and the main events are in the past, a matter for recollection.

I was fortunate my life path crossed his. My own life would have been different and certainly less eventful if I had not met this man, though probably not as hard as it has been.

He lived on in my heart for many years while being far away. I was neither a close friend of his, nor a total stranger. He was invariably amiable and good-natured whenever we met during the twenty years of our acquaintanceship—from 1938 to 1958, the last year of his life.

That kindness was not a reward for any of my merits, but a reflection of his sensitivity and tact, the kindness of his soul. He was no angel. At times he was harsh to the point of ruthlessness. With his explosive temper he was prone to anger, but was never unfair. I thank my lucky stars I was never a cause for an outburst of his righteous wrath.

The name of this man is Ivan Efimovich Petrov. When I first saw him in 1938, he was in army uniform with a brigadier's insignia on his collar tabs. His face was tanned, waist strapped with a broad officer's belt, its buckle emblazoned with a large star, a leather strap over his right shoulder and jackboots polished to mirror lustre. An unexpected pince-nez on the bridge of his nose completed the portrait. In fact, during my long years of army service I have never seen a commanding officer wearing a pince-nez, though many wore spectacles.

Brigadier Petrov was commandant of the Tashkent Infantry School housed in the building of the former Cadet Corps close to the River Salar, where Parkent Street, now bearing his name, began.

The next building on the street was the secondary school No. 61, which I attended along with children of many of the infantry school's officer teachers. Yuri Petrov, the brigadier's only son, was one of my class mates. Once he invited me to his home, where I met his father and mother Zoya Pavlovna.

Lean of body and fast-footed, always cheerful and sociable, Yuri was invariably the mastermind of schoolboys' mischief, which, however, they never carried too far. He was a good pupil, straightforward and frank in his relations with friends. Now he is no longer alive. Yuri was a Lieutenant Colonel when he died tragically in Ashkhabad in 1948.

Much water has flowed under the bridge since then, and we have witnessed and taken part in great historic events. Ivan Petrov was promoted to the rank of Army General and many times led troops into fierce battles. He commanded Army Groups and was awarded the title of Hero of the Soviet Union, the supreme distinction for valour, and numerous war medals.

In the period of his military service he experienced both sudden ascents and unexpected falls. Unfair destiny followed in the footsteps of this good man for years. There were quite a few unravelled mysteries in his life.

My book shelves are stocked with memoirs of Soviet World War II heroes. Among them are books by the celebrated Marshals Georgy Zhukov, Alexander Vasilevsky, Konstantin Rokossovsky, Ivan Konev, and Ivan Bagramian, to mention but a few. Ivan Petrov was their close associate and comrade-in-arms, and they have devoted many warm recollections to him.

Novorossiisk, Kerch, Moscow, Leningrad, Stalingrad (Volgograd today), Sevastopol, Odessa, Kiev, Minsk, and Brest are a brilliant constellation of Soviet heroic cities which attest to the courage and self-sacrifice of Soviet men and women in war time.

General Petrov was one of those in command of the Soviet forces which put up a stiff resistance to the Nazi Wehrmacht in the Battle of Odessa and the Battle of Sevastopol, and liberated the cities of Kerch and Novorossiisk on the Black Sea. In other words, he led Soviet troops in the battle for four of the ten Soviet heroic cities. It is a splendid record for a general, indeed.

In this book I will attempt to describe to the best of my ability his tactical skill and strategic foresight. I do not overestimate my competence, of course, nor do I intend to pronounce peremptory judgement on the merits or faults of General Petrov as a military leader, nor on combat operations which he directed in the war. I rely in my judgement on documents, books and reminiscences of top-ranking military officers who were at different times his superiors or equals both in rank and in levels of tactical and strategic competence and foresight.

General Petrov died in 1958 following a long and severe illness. He left no memoirs in print. In his declining years, it is true, he wrote recollections, but all my efforts to find his manuscripts have been futile. His wife Zoya Pavlovna did not survive him for long, and left no archives either.

This book is not General Petrov's biography, nor is it a book of my own memoirs, but simply a tribute of respect and gratitude to the man I admired. He was a model of integrity, courage and dedication to duty for me, although he himself had not the slightest idea of the unique role he played in my life.

I wish again to relive with General Petrov the many events of the Soviet Union's war against Nazi Germany, which is known as the Great Patriotic War in my country, and to shed light—for my own better comprehension, for the edification of his friends and, perhaps, for the benefit of history itself—on those complications and understatements interspersed with open malice that so unfairly clouded his life.

I have been collecting material for this book for a good ten years, recalling and musing over and over again on my meetings and discussions with General Petrov. I have read dozens of books in which certain events of his life are mentioned, found many of his wartime friends and comrades-in-arms and his colleagues of later days, and I have put on record their stories of the late General.

I have gone out of my way to let them speak freely from the pages of this book, because their first-hand experience cannot be supplanted by imagination. I, for my part, have searched far and wide for documents that would guard me from error in my story.

In a nutshell, this story is a mosaic of known facts, unknown episodes, documents and what is called personal observations and first-hand impressions.

There are a host of quotations in this book, which are to me a means of artistic expression, like bits of coloured glass and stone in an inlaid pattern. These, I hope, will help revive the General's personality, as well as to reproduce at least an overall outline of the time, the main events and influences that were to transform an ensign of the Imperial Russian Army into a high-ranking Soviet military officer, a leading authority on the art of warfare, a Soviet patriot utterly dedicated to his country.

This is the life story of a man who performed many splendid deeds but who also made mistakes, who found himself among persons noble or vile, a man who was pained by whatever disaster befell his people and country, who shared the joy of our common triumphs and knew the joy of personal success. He will be seen in the midst of those he was destined to meet in the course of his life.

This man loved life and loved people and his love was returned. However, besides true love with which every human being is blessed with, he was affectionately admired by the thousands of officers and soldiers under his command, by natives of all Republics of the USSR, and especially by the natives of the Central Asian Republics where his name is surrounded by legend to this day.

He was not a stranger to whatever is human, but he was endowed with merits that are denied to many.

As far I am concerned, I rest my hopes in this Latin saying: "feci quod potui, faciant meliora potentes"—"I have done my best, and may others do it better."

Vladimir Karpov

The Battle of Odessa

July 1941

. . . It was early morning. A passenger train drawn by a steam locomotive was chugging along on its way to Odessa, and the city was steadily moving into broader view. The sun was already fairly high above the skyline, and the weightless white wisps of vapour were seen flitting past the carriage windows as the train picked up speed, drawing closer to its destination. There was not a single cloud in the serene sky.

The continuous booming of distant thunder way ahead of the train was a strange thing to hear on that clear sunny morning. This was no thunderclap of an instant shower in midsummer that is shortly followed by a new crop of mushrooms, but the thunder of bomb explosions in the city and the thunder of anti-aircraft guns. A German air raid over the city awakened its residents.

The locomotive slowed down, moving cautiously as though groping its way, lest the tracks be damaged enough to derail it. Passengers were popping heads out of windows and gazing fearfully at the sky and the city sprawling ahead. As trails of black smoke soared from the ground and the drone of aircraft bombing the city reached their ears, the train drew to a halt and waited. Indeed, the German airmen might well choose it for another target on which to drop their lethal cargo.

Major General Ivan Petrov was a passenger on that train. A short while earlier, before the war broke out, he had been summoned from his Central Asian military district to a headquarters in Moscow to receive a new appointment, this time in the Odessa Military District.

There were three war medals on the General's chest, which was a rare thing to see so early in the war: three much-coveted Red Banners, one of the USSR, the other two of the Turkmenian and Bukhara Republics. Another medal commemorated his twenty years' service in the Red Army.

At the time of his assignment to Odessa he had just turned forty-five. The General was lean of body and of medium height, his face was tanned, his soft hair touched with grey was parted in the middle, and his belts were slung over his shoulders in cavalry fashion to complete the typical portrait of a professional soldier, but for one unusual detail: his eyes behind the incongruous pince-nez were the kind eyes of a doctor.

1

... After several attacks the German bomber force turned westwards and slowly disappeared in the haze, followed by its fighter escort. The sirens stopped wailing to call off the air alert.

The train slowly pulled in to the railway terminus. The platform was totally deserted. Trails of smoke were still rising from a few bomb holes in the station building, the ground was strewn with debris of broken glass, bricks and plaster, and a few walls had collapsed.

Nobody came onto the platform to meet the train, which was strange to see, raid or no raid. After a moment of confusion, passengers hurriedly got out of the carriages lest they be caught in a new raid, should the Germans decide to come back, and, forgetting the weight of their suitcases and bags, quickly dispersed into the surrounding streets. The station was empty in less time than it takes to tell.

General Petrov, flanked by two army officers he had met on the train, stood on the platform, inspecting the damage.

"Where are the station master and staff, I wonder? Do you have any ideas?" he asked his companions. "It's unlikely all of them got killed."

An assistant cautiously appeared at last. He was obviously confused and took off his red cap for some reason, whilst answering the General's questions absentmindedly. Petrov instructed him to find the station master, and the latter soon stood to attention before him, listening to his rebuke.

"The raid's over, man, and life is going on. It's war and you need to get used to it. Telegraph and inquiry desks should work without a break in times of crisis. You have loudspeakers here to announce a change in train schedules and calm passengers unless you want a panic on your hands. Your staff should do their duty, not flee to safety. Is that clear?"

The station master looked ashamed. The General certainly knew how to handle a crisis like that but it was new to a civilian. Presence of mind was something he was yet to learn. The General read his mind and did not dwell on it.

"Alright, take it easy, man. War is a good teacher, but one must be a good learner to win it."

His lenient tone carried the authority of wisdom and experience. The General stayed on the platform for some time, watching station personnel coming back to their different posts. Not until he knew they would carry on without his advice did he leave the station and go to town. A railway was an artery vital to defence, and he knew he had not wasted his time here.

... There were crowds on the streets excitedly discussing the raid. Odessa townsfolk are a cheerful and temperamental lot, and now they were gesticulating wildly, exchanging their impressions and announcing proudly that a few German bombers had been hit by anti-aircraft defences and crashed in flames outside city limits.

It appeared, however, that the German air raid had not caused much destruction in the city. The main targets of the German airmen were the railway station and tracks.

The Years 1939–1940 in Retrospect

From September 1939 I saw Petrov almost every day. I was a cadet at the Tashkent Infantry School of which he was commandant with the rank of divisional commander and, after the introduction of Generals' ranks, with the rank of Major General.

The first time we saw him was in the morning, while doing our daily dozen. He did not take part in the exercises or come to watch how we did them. By the time we had left our warm beds and had assembled in the stadium, General Petrov would return from horse riding. His wife Zoya Pavlovna would complete her morning chores, washing the steps of the little porch of their cottage hidden in the shade of the trees near the school gates.

She was a stickler for cleanliness and a terror to whoever was negligent in matters of hygiene. Whenever Yuri and I dropped in at the cottage whilst we were class mates, she levied her critical gaze at our feet, lest they should leave footprints on the spotless painted floor boards.

Ivan Efimovich treated us boys with kindness and helped our school to cope with its problems. Once, when I was already in my teens and taking lessons in boxing, he told me something that made my heart melt. Patting my back, he remarked amiably: "You're a strong lad, Vladimir, and could make a good officer. Has such an idea ever crossed your mind? Think about it."

In fact, he had read my mind: it was my cherished dream to become a military cadet. At that time it was a dream of many boys like me; it was not a fashion but an expression of infatuation with the romance of a military career. Boys dreamt of becoming lieutenants of artillery, or the tank forces, or—the most coveted goal of all—air force pilots. These were idols no less popular than cosmonauts are in this present day.

In those prewar years members of the armed forces were surrounded with unusual respect and affection: people seemed to anticipate the hardships of a great war which lay before the men in uniform who would defend their country against a formidable enemy.

Petrov was the school commandant from January 1933 to June 1940. The cadets and officers loved him, and he enjoyed wide renown and respect among the people in the Central Asian Republics. His name was known in the most distant mountain and steppe villages of Turkestan.

He won this fame by his exemplary courage and fighting skill demonstrated at the time of wiping out the hated *basmach* gangs in Central Asia, which raided villages, terrorized and robbed their inhabitants, and by his strenuous work to ease the plight of local peasants caused by the ravages of war. He was thankfully remembered by all old-timers there.

In 1939 an important event took place in the life of all servicemen of the Red Army and, by definition, in Brigadier Petrov's service routine. The Presidium of the USSR Supreme Soviet introduced by special decree a new ceremony of taking an oath of allegiance to the colours. It was now to be taken by all members of the armed forces simultaneously on February 23, that is on Red Army and Navy Day. Every serviceman was required to read his oath aloud in front of his unit and sign it.

On the morning of that memorable day the cadets drew up ranks in front of the school. Commandant Petrov, with the inevitable pince-nez on the bridge of his nose and a neat row of medals on his trim tunic, faced the formation. He was flanked by the regimental commissar Feighin, a short and heavily built man.

Petrov was obviously trying not to betray his excitement. He made a brief speech and came up to the table draped in a red cloth. As he read his oath his voice was loud and clear, and we admired the way he enunciated every word of it.

Commissar Feighin was the next in turn to read the oath and was followed by the other officers.

When all the cadets had read and signed their oaths, Brigadier Petrov addressed them with these noble words:

"We have sworn allegiance to our nation. We will be faithful to this oath as long as we live. We will cherish it in our hearts to the last hour, and we will live up to its every word. Should any of us be destined to give our lives for our country in battle, may we do it without fear of death and may we proudly say these final words: 'I have done my duty.'"

The cadets responded with a thunderous "Hooray!" Our love and affection for our commander was infinite. His stern manner and fastidiousness in matters of military training never misled us. We knew that he loved us dearly. He sometimes cracked jokes and made ironic remarks about our faults but his frankness never went as far as familiarity since he certainly realized that an exacting attitude was beneficial to our success.

I remember well Petrov's last day in our school. We cadets assembled for the send-off ceremony. Petrov had been appointed divisional commander in July 1940. He was now a General with gold stars in the red collar tabs of his tunic. Generals' ranks had been introduced shortly before.

There was something unofficial in his bearing. He watched us affectionately and was seemingly holding his breath lest his voice break off and betray his feelings. There was dead silence as he finally spoke. I remember what he said almost word for word.

"I have been in charge of your school for eight years, and you are like my own family to me. I am very sad to leave you. My dear boys, remember that you are Leninists! You must equal this noble name wherever you may be and whatever duty you may perform."

We were deeply moved, and our hearts went out to him. We eagerly desired to escort him to his home but we were under orders to stand to attention. That seemed a sad parting to me and my comrades. We did not know that the last three years had been a hard time for our commandant, that he had been slandered and his life was at risk. He had never spoken of the reasons for his transfer. The crisis in his life at that time is the subject of a further story, and now we shall return to Odessa besieged on all sides by enormous enemy forces which were relentlessly pressing its defenders towards the sea.

July 1941

In the Army HQ General Petrov reported his arrival to Lieutenant General Nikander Chibisov, commander of the Maritime Army. General Chibisov, a broad-chested man, slightly overweight, with black moustache turned up at the ends, was issuing orders to his units holding off the invading forces on the border. He was too busy for a detailed discussion of developments and his instructions to Petrov were curt:

"A cavalry division is being formed here in Odessa. Take it under your command and complete its formation. I request you to complement its regiments with men, weapons and horses as soon as possible. There is no time to be lost, and you may be required to join battle at short notice. You will be briefed on the situation by the Operations Group. You will hardly need to know the details for the time being, however."

When he was still on the train, General Petrov had mused a lot on the Red Army's first setbacks on the Western front. Like other high-ranking officers he had been firmly convinced that the Red Army should conduct active operations and defeat the aggressor on his own territory, without surrendering an inch of Soviet territory and would achieve victory without much bloodshed.

The actual tide of hostilities, however, was a far cry from those concepts. That was simply incredible; it was hard to believe that the doctrine in which spirit he had been raised and which he himself had taught to his subordinates had suddenly been proved wrong.

General Petrov realized that the Nazis had a fully mobilized army at their disposal and had formed strike forces for breakthroughs, that in the initial period retreats of Soviet troops under pressure from superior enemy troop concentrations in individual directions were possible. At places the enemy might even wedge himself deep into Soviet territory.

It was time devastating strikes were dealt under the bases of these wedges to cut them off, encircle and wipe out the invaders.

However, judging by the war communiqués broadcast and published in the newspapers that time was yet to come.

Needless to say, it would take some time to mobilize the army, put units into combat readiness, and bring them to the front line. Therefore, Petrov expected a reversal in the tide of hostilities any day. However, news that reached him from friends and colleagues, not only from war communiqués, was extremely alarming.

. . . Major General Vorobyov, Chief of Operations, looked harassed and played out, but he greeted Petrov with a smile and briefly described the situation at the front.

"Thank God, we are still holding our positions on the state border. At places we have even counterattacked, though with small forces and on a local scale."

"Well, at least in your area things are not bad," Petrov remarked with a sigh. "But, you know, they are going from bad to worse north of you."

"I hate to upset you or sound pessimistic but we can hardly hold the border much longer. Our troops are heavily outnumbered and have suffered severe casualties. I feel we may soon be in trouble, too. We are able to hold our ground on the border, but troops north of us are in slow retreat. In fact, we are being outflanked by enemy forces. . . ."

It was in that situation that Petrov got down to work, aware that the division he was to form might be committed to battle in the coming few days.

Petrov was to complement his cavalry division with recruits from Odessa and neighbouring districts. They varied widely in age from youngsters who had just reached military age to staid elderly men who had long been listed in the reserve.

There were war veterans who had volunteered to join the division, some of them wearing cavalry helmets they had kept at home as relics since the Civil War. General Petrov was the right commanding officer for these battlewise cavalrymen. With leather straps across his shoulders, trim, slender and agile, he was the very picture of a fighting-fit cavalryman.

Here is what General Petrov wrote in an article about the recruits of his division:

—Some regarded Odessa's townsfolk as an unsteady lot prone to panic. That proved a mistaken view. Needless to say, there were more idle elements in Odessa than in any other Soviet city, as well as individuals of uncertain and at times very doubtful professions. It was these elements that were to blame for the nasty rumours. In fact, idle elements were just a handful in Odessa's large population. At the first signs of danger all this scum fled, whereas the mass of Odessa's working people, who were fond of their native city and dedicated to their country, gave enormous assistance to troops in strengthening the defence lines.

From the early days of their service under General Petrov's command his cavalrymen became deeply attached to him. And small wonder. He was not only a man experienced in the art of warfare but also a past master of horsemanship familiar with all the subtleties of equestrian art and the care of horses.

Perhaps in all armies of the world there exist, besides official dossiers for every officer, what one may call "folklore files". An officer arrives at his new place of service, the official dossier with references and recommendations is still in transit, but the men of his new unit are already informed about his habits, merits and demerits, and know what kind of person he is.

Needless to say, such grapevine information is available only on officers advanced in years and known to somebody in their new garrison. In this way good or bad fame, however well deserved, goes ahead of them.

Before his assignment to Odessa Ivan Petrov had served in the army in various posts for many years. Since rumours and gossip, even among officers, are based on information not very authentic, let us look at Petrov's biography based on more accurate—documentary—sources.

. . . Doing his work in forming the regiments of his division, Petrov stayed in the city. One early morning, when he had an hour of leisure, he went to the harbour. He had long been attracted to the sea and ships which were so near at hand but could not afford the time to visit the waterfront. Now he was here at last.

He descended to the pier and watched the waves gently lapping its side, inhaling the intoxicating tang of the sea, tar, ropes and fish. His head swam. He closed his eyes and stood still for a long moment, wondering why he felt so happy. Another scene as vivid as the one before him floated into his mind. It was a scene from his childhood, now half forgotten, and the same smell of tar, ropes and fish.

The Years 1896–1924 in Retrospect

Trubchevsk is a small town on the River Desna. Ivan often went with his friends to the pier and they watched the busy life on the river for hours. From here steamships and barges sailed off downstream to large cities, such as Kiev and Odessa, or upstream to the north, carrying their cargoes of hemp, ropes and hawsers.

The air smelled of pitch and tar and fish, and there was a constant noisy hustle and bustle of people from all walks of life, from rich merchants to tramps and thieves. Deep hoots of steamships called the boys to distant lands and stirred their dreams of travel.

The town had about 7,000 inhabitants. Their main occupation was work at small local hemp-processing and churning factories. The hemp grown by local peasants was considered the best in Russia. The town was surrounded by woods. Its residents crafted sledges, carts, spoons and toys from the wood and also obtained tar and pitch. Shipwrights built boats and barges that ploughed up and down the Desna. It was a typical provincial town where life was uneventful and ran at an unhurried pace.

Trubchevsk was Ivan Petrov's birthplace. His father was a shoemaker and his mother an ordinary housewife. He had two sisters and a brother, and with only one breadwinner to feed that large family their life was hard. His father died in 1906 when Ivan was only 10.

Their illiterate mother took odd jobs to earn a living barely enough for her children to survive. Always preoccupied with the problems of getting food and clothes she could not teach them much. His older sister Tatiana, however, understood the value of education and at a young age became a school teacher. Ivan learned very much from her. In addition, she was kind-hearted and fair, frank and bold and very charitable.

Ivan Petrov often remarked that she had been a second mother to him, who had influenced him greatly. On her insistence he entered a teachers' college at Karachev where he lived on a meagre allowance granted to very poor students.

Karachev had 20,000 inhabitants and also had a railway station. In addition to hemp-processing factories there were brick factories, a vodka distillery, two hospitals, a Red Cross society and a volunteer fire brigade. Not much to boast of by any standards but to a young man from a backwoods community it seemed a civilized centre of industry and culture in its own right.

In 1914 the First World War broke out, and Russia sided with Britain and France against Germany. News of the hostilities reached this quiet town and aroused a surge of patriotic feeling in some and an uneasy anticipation of disaster in others. Ivan knew of the war and its causes only from what he read in the newspapers and learned in conversations with knowledgeable veterans. His heart melted in admiration for the daredevil Cossacks when he was reading the stories of them charging the Germans in cavalry attacks and putting them to flight with their deadly sabres. The war seemed a distant and romantic adventure, and he regretted he was too young to bear arms and stand up for Mother Russia on the battlefield.

At that time he was not yet aware of revolutionary ideas of social justice and had naïve faith in official declarations. Imagine the sentiments of a youngster sick and tired of the drab monotony of provincial life reading the Tsar's Manifesto on Russia's commitment to the war with its grandiloquent lines about "Russia's historic behests", "the Russian people's feelings for their Slav brothers", "the honour, dignity and integrity of Russia and her position among the Great Powers", "the threatening hour of trials. . .", and so on.

It can be presumed that far from everything in the country's social order satisfied him and he desired a change for the better in his native Russia. This is suggested by his social standing but is merely a conjecture. A person's views and beliefs are best seen in action, and we have no information on any steps he might have taken in search of contact with revolutionary circles.

He was eager to go to the firing lines as he was supposed to do as a "loyal son of the fatherland". In 1914, however, he was too young to be enlisted, and in 1916 when he had reached military age his service was postponed to let him graduate from college. Under the scheme of officer training in war time teachers were commissioned after a crash course of training at military schools. The war which had been going on for two years was indiscriminately snuffing out the lives of privates and officers.

In the autumn of 1916 the Karachayev teachers' college turned out its annual batch of graduates and promptly distributed them among various military schools. Ivan Petrov was enrolled at Moscow's Alexeyev Military School in January 1917.

That was a crucial period in shaping his moral principles and political views, so I shall briefly describe some events which undoubtedly influenced them.

Petrov had come to Moscow shortly before the March Revolution of 1917. He was still adapting to his new surroundings and trying to understand the meaning of recent developments when news of the Tsar's abdication and the formation of the Provisional Government was announced. The new government issued a torrent of instructions but was practically impotent.

On March 1, workers' detachments and revolutionary units of the garrison in Moscow took over the post and telegraph offices, the State Bank, police stations, the Kremlin, the arsenal, and freed political prisoners. Moscow was in the hands of the insurgents.

The command of the Alexeyev Military School still obeyed the orders of the official authorities, that is the Provisional Government. However, another, revolutionary, government was already functioning.

Petrov stayed in Moscow for only five months. On June 1, 1917 he was commissioned as an ensign and posted to serve with the 156th infantry regiment in the city of Astrakhan. His military career, however, had a bad start. Famished by the meagre Moscow rations, the young man evidently helped himself to the fruit and vegetables plentiful in the Astrakhan markets and had to pay a dear price for it. He was afflicted with dysentery and was bed-ridden for six weeks, at the end of which he was so emaciated and weak that he was granted a two-month leave of absence for recuperation.

He went to Trubchevsk to stay with his family in the care of his mother and sisters. On his return to Astrakhan he was discharged from the army for health reasons and returned to his native town.

Then the October Revolution happened. The country was in turmoil, everything was on the move, though not necessarily in the right direction. People without strong political affiliations or a clear idea of the nature of developments were at a loss as to where to go or which side to join. All parties seemed to be championing for a better life, for the welfare and prosperity of the Motherland. But who was right? Whose struggle was really just? That was not easy to understand in the whirlwind of events.

Ivan Petrov was one of those faced by these questions. "I had a vague idea of political developments in the country and did not understand much about them", he was later to write in his autobiography. "In particular, at the time of the October government takeover and the peace talks with Germany I was opposed to peace. However, I have never joined or had links with any organization hostile to the Soviet government."

When the peace talks with Germany at Brest-Litovsk had been broken off, the Kaiser's troops mounted an offensive, and the front line began to draw nearer to Trubchevsk. One thing was clear to Petrov: his duty was to defend his country. He decided immediately to rejoin his regiment in Astrakhan where, he supposed, units for a rebuff to the enemy were to be formed.

On his way to Astrakhan Petrov met some fellow officers from his regiment. They now served in the Red Army. They told him of developments at the front and in the country and of a change in their own views. On short reflection Petrov decided to enlist in the Red Army as a volunteer and went to Samara together with his comrades.

It was in the ranks of the Red Army, in the midst of the people who had taken up arms in defence of the Soviets, in conversations with friends better informed of developments in the world, that the ex-ensign Petrov realized with crystal clarity that the cause of remaking Russia upheld by the Bolsheviks was consistent with his personal desires for change. He had dreamt of such transformations but had been unable to formulate his thoughts.

Now that he felt enlightened, he joined the Bolshevik Party in the first month of his service. In May 1918, along with other convinced Communists, he took part in suppressing an anarchists' riot in Samara. Then, as a member of the First Samara Communist Detachment, he fought the mutinous White Czech troops in the vicinity of Syzran, Samara, Melekes and Simbirsk.

Thus, an ex-ensign of the Tsar's Army had found his true calling as a Red Army commander.

After the suppression of the mutiny of Czechoslovak troops in 1919 Petrov fought the White Cossacks in the Urals. It was a good thrashing he gave them but his young heart could not resist the charm of a Cossack maiden, Zoya Pavlovna Eftifeyeva. He fell in love with her and soon they married. Their love story could be the subject of a novel, because his young wife's father and two brothers served with the Whites. It was not unlikely that their new relative had more than once clashed with them in fierce sabre duels.

In 1920, Petrov served with Soviet troops fighting the White Poles on the Western Front. In May 1922 his 11th Cavalry Division was transferred to Turkestan where it was to wipe out the *basmach* gangs. In 1924, the Petrovs had Yuri, my future classmate, born to them.

A letter I received from his niece Ekaterina Trofimovna Maslova paints his portrait in private life:

"I first saw my uncle at the time of the Civil War when he was a squadron commander in Semen Budenny's First Cavalry Army fighting the White Poles. My mother was the principal and teacher of a village school in Byelorussia. Our grandmother Evdokiya Onufriyevna (Ivan Petrov's mother.—V.K.) lived with us, and in 1919 Zoya Pavlovna—Aunt Zoya—joined her.

"We lived as one family for three years, and our uncle never missed a chance to see us. With his pointed cavalry helmet, long trenchcoat and tunic with scarlet arrows across his chest he seemed a warrior from a legend to us. He was always friendly and cheerful, radiating sparkling joy that was infective. He cracked jokes and teased us good-naturedly, and his inventiveness and wit were inexhaustible. Uncle Ivan sang fairly well, was an elegant dancer, and could play the guitar and the mandolin. He was full of youthful pep."

July 1941

As Petrov was going about his business of forming the regiments of his cavalry division in Odessa, his duties often took him to the Army HQ. There he met a man who was to become his life-long friend. That was Colonel Nikolai Ivanovich Krylov, a deputy chief of the Operations Group of the Maritime Army. Krylov, who would in time rise to the rank of Marshal, would later write about his first meeting with Petrov in his memoirs.

—General Petrov wore a cavalryman's waist and shoulder belts and a pince-nez that sometimes twitched on his nose from the involuntary motions of his head, the after-effect of a shell shock, as I would later learn. His impressive looks and delicate manner combined the traits of a born soldier and an intellectual, which, incidentally, was true to fact.

—He was one of those charismatic persons who command respect and win favour and trust immediately.

—He was able to assess a person unmistakably from a few phrases, to discern his giftedness or narrow-mindedness, to see if he was honest or secretive, whether his competence in military matters was real or sham.

Colonel Krylov, a strapping man with the large features of a typical Russian face, favourably impressed Petrov in their very first conversation by his simple manner and friendliness. A thoughtful man well versed in the art of warfare, Krylov was quite outspoken in his assessment of the situation in his sector of the front and in the country as a whole. His easy manner, however, was expressed only in his free judgement. As a professional soldier he knew his limit, so his frankness had no shade of familiarity. That was a matter of course with him even in relations with those whom he knew well. He was a simple man in the highest sense, not a simpleton.

One evening when there was a lull at the HQ, they had a more detailed discussion than usual.

Petrov wanted a full story of the outbreak of hostilities on the southern front and what had enabled Soviet troops to hold off the invaders there.

This is what Colonel Krylov told him.

—As I see it, the reason is simple: we had done something to forestall the invasion. Major General Zakharov, Chief of Staff of the Odessa Military District, went out of his way to make that possible. He had no delusions about the enemy intentions and in the last prewar days he had taken vigorous steps to prepare Soviet troops for combat.

—He personally informed the General Staff of growing enemy troop concentrations right across the border. On June 6, 1941 Zakharov spoke to the Chief of the General Staff and persuaded him to urgently move Malinovsky's 48th Infantry Corps closer to the border.

—The Staff of the Military District planned a field inspection tour with communication facilities in the latter half of June. Zakharov felt that the situation was critical and argued with General Cherevichenko, Commander of the Military District, that he cancel the tour lest the Staff break away from the troops.

—A man of discipline, Cherevichenko felt reluctant to call off a plan endorsed by the People's Commissar of Defence and was hesitant. General Zakharov knew only too well that an emergency mattered more than friendly relations and formally demanded that the District Commander immediately transmit his apprehensions to the People's Commissar. Cherevichenko complied, and Marshal Timoshenko phoned back his agreement with Zakharov's opinion.

—Now that he had support from the People's Commissar of Defence, who was evidently haunted by similar misgivings, Zakharov requested the District Commander to alert the Army Command and quarter it in Tiraspol by way of verifying the plan of mobilization preparedness. General Cherevichenko agreed.

—Shortly before the invaders attacked, the Army Command had moved to Tiraspol and got down to work.

—Zakharov had also assumed responsibility for another measure of crucial importance.

—Before the outbreak of hostilities strict orders had come from the High Command not to respond to enemy provocations or do anything that would allow Germany to conclude that Soviet troops were preparing for battle. In defiance of these orders, however, General Zakharov placed headquarters and troops on combat alert, and ordered them to leave populated localities and take up positions in the areas indicated in the mobilization plan.

—In the first massive German air raid the barracks in which these troops had been quartered were completely destroyed. If Soviet divisions had stayed there, they would have suffered enormous casualties. In fact, they were entrenched along the border and gave an effective rebuff to the invaders. . . .

For the information of readers unfamiliar with military affairs, I should tell them that General Zakharov had a spectacular record of victories during the war. In the postwar period he was awarded the rank of Marshal of the Soviet Union and was Chief of the General Staff, the brain of the Soviet Army, from 1960 to 1971 (with an interval).

This is beyond question a high and honourable post filled by the most talented and best educated general.

However, there is another post in the Armed Forces the assignment to which is not announced in the press. There is not much to be heard about this sensitive area of military service where work is directed by a highly competent general. In addition to a brilliant and inventive mind, he had a quality superior even to such laudable merits as "bright, resourceful and brave". I have in mind his capability to direct intelligence work. General Zakharov was in command of this service for some time.

The unofficial "grapevine" file I have mentioned above is perhaps one of the most favourable ones as far as Marshal Zakharov is concerned: he was highly regarded by his colleagues and all officers and men of his Army.

But let us go back to Krylov's story.

—Zakharov ordered dependable communications to be established with border units and troop movements to be carried out in accordance with the border defence plan.

The Colonel smiled wryly, recalling a curious episode. General Zakharov had a heated exchange with General Michugin, the district air force commander. Zakharov ordered him to remove all aircraft from the main bases and disperse them among reserve air fields.

—The Air Force Commander realized the serious implications of that order and took it with a grain of salt. After a moment's hesitation he said: "I request your written instructions for such an important dislocation."

—General Zakharov was aware of the risks involved in ordering a complete relocation of all air forces of the military district, but he was not afraid of the responsibility. He wrote an order and handed it to the air force commander.

—All aircraft flew over to reserve airfields. As a result, the losses incurred by the air forces of the Odessa Military District in the first surprise air raid by the Luftwaffe were negligible. German bombers had dropped their cargoes on the main air bases known to the German Air Command. These, however, were almost deserted, and only three planes were lost in that first German air strike.

—Soviet fighters were scrambled at short notice and engaged the invading armada in organized fashion, bringing down twenty enemy planes on the first day of hostilities.

—Soviet troops in position along the state border staved off the enemy and even carried the fight onto his territory in some places.

—All in all, until the end of July we had held a bridgehead seventy-six kilometres wide from the mouth of the Danube to here. Further to the north, however, the balance of fighting tipped in favour of the invaders. For some time our troops held the border in that area as well, but then superior invading forces concentrated in a narrow sector of the front burst through the junction point between the 14th and 35th Infantry Corps. Here they crossed the River Prut, seized a foothold on its eastern bank and started to bring up reinforcements there. Before long more than three divisions were moved in.

—Hence the danger is greatest precisely in that area, as I see it. If we dislodge the enemy from that bridgehead to prevent his breaking out of it for a further drive onwards, we shall be able to hold the border. If we don't, that breakthrough will cause us no end of trouble.

—It's too bad that General Zakharov has been taken away from us. He has been appointed Chief of Staff of Marshal Voroshilov's North-Western Army Group. There's talk that our own Army Commander, Lieutenant General Chibisov, is to leave us soon, and a new man will take over. This is exigency, of course, but still I doubt the benefits of reshuffling the top echelon during a battle. It's changing horses in midstream.—

Krylov drew an allegory to illustrate his idea of active defence.

—Let us imagine Hercules with his back to the wall surrounded by enemies throwing stones. What happens if he simply evades hits without attacking his enemies? Sooner or later a stone will hit his head and strike him down.

—Doesn't our stand at Odessa look the same? Passive defence is always questionable, but in our circumstances it is simply disastrous.—

"Your parable hits the right nail", Petrov said thoughtfully. "Indeed, fighting back is not enough." Later, in the days of fighting for Odessa and Sevastopol, he often recalled that allegory.

At the end of their conversation Krylov told him about his earlier service.

—I was posted to the Odessa district recently. Before that I had served in the Far East and the North Caucasus.—His face grew dark.—My wife, two sons and daughter arrived on June 20. On the next night I received an emergency call to report for duty. The last time I saw them they were climbing into a lorry along with other children and wives of our commanding officers. We barely had time to say good-bye. They drove eastwards, and I don't know where they are now.—

... Shortly afterwards, on July 31, Lieutenant General Georgy Sofronov, the newly-appointed Commander of the Maritime Army, arrived in Odessa. Taking over duties from Chibisov, he acquainted himself with the units, their disposition and the overall situation. Touring the positions of troops, he met General Petrov one day. Their destinies had something in common: Sofronov had also been an ensign during the First World War. Their later careers were also similar in certain respects.

His inspection over, he stayed on to dine with Petrov and told him something in confidence about his assignment to the southern sector.

—I was Deputy Commander of the North-Western Army Group. One day I was summoned, quite unexpectedly, by the Chief of the General Staff, General of the Army Georgy Zhukov. As soon as I arrived at his HQ, Zhukov told me straight away of my appointment as Commander of the separate Maritime Army. That, as I realized, had been settled in advance. Zhukov briefed me in a few words, telling me that the Maritime Army consisting of three infantry divisions had been detached from the 9th Army and would be enlarged to include five or six divisions.

—It is hard to predict the tide of hostilities, but measures are needed to prepare for defending Odessa against encirclement. Should that happen, the land forces should hold the enemy troops fixed in co-operation with the Black Sea Fleet. In the event of a counter-offensive by Soviet forces, the Maritime Army could effectively assist them from behind the enemy lines, taking advantage of its flanking position.

—And now I am here. Unfortunately, the Maritime Army is not what Zhukov told me. As you know, only the Chapayev 25th division and the 95th infantry division have remained on its strength, while the 51st division was transferred by the Army Group HQ to its reserve yesterday. We shall also have your newly-formed cavalry division. I am pinning great hopes on it as a force to protect our right flank.

—The Germans have already driven a solid wedge between our Army and the right-flank units. We need forces to stop this breakthrough. Now we must hold off the enemy on the Dniester at any rate. We have not enough manpower however. The Army Group Commander can promise no aid for the time being.

—Fortified lines for defending the city itself should be built without delay. With our units holding the enemy on the Dniester and in defensive fighting elsewhere, we shall have time to complete this work. As Chibisov told me, this work is already in progress, but the lines should be equipped as soon as possible. I must inform you, just in case, that my reserve command post will be at Chebanka near Odessa.—

Sofronov could not afford to remain longer and take a rest; he was worried by his numerous difficulties and problems cropping up by day and by night.

Much has been written about Soviet setbacks in the summer and autumn of 1941.

Petrov had his own opinion of the first battles fought by Soviet troops. I heard him speak his mind on this subject with my own ears. This is how it happened.

The Year 1945 in Retrospect

In September 1945 General of the Army Petrov was appointed Commander of the Turkestan Military District. Other officers accepted posting there with reluctance; the sweltering heat, remoteness, sun-scorched deserts, and mountains of that forbidding area—suffice it to mention the Kara-Kumy desert and the Pamirs alone— were a scare to many.

Petrov, however, was happy with his appointment. Turkestan was a place reminiscent of his youth, where every trail was familiar to him and many people he knew and respected would be glad to see him. His own mother and sister and many of his close friends lived in Turkestan.

At the end of September Petrov arrived in Tashkent and settled in a small detached house on Pushkin Street, which had been the traditional residence of all his predecessors.

At that time I was staying with my parents during my holiday leave of absence from the Frunze Military Academy in Moscow, where I was a student. On learning of Petrov's arrival, I decided to visit him. I went to his house and stopped in front of it hesitantly. Would he receive me? Would he remember me? There had been a long war and he was now a five-star General in command of a large military district, while I was a plain Captain.

I suppressed my doubts and came up to the sentry guarding the gate.

"Is the Commander in?"

"Yes, he is."

"Could you tell him Captain Karpov, his former cadet, wants to see him?"

The sentry looked at my chest respectfully, and the Gold Star evidently proved the decisive argument.

"I'll try, though it's against regulations. I'm on duty."

Unwilling to cause trouble to the soldier, I suggested:

"Let me in and I'll do it myself, if you please."

"No, I can't, Comrade Captain. But there is a button on the door over there, and you may call him."

I climbed the steps of a little porch and pressed the white button. I heard approaching steps, and the heavy door opened. The General himself in pyjamas and slippers stood in the doorway. He looked at me closely and smiled. I felt a surge of joy: he had recognized me. Finally, he spoke slowly, as though confirming what he saw:

"A Captain. A hero. Tin shop medals. And, most important, alive! Bravo! Now, Vladimir, let me kiss you."

He hugged me and kissed me three times on both cheeks in the Russian fashion. I caught sight of the sentry's face grinning broadly. Petrov waved his hand towards the door and exclaimed:

"Come on in. You couldn't have chosen a better time!"

We entered the house. The rooms were not furnished yet, there were tied-up stacks of books on the floor and a pile of boxes in a corner. In the spacious dining-room I saw a long table with a solitary fancy cake box upon it. Petrov explained:

"I've just arrived, alone. Zoya Pavlovna and Yuri are still in Moscow. So I have to fend for myself. Incidentally, today is my birthday. I have turned forty-nine. Nobody knows about it. Only one queer fish has remembered and sent me this cake. Do you like sweet things? It looks delicious, and we may help ourselves to it. I have some booze here, too. Let us celebrate. You've come at the right time."

Turning to the door, he called: "Nesterenko!" A sergeant promptly appeared from the next room: "Yes, sir."

"Please look into our stores and bring us some bottles and whatever else you'll find for a bite to eat."

It was like a dream. General Petrov spoke to me as if I was his old friend and equal. Since I was neither of these, I felt awkward, wondering if I was not simply an intruder. Perhaps guests would come. Some generals. It was unlikely they had overlooked their new commander's birthday.

My host evidently sensed my predicament and asked me to make myself comfortable.

"Unbutton your jacket. It's hot here."

He smiled cheerfully as he was laying the table and giving instructions.

The sergeant came back, carrying a cluster of bottles in his hands.

"Comrade General, I don't know which of these is good for you. The labels are foreign."

"Never mind. We'll find out. Leave them here."

When we had sat down to our meal, I formally congratulated the General on his birthday and wished him, as is the custom, good health and success in his work. Then we talked of some every-day affairs, and finally came to the experience of the war. What he told me is impressed on my mind.

—That's good that you've enrolled in the Academy. I've advised Yuri to do the same: the war experience should be analyzed, summed up and put on a theoretical foundation. Then you'll be invaluable as military officers. Many commanding officers of my generation were, in effect, self-trained practitioners. Our alma mater was the Civil War. Add to that various advanced training courses and routine study on the job and that's all there was to it. Only a few lucky ones got an academic education. One won't be able to do without it in the future. Everything—people, weapons, the art of warfare—is getting more sophisticated. There won't be time enough to remedy mistakes in a future war. Its outcome will be settled at once, in the opening battles. A retreat to the Volga and a return to the border wouldn't work this time.—

He mused a little and continued:

—In the last war, too, it had been possible to prevent a deep enemy invasion. The Nazis had demonstrated their blitzkrieg tactics of large troop concentrations in narrow sectors, deep thrusts mostly along roads and other things of this kind in fighting with Poland and France for all the world to see.

—Our army should have been trained to deal with such breakthroughs. Trained to cut off such wedges! Not to retreat between roads overrun by Nazi tanks and mechanized infantry but to attack them from the flanks, to interrupt their supplies. Our armies, however, steadily retreated, trying to establish a new continuous front line.

—But why so? They failed to take advantage of the Nazi tactics, though they were familiar with them. Our commanders and troops should have been taught the experiences of fighting in Europe. Then, unafraid of encirclement, they could have calmly throttled fuel supplies to the enemy forces forging ahead. The momentum of the German offensive would have soon petered out.

—In addition, defence lines should have been arranged in depth and troops moved into field positions to entrench themselves, build fortifications and lay mine fields. In the Battle of Kursk, for instance, we had a model echelonment in depth, and the Nazis broke their teeth on it, and we put them to flight.

—Our experience in fighting for Odessa and Sevastopol has proved that even vastly superior enemy forces can do nothing against good defences. If we had had enough ammunition and normal supplies the Nazis would never have seized Sevastopol or Odessa. They could have been stopped on the Dnieper line.

—That opportunity was missed. Victory in war is prepared in peace time. We have eventually defeated the invaders. In 1941, however, I began to doubt our doctrine. Do you remember how Stalin worded it?

"We want no foreign land, but won't yield an inch of our own to anybody." And more: "Should we have to fight a war, we'll carry it to the enemy immediately and win it with little bloodshed aided by our class comrades in the enemy rear."

—During the retreat of 1941 all that seemed wrong. The value of a doctrine, however, is judged by the whole course of a war and its ultimate result. Well, viewing the matter from this angle, we may put it this way: we have routed the aggressor in his own territory, for which we had to fight our way through half of Europe; our class comrades, progressives and all who hated the Nazis have helped us, and we have not yielded an inch of our own territory.

—However, the prediction about "little bloodshed" and "immediateness" did not come true: the war was long and fought in our territory, the bloodshed was terrible and the losses were heavy. Too heavy! To sum up, however bitter and unpleasant this may be, one should admit his errors and learn his lesson lest such disasters ever happen again.—

Today much literature is in print about the lessons of the war, and they are analyzed in detail during the study of tactics and operational skill at military academies. It should be borne in mind, however, that Petrov was one of the first critics who spoke their minds shortly after the end of the war. His opinion was unpalatable to many, since the shortcomings and omissions which had caused our setbacks in 1941 were on the consciences of those who were in positions of authority at the time.—

We wandered in conversation to many subjects. At about 9 o'clock the General called for a car and together we went to see my parents. He had a cup of tea with them, and even wanted to send his driver for what remained of the fancy cake to be brought over, but my mother protested. In fact, on the occasion of my homecoming, she had baked an enormous quantity of little pies and now she was happy to give the "poor loner" Petrov a full bag of them.

The General thanked her cordially and said something that again left me wondering about the limits of his memory.

"You have a kind heart, Lidiya Loginovna, and I wish to thank you again for helping my old mother. She told me of how well you cared for her in wartime. I will never forget it!"

Now I knew he remembered everything. During the war I had a ten-day leave of absence to recover from a wound and visited Petrov's mother, who lived in a room on the grounds of the military school. Evdokiya Onufriyevna, which was her name, told me:

"I'm all right. I get help and even meals from the cadet canteen." She added after a pause: "I'm old. Soldiers' food is too crude for me. I'd like to have some porridge, but I've nothing to make it with."

When I came home, I told my mother about it. Times were hard, and food rationing was still in effect. My mother, however, had providently stowed some stocks away for a rainy day. She promptly brought out two small cloth bags and we inspected their contents. There was about a kilo of rice and just as much semolina."

"Take this to Evdokiya Onufriyevna. I'll give her more when I can."

That was what the General thankfully remembered. I recall his mother's cherished hopes that she shared with me in those days.

"I'd hate to die before the war's over. I'm determined to live through to see victory. I must see my darling boy come back. Just one little look, and then I'll be ready to depart. I dream of a funeral with a brass band and my dear boy present. And a church service, too. I'm a believer, you know."

Her dream came true, just as she wanted. There was an orchestra at her funeral and many wreaths. General Petrov followed the hearse on foot all the way through town to her last resting place. Now there are two graves near the church at the Tashkent cemetery: his mother's and his son Yuri's.

August 1941

On August 5, Marshal Semen Budenny, Commander-in-Chief of the South-Western Army Group, issued an order: "Odessa is not to be surrendered and must be defended as long as possible, relying on the assistance of the Black Sea Fleet." The Marshal, in fact, had duplicated an order from the General Headquarters. That day marked the beginning of the heroic defence of Odessa sea port.

Now the front line was an eighty-kilometre arc with its ends resting on the sea coast. At its right flank this arc was roughly thirty kilometres away from the city; at the left flank and in the centre forty kilometres away. The commander of the defence area and unit commanders were drawing up to this arc whatever forces had survived earlier battles. Soviet troops were not simply retreating but fighting back the enemy units closing in on the city.

The cavalry regiments of Petrov's division trying to link up with their neighbours on the right flank burst far ahead of the firing lines and some of them found themselves in the enemy rear. Now they had to fight their way back through the lines of Rumanian and German troops that had cut off their paths of retreat. During those days of continuous fighting Petrov drove back and forth across the steppe in search of scattered units of his division to align them along a new line of defence.

In the early period of the war radio communication was used on a limited scale. Telephone lines were, of course, also of limited use in mobile battles. Therefore, Petrov had to rely on the assistance of his HQ officers and drive from place to place himself to collect his troops. In these trips he had a few encounters with enemy forces. His earlier experience in fighting *basmach* gangs in Central Asia stood him in good stead.

Finally, Petrov gathered almost all units of his division; only the whereabouts of Captain Blinov's 5th cavalry regiment were not yet known. Petrov himself went off in search of the missing regiment. He discovered it near the village of Sverdlovo. The scene he saw surprised him. The regiment was lined up, and a few enemy tankmen stood in front of it. The regimental commander Blinov was speaking to his men.

A short story of the preceding events is needed to explain what had happened. To break out of the enemy encirclement, Blinov had ordered his regiment to fall into battle formation: the cavalry squadrons in the vanguard, the staff and special units in the middle, and machine-gun carts providing cover in the rearguard. In this formation the regiment pierced the enemy lines. The Nazis had moved in tanks to stop it. The regimental artillery knocked out a few tanks, and their crews were captured. They were Germans, not Rumanians. To build up the morale of his officers and men, Blinov ordered the prisoners to be brought up in front of the regiment and made a short speech.

—Look at these Nazi thugs. Look closely, comrades! See these warriors shaking with fear. All of them are like that—treacherous cowards. You are fit to defeat them, I am sure.—

At that moment Petrov came up to the regimental commander. Blinov stood to attention and reported the arrival of his regiment. Petrov hugged him and kissed him on both cheeks and then congratulated the cavalrymen on their courage and exemplary fighting skill.

Organizing the defence of Odessa, Lieutenant General Sofronov, Commander of the Maritime Army, divided the city defences into three sectors. Each sector was to be defended by a division.

The Eastern sector was placed in charge of Brigadier Monakhov. This sector had not enough manpower for a division and was defended by various units, some of which had been formed but recently and lacked the necessary training: the 1st regiment of the Marines, a composite regiment of the Interior Force, and the 54th Razin regiment of the Chapayev division, which had moved into this area in the course of hostilities.

These scattered units put up a heroic resistance to the advancing troops of the Rumanian 15th and 13th infantry divisions, the German 72nd infantry division, a Rumanian cavalry brigade, a motorized infantry brigade, which were supported by numerous artillery and tanks.

The Western sector was under the command of Major General Vorobyov, commander of the 95th infantry division which was opposed by a Rumanian army corps and two Rumanian infantry divisions with armoured support.

The Southern sector was defended by the Chapayev 25th division (short of one regiment) under the command of Colonel Zakharchenko and a composite machine-gun battalion.

General Petrov's cavalry division which had sustained heavy casualties in earlier battles was withdrawn into the Army Commander's reserve.

The division of the defences into independent sectors was perhaps the wisest measure under the circumstances since the natural terrain of the defended area suggested that. The eighty-kilometre arc of the defence lines was protected at the flanks by salt lakes extending far inland: Lake Dniester in the west and Lake Hajibei in the east. Inside this arc there were several other salt lakes also extending from the sea to the front line: Kuyalnitsky, Ajalyksky, Tiligulsky, and Sukhoi. They cut the entire defence area of Odessa into sectors and, what mattered most, hampered freedom of manoeuvre inside the area. The division into sectors enabled Soviet troops to hold out against enemy attacks independently, to make rapid movements inside a sector and secured dependable direction of troops.

Odessa's defenders had no tanks and very few aircraft. But, to make up for it, all coastal artillery and the huge guns of the warships anchored in Odessa harbour unleashed their firepower on the invading forces.

At the time of fighting on the approaches to Odessa many of its residents had joined the Red Army, and when the enemy advanced on the suburbs 12,000 Communists and 73,000 Komsomol members went to the firing lines. That was the opening page in the story of the siege of the heroic city cut off from the rest of the country by the sea and the ruthless enemy.

On August 19, General Headquarters issued an order to establish the Odessa defence area subordinated to the Black Sea Fleet. Rear Admiral Gavriil Zhukov, commander of the naval base, was appointed to command the defence area. Thus, the Maritime Army was placed under the command of the Navy, although it remained the backbone of the land defences.

The Navy and the Army, after some misunderstanding at the initial stage, put their heads together to work out a defence plan for Odessa. Their further efforts were a model of teamwork for the common cause. That was only natural, since the men in key positions responsible for the defence of the city were experienced generals, and communist patriots. General Petrov would later direct combat operations for many days jointly with Rear Admiral Zhukov, whose biography was also typical of a high-ranking Soviet military officer.

At the age of 18 Zhukov had joined the Red Army during the Civil War and as a member of sailors' units had taken part in fighting the White Guards and foreign intervention forces near Astrakhan. In 1919, he joined the Communist Party, and in the same year he was decorated with the Order of the Red

Banner for courage in battle. After the Civil War Zhukov graduated from the Leningrad Naval School and served with the Navy in the Baltic and on the Black Sea.

Zhukov had fought as a volunteer against the fascists in Spain. Since 1940 he had been in command of the Odessa naval base. In the days of fighting for Odessa he displayed great presence of mind and competence in the art of warfare. He was known as an exacting commander keen on military discipline. He was a man of principle and at a critical moment took a noble stand in relation to General Petrov, exposing his own career to great risks, as will be shown later in the story.

The days when the Odessa defence area was established were a difficult time for the city's defenders. On the morning of August 20 the enemy committed to battle up to six infantry divisions, one cavalry division, and one armoured brigade and made a breakthrough in the sector of Kagarlyk–Belyayevka. Enemy troops burst into Belyayevka, where the head installations of the Odessa waterworks were now in danger of falling into enemy hands. Odessa's population of 300,000 would be left without a water supply.

The order of General Headquarters prescribed "... Rear Admiral Zhukov to assume command of all units and services of the former Maritime Army. ..." Zhukov interpreted that clause as disbanding the Staff of the Maritime Army and took over direct command of the divisions. In view of its critical situation he allowed the Chapayev 25th division to withdraw from the Southern sector to a new line of defence. That entailed the retreat of the 95th division in the Western sector to avoid the risk of its being outflanked and encircled. Major General Vorobyov, commander of the Western sector, and his men had done a great deal of work to fortify the defence line of the division, which it could have held for a long time, but for the events in the Southern sector.

The 25th division had retreated in disorder, and its command had lost control of its units. The situation rapidly deteriorated, and new, more fierce battles were to be fought. In that situation the divisional commander could not be expected to correct his mistakes, so prompt and resolute action was necessary. On the same night, therefore, the Military Council appointed Major General Petrov commander of the Chapayev 25th division. Brigade Commissar Stepanov was appointed divisional commissar for political affairs, his second-in-command. The cavalry division was temporarily left under Petrov's control, so that he could check the enemy advance in the Southern sector.

General Petrov began his duties of commanding the Chapayev 25th infantry division in an unusual way. That was not, of course, motivated by a desire to impress anybody. The reason was simple: Petrov was a battlewise commander with his own mature views on the conduct of fighting. At dawn on August 21, the first day of his new commission, he arrived with his aide-de-camp at the positions of Major Sultan-Galiyev's 287th infantry regiment to acquaint himself with the situation at first hand and meet the unit commanders. It was a hard-and-fast rule with him that he should know personally all commanding officers he was to serve with, from platoon commanders up. Therefore, his first visit was to the firing lines. He knew that his appearance here at a critical time of the enemy offensive would encourage his officers and men and strengthen their fighting spirit. He was not mistaken.

In fact, the enemy launched another attack at dawn. At the height of the battle, when his troops were fighting fiercely to hold off the attackers, Petrov left the relative safety of regimental headquarters and went over to a battalion command post. Here the battlefield was right in front of his eyes. He saw the attackers forging ahead, hauling artillery with them. They stopped from time to time and fired at Soviet machine-gun posts to support their infantry. Then they moved onwards again. Attacking with artillery like that was, of course, risky but they were evidently sure of themselves and determined to seize the Soviet positions.

Petrov was not taken in by that show of mettle. He called out to the battalion commander:

"Hey, these cheeky bastards need a lesson. Seize those guns! Over the top!"

The Soviet defenders charged, the commanding officers leading the way. Scared of hand-to-hand fighting, the attackers took to their heels, abandoning five pieces of artillery and ammunition. The enemy advance in this sector was stopped.

Wasn't General Petrov too careless to come to the battlefield and risk his life when he had a full division on his hands to take care of? Wasn't it a bravado intended to impress his subordinates? Or was it contempt for the traditional formalities of handover and takeover of command?

None of these questions hits the mark. His reasons were practical: to hurl the enemy back and to stabilize the front line in his sector. Indeed, what could he do at his headquarters? Accept and sign papers? Inspect units? But he had only two infantry regiments under his command, both in the firing lines, and the third one was in the Eastern sector. He had no reserves. The cavalry division under his operational control was familiar to him as its ex-commander. What else then?

Needless to say, there was much routine work to be handled by a divisional commander but this might be left to his deputies and Chief of Staff, who knew the details of their business. The main thing now was to stop the enemy! This takes knowing the enemy's whereabouts, strength and intended thrusts. He had to know how much manpower and firepower he had at his disposal.

Since all his troops were in the firing lines, he had to join them immediately. What kind of men were in command of the regiments, battalions and platoons? He knew only too well that very much depended on a commanding officer in battle. If he is resourceful and brave, his unit is in dependable hands and can be relied upon in fighting. If he is sluggish and unsure of himself, his unit may falter, too.

So Petrov knew what to do first. He had a brief exchange with his Chief of Staff and divisional commissar; there was no time to be lost. He called out: "Chief of Artillery, follow me!"

They climbed into his car and drove off.

Artillery was the chief weapon the General could wield to influence the outcome of fighting at that stage. He had neither tanks, nor support forces to influence the outcome of battle.

On their way to the front line Petrov discussed this problem with his Chief of Artillery. Before the war Lieutenant Colonel Frol Grossman was a teacher at a military school. His repeated requests for a transfer to the fighting forces were finally granted, and he replaced the Chief of Artillery of the Chapayev division disabled by a wound. By the time of Petrov's appointment as divisional commander Grossman had gained an illustrious record as an artillery officer.

Soon they reached the positions of the 287th infantry regiment, where Petrov took over the direction of combat and achieved his first success.

Marshal Krylov, who was Chief of Operations in the Maritime Army, writes:

—There are different views as to whether the commander of a large formation fighting a battle can afford to delegate his duties to his deputy and leave his command post to see his troops in the front lines. Evidently, there is no general rule to this effect. Vasily Vorobyov, for instance, almost never left his command post but efficiently directed his troops. Petrov, however, preferred to see with his own eyes the combat performance of his regiments and battalions. That was probably due to his state of mind and the experiences of his earlier service. It was not long before he could recognize by face and address by first name and patronymic every platoon commander in the Chapayev division.

—I believe that whenever Petrov analyzed developments on a battlefield he relied in his judgement on his knowledge of the personal qualities of his officers and men. That knowledge guided him in taking decisions and setting combat tasks to his troops.—

Within a few days Petrov's troops checked the enemy advance in the Southern sector and entrenched themselves on a new defence line. They had achieved that success by defensive action and frequent counter-attacks. That was Petrov's principle of combat. Sometimes Soviet counter-attacking units took up positions in a captured area and shifted to circular defence. By holding these positions, they fragmented the battle order of attacking enemy troops. Unable to advance all along the front, the latter lost the advantage of a massive offensive and had to call a retreat.

Petrov also skilfully employed the cavalry under his command. Under cover of night they moved into tall fields of maize to conceal their concentration and then launched surprise attacks to drive enemy troops out of villages. In a swift counter-attack one of his regiments encircled a battalion of the enemy's 14th infantry division and wiped it out. Two other enemy battalions suffered severe losses and fell back. The Pugachev 31st regiment pushed the enemy backwards in a fierce counter-attack and burst into Franzfeld. The Army Commander phoned to General Petrov and congratulated him on that success.

. . . The divisions defending Odessa were decimated by continuous fighting. Units cut off from the country and the main forces of the Red Army could not, of course, receive replacements regularly. Sometimes, groups of volunteers from the crews of merchant ships joined the defending forces. Most of the replacements, however, came from Odessa. During the siege very young Komsomols, veterans too old to be enlisted and those who were unfit for active service for health reasons volunteered to join the army. They were staunch and brave soldiers and they fought for their city to the last.

Here is an eyewitness account I heard from Yakov Vaskovsky, who served with the Razin regiment of General Petrov's division.

—The next attack of fresh enemy troops was dogged and fierce, and they came in close to our trenches. We kept firing at the attackers, but our machine-gun on the left flank was silent.

Battalion commander Sergiyenko shouted into his phone angrily: "What's wrong with the machine-gun? Find out and report immediately!"

Lieutenant Grintsov, platoon commander, ran to the left flank. The machine-gun crew there was new; he had not yet time to talk with them before the fighting broke out.

Grintsov found them alive, and the machine-gunner spread on the ground and watching the battle scene through his sights.

"Why aren't you firing?"

"They're too far yet. Let them come nearer," the gunner answered calmly.

"But they'll wipe you out with hand-grenades. Fire!"

Grintsov was about to push the stubborn gunner out of the way when the latter opened fire. Lines of attackers were cut down by accurate hits.

"Well done, boy! You deserve a medal," Grintsov exclaimed.

The gunner finally looked back, and the lieutenant saw a girl with a boy's haircut. She screwed up her eyes in a grin.

"That's a good idea, Lieutenant. But I'm not keen on medals. I'm fighting for my home city."

When the battle was over, battalion commander Sergiyenko came to meet the intrepid lady gunner. Her name was Nina Onilova.

"You're just like Anna the gunner in the film about Chapayev. And yet you should keep your distance and out of point blank range. If your gun jams or if you're within reach of a hand grenade the enemy may overrun your trench in the next moment."

"Yes, Comrade Captain!"

Rumours of the valiant gunner reached General Petrov's ear. Before long he received a recommendation for awarding her a decoration. The General for some reason did not sign the paper immediately and sent for her to be brought to his headquarters.

She came promptly and stood, silent and shy, before the General. Short and slender, she was dressed in a soiled quilted jacket and her face which she had obviously washed hastily bore traces of gun oil and soot.

"Well, young lady, could you tell me of your battle exploits?"

"There isn't much to tell, Comrade General. I was doing my duty like everybody else."

"But you were doing that at point blank range, weren't you?"

The girl lowered her eyes guiltily.

"I couldn't afford to miss my target, Comrade General. There were too many of them. And I hate to waste ammunition."

The General said cheerfully:

"That's a good answer, my brave lady. You've earned a promotion. Your new rank is sergeant, 1st class."

The girl forgot to stand to attention and looked at the General in confusion. He stood up to shake her hand, which she extended timidly like a child.

Petrov released her and remarked to Captain Kovtun, who had heard their conversation:

"A very remarkable girl. She deserves a higher award than the Red Star. Recommend her for a Red Banner. So young and fearless! I must confess I wanted to see if she is not just a favourite of one of our commanders. Now I see she is a real fighter and a very modest one at that."

Sergeant Onilova showed her unusual courage in many other battles and her name became famous among the defenders of Odessa. A native of Odessa she had been raised at an orphanage, worked at a knitted goods factory, and volunteered for front line service along with many other girls. She was very proud of her enlistment in the Chapayev Division.

From the first few hours of controlling the defence of the Southern sector General Petrov found himself at one of the focal points of the Battle of Odessa. The tension of fighting here was growing steadily.

There were casualties in Petrov's division. The Commander of the 287th regiment Sultan-Galiyev was wounded and taken to hospital. That loss caused the General a lot of worry. The 287th was a new regiment in the celebrated Chapayev Division. During the battles on the Dniester it had been incorporated in the division to replace the Frunze 263rd regiment. In the whirlwind of fighting the latter had found itself within the battle order of another division which then retreated with the 9th Army. Now that the 287th regiment was left without an experienced commander, Petrov had to find a worthy replacement urgently.

It is never easy to replace a commanding officer, especially with high casualty figures among command personnel. Besides, all of Petrov's officers had a short record of joint service, and their fitness for taking an important command post was not known well. Petrov had to rely, therefore, on his own intuition and ability to appreciate the merits of other persons instantly and discern their potentials.

The prevailing situation would not allow long discussions, instructions or advice, so he needed a man who would be quick in the uptake and act without hesitation. Kovtun was the right man for him, as he had concluded from several previous conversations.

Petrov rarely erred in his judgement of people, and he was not mistaken this time either.

Here is an illustration. Another eyewitness I interviewed was Colonel of the Reserve Ivan Bezghinov, who had served as Captain with the Operations Group of the Maritime Army. He was at the headquarters of the 287th regiment at the time when Kovtun assumed command.

—He was received with a measure of caution—the Colonel told me. He was a Captain and not young for that matter. Sultan-Galiyev had been popular with his men. However, after Kovtun had led a counter-attack against enemy troops assaulting the regimental command post and taken part in hand-to-hand fighting along with the men of a battalion whose commander was killed, his reputation was established for good. As if by general agreement, he was now addressed respectfully as regimental commander, not as Captain. After all there were many Captains in the regiment.

In his reminiscences Marshal Krylov quotes a report from Kovtun's regiment:

—The 287th infantry regiment had repelled fierce enemy attacks until dark. By nightfall only 740 men had remained on its strength. The units of the regiment are firmly holding their ground. Commenting on these terse lines of a battle report, Krylov writes that the 287th regiment "performed a heroic exploit. . . . 740 men are merely a battalion in terms of numerical strength. A regiment, however, remains a regiment if it holds on to its positions regardless of its losses."

Kovtun himself gave the following account of the fighting in the early days of his command.

—I can't recall how many attacks we repulsed on that ill-fated day; we lost count of them. . . . Petrov phoned us from a neighbouring regiment from where our right flank could be seen. He said: "You're fighting well. Hold on! The whole division is staunchly holding its ground." Of course, we had to hold on. I knew that "the whole division" was us and the second regiment, our neighbours. In my regiment casualties were mounting, and the regimental commissar Balashov was wounded at the end of the day.

—His wound was bandaged, and he stayed on with me at the observation post. He was bleeding and could hardly stand on his feet, but would not agree to be taken to hospital. He stubbornly objected to all my arguments by saying: "It's my duty to stay on." He kept calling the battalions on the phone to give instructions and, what is most important, to let them know he was alive. I felt very thankful to him for that. A commissar's word said at a critical time was of paramount importance. At nightfall I counted our dead and wounded and was horrified. I wondered about our fitness to keep on fighting the next day. I went to see the men in the trenches and found them utterly exhausted. I ventured a question: "What about tomorrow boys?" A few chuckled and a voice said: "Before tomorrow we'll take a nap, have a bite to eat and a smoke and be ready for another fight." So I wrote in my report that we were determined to hold our positions.

The General Situation in the Autumn of 1941

To understand the causes of those fierce battles one should take a broader view of the situation than what the defenders of Odessa could see at the time. In matters of war it is nearly always the general rule that the combatants have no complete and accurate information about all the circumstances and factors that influence the course and outcome of a battle. The full picture of hostilities is revealed only when a battle or a war as a whole is over. It is composed by researchers, historians and the generals themselves in their memoirs. In the heat of battle, however, at times three-quarters of what a commanding officer needs to know for taking a competent decision is unknown to him. It is not easy for a commander to obtain timely, authentic and complete information about his own forces, let alone the enemy who is making every effort to conceal information about himself, to mislead the opposing side by spreading disinformation about his forces, intentions, timings and directions of strikes. All this was true of the units of the Maritime Army as well.

Towards August 20, when Petrov was appointed commander of the Southern sector, the Battle of Smolensk was at its height. Leningrad had been under siege for a full month. Moscow was repulsing German air raids. The defenders of Odessa were aware of those events but they did not know that the Nazis were confident of their victory and thought it was close at hand.

In those days, General Halder, Chief of the German Army General Staff, wrote:

—The task of defeating the main forces of the Russian Army in front of the Western Dvina and the Dniester has been accomplished. It would be no exaggeration to say, therefore, that the campaign against Russia was won within 14 days.—

In that way, quickly and simply, the Soviet Union was struck from history, and not by Goebbels in a frenzy of propaganda but by one of the top leaders of the Wehrmacht, manipulating facts and figures.

Now the world knows how grossly they had miscalculated and what a price they had to pay for that.

To make their plans come true, the Nazis had to supply their forces of invasion with whatever they needed to fight the war. Odessa was a formidable obstacle to the invaders' efforts to gain control of the Black Sea and its coast. The Black Sea could provide excellent lanes for German transports to bring in supplies to the troops operating on the southern flank of the Soviet-German front, which was required, in particular, for implementing the plans of advance into the Caucasus.

Transports with cargoes of ammunition and equipment for the Wehrmacht anchored at Rumanian and Bulgarian ports were waiting for a signal to set sail for Odessa. General Halder wrote on August 15:

—The troops operating in the Dnieper area and at the approaches to Kiev require an average of 30 trainloads of supplies daily. . . . It is a matter of first priority to deliver to Odessa and Kherson 15,000 tons of ammunition, 15,000 tons of provisions, 7,000 tons of fuel for the 11th and 17th Armies. These supplies should be delivered within 10 days of taking Odessa.—

Thus, everything had been planned, calculated and prepared. Only one thing was lacking: they couldn't take Odessa.

Odessa was besieged by the whole of the Rumanian 4th Army, and after a few days 12 Rumanian divisions, including one armoured division, another seven brigades, and also units of the German 72nd infantry division embarked on an offensive. A 300,000-strong army supported by a large number of tanks and more than 100 aircraft was advancing towards the city.

They were opposed by three divisions of the Maritime Army and a few separate sailors' units. These divisions had already been heavily depleted in fighting during their retreat from the Soviet border.

According to the theory of warfare, the offensive forces need a triple superiority in numbers to defeat the defensive forces. In the Battle of Odessa the enemy had a far greater superiority and in some sectors outnumbered the defenders ten to one. There is a document illustrating the enemy's admission of his inability to take Odessa despite his vastly superior strength. It is an order to the 4th Army signed by Antonescu which was discovered on the body of an officer killed near Odessa.

—Many commanders have informed me that our infantry troops refuse to stand up and follow their officers, as it exactly happened in the 11th division. . . . I blame this on their commanders, if they failed to execute on the spot those scoundrels who bring disgrace on their nation, their ranks and their names.

—I also regard as guilty all commanders of large and small units who evacuate those wounded in the hands and toes. With rare exceptions their wounds are self-inflicted, and they should be executed on the spot.

—I demand moral staunchness and energy from all. . . . You are scared of tanks. Whole regiments, such as the 15th infantry regiment, fled 4 to 5 kilometres in panic from the appearance of three or four enemy tanks. . . . It is a disgrace for an army which outnumbers the enemy four or five to one in manpower and has superior armaments . . . to be held in check by small Soviet units. . . .—

August 1941

The tanks mentioned by Antonescu were, in fact, dummies built in Odessa. They were ordinary tractors protected with steel sheets imitating the shape of a tank. They produced a demoralizing effect on enemy troops but could not do much more. Odessa townspeople cracked jokes about these mock-ups, calling them "SC tanks", SC spelt out as "scarecrow". Indeed, supporting Soviet counter-attacks, they scared the enemy with the roar of their engines, the clanging of their plating and the rumble of their caterpillar tracks.

In one battle three such machines moved out to repulse attacking enemy infantry. Their mounted machine-guns rattled away. The enemy troops retreated and hugged the ground but enemy artillery opened fire at the "tanks". Now they were having a hell of a time. One of them was hit and stopped. If it were not for our infantry who came to their rescue, the crew might have been taken prisoner. The "armour" of the "tank" was damaged by bullets and shell splinters, and there was a gaping hole in its side.

Soldiers chuckled and joked, inspecting the crippled vehicle. Someone remarked to its desperate crew:

"It takes guts to fight a war in this tin can."

The crew commander, a Lieutenant, smiled: "You're a sceptic. This is a wonderful battle machine. In an ordinary tank a shell explodes and makes a dreadful mess, God only knows what a mess! My van, however, is pierced so easily that the fuse fails to go off. I can be killed only by a direct hit. According to the law of chances, the enemy will have to expend more than half of his ammunition to hit me. As for two such tanks—they have not enough shells to knock them out."

Forcing their troops into battle, the Rumanian command played on their sentiments, deceiving them shamelessly. Once the Chief of Reconnaissance brought Petrov a leaflet retrieved from Rumanian POWs. The General read it and commented, smiling ironically:

"At all times military leaders knew the value of the factor of morale. They fortified and enhanced the fighting spirit of their troops by various ways and means. Some appealed to their religious feelings, others encouraged them by keeping their bellies full, still others promised them a generous loot.

"That usually pepped them up though not for long. Except, perhaps, in matters of religion. Religion was the most effective means of boosting morale. The strongest base for the fighting spirit of troops, however, is not faith in God, or chauvinism, or a craving for wealth but an awareness of the justness of the war they are fighting.

"This Rumanian leaflet was written by an experienced hand. At first it gives a correct picture of the situation on the front. This is intended to win the soldiers' confidence. But what comes next? Empty verbiage, lies, and vulgar appeals to nationalist ambitions. Just listen to this." And he read the leaflet aloud:

—Soldiers! The enemy is weak. He is exhausted by the war, which has lasted for two months without a respite, and has been routed all along the front from the Prut to the Dniester. Make your final effort to complete this struggle, do not retreat before the enemy's fierce counterattacks. He cannot win, because we are stronger. Keep up your offensive! In two days you will take the biggest port on the Black Sea. This will cover you and your country with glory. The whole world is watching you and expecting to see you in Odessa. May you be equal to your high destiny!—

The Chief of Reconnaissance said: "They have announced a military parade on Cathedral Square to celebrate the taking of Odessa and a thanksgiving service at the Assumption Cathedral on August 23."

"Bastards!" Petrov's head twitched nervously, and his pince-nez glistened coldly.

"We'll make them eat dirt instead of parading."

Infuriated by the stubborn resistance of Odessa's defenders and the cowardice of their own troops, Antonescu and his generals went to extremes. Ignoring the changes in weaponry and tactics that had taken place in the last few years, Rumanian commanders resorted to "psychological warfare".

On August 23, the commander of the 31st regiment reported to Petrov by phone about an unusual enemy attack. The General hastened to his command post, from where he saw columns of enemy infantry marching across the field. It looked like the scene of a White Guards' attack in the film about Chapayev. The officers were goosestepping with swords drawn and the soldiers were holding their rifles atilt. They were followed by a brass band with shining trumpets playing a march. The enemy columns were stamping their feet on the ground as if on a military parade and steadily approaching the Soviet positions.

That was a strange and spectacular scene. "Well, that's not a sign of good fortune at war", Petrov said. "They've lost hope of defeating us in conventional battles, and are trying this as a last resort. I wonder if they realize that with modern weapons an attack like that is suicidal."

The General silently watched the marching troops, as though fascinated by the sinister beauty of their faultless formation and the strains of martial music.

It was a sunny day. The enemy lines were swaying rhythmically, the polished jackboots of officers and the swords in their hands flashing in the sun. All was quiet and nobody fired. Only the music disturbed the silence. Everybody stood still, amazed by this parade of death.

"Good marchers!" Petrov commented at last. Those were exactly the words Chapayev had said, watching the columns of Kappel's White Guards. "But stupid. Very stupid indeed. I even feel sorry for them, even though they are the enemy. Well, we haven't invited them here after all. Chief of Artillery!

Open fire! Disperse and wipe out this gang of dandies!"

Artillery thundered. It was strange and terrifying to see shells exploding, black cones of earth and flames rising near the columns and then in the midst of the marchers. Their ranks broke up and they stopped in confusion. There were a few more direct hits, and the soldiers scattered over the field. The brass band was also caught up in the explosions and fell silent. Officers were waving their swords and shouting at their men, driving them forward, but then Soviet machine-guns opened up and were joined by rifle fire.

Here and there men were hit and fell, dead or wounded. The survivors finally turned back and ran for their lives, but bullets found more and more victims in the fleeing crowd.

Only a few made it to their trenches. The cries and groans of wounded men left in the field were heard for a long time. There was no one to help them. Those who had learned their lesson from Soviet arms in that psychological attack did not venture to return to the battlefield. It was only at night that the Rumanians started to rescue their wounded. Soviet troops heard that work going on in the field but did not open fire.

Petrov was satisfied to know that another offensive had been beaten off but wondered with a touch of compassion why Rumanian commanders were wasting their troops in modern combat so thoughtlessly. It was not long before he learned the reason from an order seized from a captive officer. It read in part:

General Antonescu has ordered that commanders of units who have failed to take determined offensive action should be dismissed, court-martialled and divested of their pension entitlement. Soldiers who have failed to fight with fervour in an attack or who have abandoned the defensive lines should be deprived of their land holdings and war-time allowances. Soldiers who have lost their weapons should be shot on the spot. If a unit retreats without authorization, its commander must set up machine-guns behind the lines and shoot deserters on sight without mercy. Any weakness, vacillation or passiveness in directing operations shall be punished mercilessly. This order is to be announced immediately to all troops under your command.—

The Rumanian troops outnumbered Soviet defenders five to one. In the past Rumanian soldiers had more than once shown courage and staunchness in defending their country, but here they were fighting half-heartedly. They went into battle under coercion, obviously unwilling to die for the goals of a war they abhorred. The political and military leadership of the Rumanian Army was not united with the mass of the soldiers by a common cause and a common determination to win the war. Rumanian generals either toadied to their Nazi masters or were scared of them, while Rumanian soldiers were generally ignorant of the aims they were expected to die for. The lands and privileges they had been promised on conquered territories were phantoms and what's the use of those lands if they had to give their lives for them?

I visited Rumania more than once after the war, collecting material for this book and searching for documents, as well as, most important of all, meeting with ex-servicemen who had taken part in the Battle of Odessa. Here I shall give some information which may be helpful to understanding the situation in the days under review.

Antonescu was an experienced general and knew that in addition to weapons the soldiers of his army needed moral incentives that would direct their efforts towards a common goal, galvanize them into action and maintain its momentum. What incentives could he offer them as the head of government?

Antonescu called the invasion a "holy war", and his propaganda machine was at work to drive it home to the troops that the war had the blessing of the Almighty, because it was being waged against the godless Bolsheviks, who spurned religion and persecuted all believers. Booklets and pamphlets widely circulated among Rumanian soldiers featured photographs showing Russians pulling down crosses and bells from churches, churches converted to warehouses, members of May Day and other festive processions dressed up in church robes clowning in mockery of priests.

Rumanian soldiers were thus called on to fight for their faith, for a cause blessed by the Lord. In those years the common people in Rumania were uneducated and religious, and such brainwashing had a definite effect. Not a very strong one, it is true, not strong enough to satisfy Antonescu at any rate; Rumanian troops were by no means spoiling for a fight.

Antonescu's Nazi masters, however, were putting pressure on him, demanding more vigorous action, and using stick and carrot to spur him on. For instance, during their meeting at the headquarters of Army Group South in Berdichev in August 1941, Hitler showered Antonescu with praise, called him "the liberator of Bessarabia", lauded his military exploits and decorated him with the Nazi Reich's supreme award—the Knight's Cross—there and then.

How, indeed, could the newly-created "knight" now report the endless setbacks of his offensive against Odessa? Antonescu was beside himself with rage on learning that his soldiers were reluctant to fight, shirked their duties, malingered and injured themselves to get out of the line. So the vindictive dictator resolved to drive his troops into battle in columns to be slaughtered like cattle.

He reasoned as follows: You don't want to fight, then you'll go to your death.

In a column all men are in view of each other and the officers; one cannot take a single step to the left or to the right or hide behind a bush; the only way is to march forward and come under a hail of enemy bullets and shells. That psychological pressure and vengeance for obstinacy pursued a reformative aim: a few battalions notorious for their inertness were sent into battle in columns as an object lesson and a warning to the whole army: this penalty will be meted out to all of you, if you fail to fight well.

Visiting Rumania in 1981, I chanced to talk with a few veterans of the Battle of Odessa. Stephan Petrescu, a stout and good-natured grey-haired man, greeted me with a friendly smile and there was a shade of apology in his eyes as he spoke:

"We took sides with Nazi Germany by some fatal historical mistake. In fact, Rumania was just like Poland or Czechoslovakia or other countries occupied by Hitler. A large and unfriendly German army, which was, in fact, an army of occupation, stayed on our soil. We were gripped by the throat. The Nazis were pumping out our oil; that mattered most of all to them. We should have fought them. If defeated like other countries of Europe, we would have at least had our conscience clear. We could have taken to guerrilla warfare, and our fuel would not have flown freely to Hitler's tanks and planes. Hitler cheated our nation."

"Foreign invasion and guerrilla warfare mean suffering and sacrifices", I reminded him.

"Other nations accepted that!" Stephan exclaimed. "We should have done that, too, and kept our honour. But what happened really? Just listen to what our Rumanian author Tudor Arghesi writes."

He took a book off a shelf, found the right page and read: "The French had the Maquis, the Russians had the partisans. The Serbians, Greeks, Norwegians, Belgians, Dutchmen, Poles resisted the occupation. . . . Let us face the ugly truth with courage and look into our conscience. Needless to say, this is uncomfortable. All of us, however, were implicated more or less in crimes that deserve a court trial. At a time when our friends, brothers and comrades were dying in jail, or living like tramps in foreign exile, we—let us not play the hypocrite—were filling our bellies with lavish meals and washing them down with delicious wines, we were laughing loudly and enjoying ourselves in overcrowded beer halls, at restaurants and balls. . . ."

Tudor Arghesi was a good and honest writer, and he painted a true-to-life picture of the shameful life-style of some circles in Rumania.

Completing my story of the situation in the enemy camp during the Battle of Odessa, I wish to make it clear that whatever belated regrets one might feel about Rumania taking part in the war against the Soviet Union this does not absolve Antonescu's Army of its responsibility for the crimes it perpetrated. His army was a loyal ally of Nazi Germany and joined it in its treacherous attack on the USSR. In the areas invaded by them, Rumanian troops committed atrocities, looting Soviet towns and villages and killing innocent civilians. The Rumanian military had a hand in the heinous crimes of the Nazis and share the responsibility for them. This is not a pleasant subject for me to write on and for our Rumanian comrades to recall today. But let bygones be bygones.

Late August 1941

On August 25, the enemy moved in more than ten divisions and went on the offensive in three sectors. This was yet another desperate effort to achieve a breakthrough towards the city. The Soviet divisions had a hard time holding positions in their sectors: they had suffered heavy casualties in earlier fighting. On that day, shells exploded in the harbour district of Odessa; before that the post had been hit only during air raids.

After August 25, the situation sharply deteriorated in the Eastern sector defended by the troops of Brigadier Monakhov. The enemy now had Odessa within firing range of its artillery and committed more and more reinforcements to battle, trying to break through towards the city by a shortcut precisely from here, from the east. The Soviet defenders were given fire support by the long-range guns of warships anchored in the Bay of Odessa. Even the coast artillery batteries in the Southern sector opened fire, and their huge shells flew over the whole city before hitting their targets. The enemy troops advancing from the east came close to the positions of the 21st coast artillery battery. It had a key part to play in the city's defences and was now in danger of being captured.

The situation became critical. There were only two alternatives left: to blow up the guns and all coastal fortifications, or to keep on firing to the last round.

The battery crew opted for the latter. However, the right moment for destroying the guns was not to be missed lest they fall into enemy hands intact.

The story of the heroic exploits of the crew was known to Petrov, and in December 1980 I learned its details from Rear Admiral Derevyanko, who had been Chief of Staff of the naval base at the time:

—I was in constant communication with that battery. Once, when the enemy was already close to it, I was talking on the phone with its operator. There was a sudden crackle and noise and a hubbub of voices in the earpiece. My first thought was that enemy troops had probably overrun the command post and it was all over.

—I shouted into the phone, calling the operator, but the phone was dead. After some time, however, I heard the operator's voice again. He uttered a phrase I will never forget: "Excuse me, sir, I had to attend to hand-to-hand fighting."

—I told him of my orders to blow up the battery and get the crew down to the shore to be picked up by rescue launches, which were on their way. After some time, however, the launches came back empty. I learned that the artillery crew had beaten off all enemy attacks with hand-grenades and held their battery. They couldn't bring themselves to destroy their favourite guns with their own hands.

—Finally, they blew them up but wouldn't agree to board the launches and stayed on with Osipov's regiment to fight the enemy as infantry men. Captain Kuznetsov, who was in command of the crew, was nominated for the Order of the Red Banner for that fighting, but he never got it. Very soon after he was killed in action. . . .—

The enemy troops continued to advance in the Eastern sector. Having captured new, more convenient, positions they entrenched themselves and opened fire on Soviet warships lying at anchor in the Bay of Odessa.

On August 26, General Petrov concluded from messages he had received by phone from various commanders and from his own observations from his command post that the enemy was preparing for an offensive in his sector on the next day. His division had not enough strength for an effective rebuff to attackers and the absence of reserves was its weakest spot. Petrov was thinking, therefore, of a way to thwart or take the edge off the next enemy offensive before it got under way. His fairly strong artillery, which could rely on the support of coastal defence guns and the Navy, was an effective means of breaking the back of any offensive, but firing at invisible targets at night would hardly score as many hits as necessary. An air raid at night would not be effective enough either, and aircraft were too few in any case. At dawn all these forces would be committed to support the troops in the Eastern sector where the enemy pressure was stiffest.

What was he to do to undermine the enemy's attack plan? General Petrov found a way to deal with that problem, relying on the combat experience of the regiments of his cavalry division. By that time they had already dismounted and were fighting the war as infantry men, but their cavalry mettle was as strong as ever. Petrov decided to take advantage of their fitness for a surprise attack and rapid thrusts behind the enemy lines.

On the night of August 26 when enemy troops were about to move into their attack positions his cavalrymen dealt them a pre-emptive blow. It was fast and resolute, and they descended upon one of the regiments of the Rumanian 14th division. They captured many artillery guns and other weapons, and, most important of all, frustrated the enemy offensive scheduled for the morning.

After a day, however, the enemy troops went over to the offensive, and, as it became clear in the course of attacks, as well as from documents and interrog- ation of prisoners, the 14th division was joined by fresh forces: the 8th, and, after some time, the 21st infantry division. The commitment of such large forces was an obvious sign of the enemy's determination to achieve decisive success. That was confirmed by the prisoners, who testified that Antonescu had demanded a thrust to be made towards the Sukhoi salt lake where artillery could be installed to bombard Odessa and the rear of the Southern sector from the west. Odessa would thus be clamped in pincers of fire.

The enemy troops delivered their main strike at Captain Kovtun's 287th regiment. General Petrov had full confidence in this commander; therefore, expecting an attack in the neighbouring sector, he stayed at the observation post of the right-flank regiment. Petrov saw the 287th regiment repelling repeated enemy attacks. He was in communication with Captain Kovtun by phone all the time.

At the day's end, when the regiment seemed too exhausted to hold the enemy off any more and it was finally clear that the main strike was directed against it, Petrov arrived at its position.

At such critical moments, some commanders encouraged their troops in a loud and confident voice, perhaps by a swear word, and sometimes by a threat. Petrov was different: he supported the spirit of his men by his calmness, respect and desire to help, and by his approval of their actions. He strengthened their confidence in themselves, persuading them that they were remarkable fighters and heroes capable of achieving what was impossible for an ordinary man.

The regiment held its ground on that day as well. Inspecting his units at night, Petrov wondered how they had managed to hold out with so few surviving men. He could see that if the enemy resumed his attacks, there would simply be no one left to oppose them. Therefore, he ordered the regiment to be pulled out for a short rest, perhaps for a couple of days, during which time it could be complemented with whatever manpower was still available. He ordered his cavalrymen to take over the positions. The General acted promptly: the very same lorries that had brought in replacements carried the men of Kovtun's regiment to the rear.

In fact, the 287th regiment was granted only one day and one night to take a rest and, with replacements of men from draft battalions and Odessa volunteers, it restored its fighting fitness. Before long it was back in the firing lines. In that way, General Petrov maintained the fighting strength of his forces by bringing units that seemed knocked out back into the line.

At a difficult moment Army Commander Sofronov arrived at Petrov's command post in the village of Dalnik. Petrov described the situation and indicated the areas of key significance. Presuming that the Army Commander would like to see them at close range and talk to the men in the trenches, he suggested:

"Mukhamedyarov's regiment is right in front of us. We can take a trip there in my pick-up lorry along this valley and then across a little patch of the field."

Stories about Petrov risking danger had already reached the Army Commander's ear. To save time, he avoided long detours regardless of risk, driving across areas exposed to enemy fire. He would stand on the footboard of his truck on the side away from the enemy lines, holding on to the open door, and sped across danger zones. Sofronov recalled those stories and said angrily:

"You are offering me to squat on the footboard just like you do and speed off to tease enemy machine-gunners, aren't you? You know, General, I'm not chicken-hearted, but I won't do that, and I forbid you to risk your life. You know quite well we are short of commanding officers. In your neighbour Vorobyev's division almost all regimental commanders have been killed or disabled. What will happen to your division if you get killed for your bravado? Just because you don't like to make detours. I want to see no more of such escapades. That is an order!"

Petrov looked down and his head jerked nervously. He said apologetically: "It's not bravado, Comrade Commander, but a way to save time. I'm hard pressed for it and have to act promptly. I have an excuse. . . ."

"I don't accept it. You are a divisional commander and must obey the regulations."

Petrov, however, did not change his ways. It was not obstinacy or insubordination. He was a man of discipline. Here, on the battle front, in the heat of fighting when a few minutes sometimes decided the outcome, he knew where and how soon he was needed most. He was an experienced commander, after all, and had a right to do what he thought best.

Staying with a unit fighting a battle, he inspired his men with his presence of mind and equanimity. He constantly followed the enemy moves and no change in the combat situation escaped his vigilant eye. He shared his rich experience with regimental and battalion commanders, teaching them to direct their troops expertly right on the spot, when fighting was in progress.

General Petrov's remarkable prowess as a military officer was seen in details that seemed of little significance at first glance. In fact, he risked his life only when he could not help it. He was not, of course, in the heat of a battle at all times but only during critical hours. Aware of the need for a clear mind to deal with the rapid change of events on a battlefield, he took good care of his physical fitness. He knew that his presence alone was not enough for his troops.

One day, when the tension of fighting was high, Colonel Krylov, who was now Chief of Staff of the Maritime Army, arrived at Petrov's command post. He had expected to see a tired and nervous man afflicted with battle fatigue after so many days of continuous fighting. To his pleasant surprise the General, who had come out to meet him, was the very picture of health. His face was well-shaven and even rosy as though after a good hot shower. Petrov smiled:

"I've taken a bath. One has to be inventive in war. I've found an old iron washing trough and bathe whenever I have a couple of minutes to spare. It makes me feel like a new man, I can tell you."

He took out a map and spread it out before Krylov.

"The enemy has captured Leninthal and has driven a deep wedge between our 31st and 287th infantry regiments. I'm worried by this new danger. I've attempted to deal with it by regaining our ground and linking up the regiment flanks as before, but we have yet to make it. The enemy has entrenched himself, taking advantage of our old trenches and digging new ones. They have many mortars and automatic firearms. This wedge contains at least two regiments of infantry, and reinforcements keep coming in. In case of an enemy thrust towards the Sukhoi salt lake, my left flank defended by Mukhamedyarov's regiment will be cut off. This wedge may cause a lot of trouble. I know it quite well. We've done our best to dislodge the enemy, but even night attacks, which were effective in the past, have so far been futile."

Krylov realized that the Chapayev division was in a fix. Petrov's words carried a hint: he wanted the 3rd regiment of the Chapayev division back. But the situation in the Eastern sector was just as precarious.

"We can't restore your regiment to you now. It's out of the question."

"I can see that. I'm not asking for it."

"But we can help you with replacements from draft units and volunteers of Odessa. The city supports us whenever we ask for aid and men. They have no arms, however. Could you give them weapons here, on the spot?"

"We will."

The cruiser *Chervona Ukraina* released 720 members of her crew who had volunteered to fight on the ground, and they joined battle immediately. There was another bit of good news: 5,000 draft replacements had sailed from Novorossiisk and were on their way to Odessa. But would they make it and arrive before it was too late? The situation was critical. Enemy troops were within a few miles of Peresyp, and the front line could now be reached by a tram. A force of 5,000 was coming to replace the casualties. On August 29, a total of 1,200 Soviet defenders were wounded and put out of action, and that in one day only!

Reinforcements came in good time, on the morning of August 30. Their arrival had been eagerly expected, particularly in the Eastern sector. Although its defenders were straining themselves to the limit, reinforcements could not be fed into that sector alone, since troops in other sectors were also fighting against overwhelming odds, and another enemy onslaught was to be expected anywhere. Therefore, the new arrivals were enlisted in the 95th, cavalry and Chapayev divisions. Their coming was very well timed, because the fate of Odessa was hanging by a thread and could be sealed in a matter of hours. These were well-trained and fighting-fit reinforcements who had come from the "mainland". Their arrival inspired the defenders of Odessa with new confidence, that the city was not isolated or abandoned but linked with the rest of the country.

Ignoring their losses, which were enormous, the enemy forces were making desperate efforts to take Odessa. They were bringing up reserves and trying new forms of combat. Early in September, to avoid well-aimed fire of Soviet artillery, they also resorted to night action, not without success, and advanced closer to the city by a few miles. Aided by its neighbours, Petrov's division attempted to push the enemy backwards but its units were now too heavily depleted, and their counter-attacks bogged down.

The city was in grave danger. There was no strength left to stave it off. The defenders of Odessa had exhausted their resources. The command of the Odessa defence district reported the crisis to General Headquarters and the Front Military Council.

September 1941

The battalions of the infantry regiments of the Chapayev division had an average of fifty men left on their strength. Whoever had been in the rear before that, including staff officers, went into the firing lines. With two machine-guns mounted on his pick-up lorry, General Petrov now and then hastened to an area where an enemy breakthrough was imminent. The situation seemed hopeless.

In the late hours of September 13, Petrov reported to the Army Commander that his 31st regiment on the left flank faced the threat of encirclement. The Army Commander was silent for a while and finally asked him:

"Have you got any suggestions to make?"

"We have to give something up. I request your authorization to withdraw our left flank to the line of the Sukhoi salt lake. That will shorten the front line, and I'll be able to hold it for some time. The fire of our supporting artillery and coastal guns will be more effective."

Sofronov did not object and said, as though musing aloud:

"But that would make the city open to enemy fire from the south as well. Our ships won't be able to enter Odessa's harbour in broad daylight since it will be within the range of enemy observation and artillery. And the enemy will get closer to the city in general. . . ."

Nevertheless, Sofronov agreed with him, so on September 14 Petrov pulled back his troops to a new defence line where they could stiffen their resistance.

On the next day a message from Moscow brought news of crucial significance for Odessa's defenders:

—Convey the request of the High Command to the officers and men defending Odessa to hold on for another six or seven days, during which time they will receive aircraft and armed troop reinforcements.

Joseph Stalin.—

General Petrov and the divisional commander A. S. Stepanov went out of their way to make that message known to every serviceman. They explained to them that the High Command highly appreciated their staunchness and realized that they no longer had enough strength to resist the onslaught of vastly superior enemy forces. Therefore, it was not an order but an appeal. They were asked to make another superhuman effort and hold their ground for another week at most. Reinforcements were on their way. The General Headquarters had promised relief, and it would make good its promise.

The fact that it was not an order but an appeal greatly impressed the defending troops. It made them feel stronger. All were eager to live up to the faith of the High Command in their prowess. And they accomplished what was impossible to accomplish by any conventional standards. They firmly stood their ground on the same lines during the next week and held the enemy in check as the High Command had requested.

The High Command did not fail them. The 157th infantry division was fresh, brought up to establishment and well trained. Its men boarded transports in the port of Novorossiisk and sailed off to Odessa.

Following through planning and preparation of an offensive strike in the Eastern sector Soviet troops went into the assault on the morning of September 22 to recover positions lost to the enemy in the area of the villages of Dofinovka and Alexandrovka and to dislodge enemy artillery from its vantage points at the Greater Adjalyk salt lake, from where it could keep the city and harbour under fire. The 421st infantry division recently formed in the Eastern sector was attacking at the right flank to facilitate and press forward the success of the initial thrust.

At 0300 hours, to dawn, a few hours before the counter-strike of the 157th division, General Petrov's units in the Southern sector had launched a counter-attack between Dalnik and the Sukhoi salt lake. They aimed to distract the enemy troops and hold them pinned down here in the Southern sector and perhaps to force them to commit their reserves, which they succeeded in doing, as later fighting would prove.

The 3rd regiment of the Marines landed near the village of Grigoryevka and made a thrust across the enemy rear towards Alexandrovka and Chebanovka to link up with the attacking forces. By its operations in the enemy rear this regiment greatly assisted the units attacking from the front. The regiment had been formed by the headquarters of the Black Sea Fleet of forces sent in from Sevastopol. The landing had been effected under the command of Rear Admiral L. A. Vladimirsky and, after his disablement by wounding, by Rear Admiral S. G. Gorshkov.

Towards the day's end the 157th and 421st divisions had fulfilled their offensive tasks, hurling the enemy backwards by more than ten kilometres.

Faithful to its pledge of aid to the besieged city of Odessa, the High Command sent in not only a regular divison and draft companies. On September 23 the transport *Chapayev* arrived at Odessa's harbour from Novorossiisk, carrying on board a new secret weapon nobody had ever known or heard of here before. It had been planned to test the new weapon on the Southern Front, and General Petrov's sector was chosen as the best site for its trials. "Katusha" rocket launchers, as they were then called, were secretly brought to their fire positions and carefully guarded. Members of the Military Council of the Odessa Defence District led by Rear Admiral Zhukov arrived at General Petrov's command post to watch the new weapon in action.

All preparations had been completed at night. At dawn enemy troops went onto the assault. Petrov had waited until the attacking lines became clearly visible and then said to the Army Chief of Artillery, Colonel Ryzhi:

"I think it is time, Colonel."

Ryzhi responded with a loud

"Guards, fire!"

There was a hissing and screeching behind the Soviet lines, then clouds of smoke shot up into the air, and blazing missiles flew out of these clouds and hurtled towards the attacking lines. They hit them accurately and exploded in blinding bursts of flame with a deafening noise. When the smoke had lifted, only a few survivors fleeing in panic were seen in the distance.

Thus, in September 1941, the enemy troops confronting General Petrov's division witnessed the formidable firepower of rocket launchers, which had first been used in July of the same year in the fighting for Orsha and were destined to open a new chapter in the theory and practice of warfare.

The Soviet Information Bureau announced in its communiqué of September 24, 1941:

"In the course of a successful operation of Soviet troops in the Odessa area the Rumanian forces suffered severe casualties in manpower and weapons. The total Rumanian losses in dead, wounded and prisoners of war amount to 5,000–6,000 officers and men, the dead accounting for 2,000. By tentative estimates the Soviet forces have captured 33 pieces of artillery of different calibres, of which a few are long-range heavy guns, 6 tanks, 2,000 rifles, 110 machine-guns, 30 mortars, 130 machine pistols, 4,000 shells, 15,000 mines, a large number of crates with rifles and hand grenades. . . ."

That was a truly great success, a great victory for the defenders of Odessa.

The Army Commander Sofronov contemplated another counterthrust to be effected by the forces of General Petrov's division and the 157th division, which would be moved into his sector. This would be a more forceful attack with the arrival of the 422nd howitzer regiment of the 157th division and its 141st reconnaissance battalion, which had 15 tanks. Both units had been on their way to join their division moved in earlier. In addition, 36 draft companies were brought into reinforce the Maritime Army.

General Petrov with his staff and his devoted aides worked round the clock, planning this counterblow and finalizing the details of co-operation between various units to secure the success of their joint action, to lend great momentum to their offensive and inflict a decisive defeat on the enemy in the Southern sector. He anticipated the powerful effect of the new secret weapon as well: the "Katusha" rocket battalion was to help him in the "softening-up" of the enemy defences.

All preparations were completed and Soviet troops were poised for attack which was scheduled for October 2. On October 1, however, Vice Admiral Gordei Levchenko, Deputy People's Commissar for the Navy, arrived in

Odessa from Sevastopol. He brought information about the developments on the other battle fronts and an order from General Headquarters, which radically changed the life of Odessa's defenders.

October 1941

In the days of writing this chapter, I often phoned Gordei Levchenko, hoping to learn the details of that event. Unfortunately, he was very ill and unable to have a discussion with me. Now he is dead. Therefore, I rely on Admiral I. Azarov's story about the conference of the Military Council of the Odessa Defence District on October 1.

—Vice Admiral Levchenko briefly described the situation:

—Under strong enemy pressure the units of the 51st Army have retreated to the line of the village of Ishun. Dependable fortifications are, in effect, non-existent there, and the danger of enemy invasion of the Crimea is real. If we lose the Crimea, we may lose Odessa as well, since it would be almost impossible to bring supplies to Odessa from the Caucasus with the Crimean airfields in enemy hands. The Fleet Military Council has informed General Headquarters of this situation and submitted its proposals. . . .

—While the fighting for the Crimea is going on at Perekop, there is a chance to pull troops out of Odessa into the Crimea and reinforce its defences. As the Fleet Military Council has reported to General Headquarters, the loss of Odessa would be the lesser evil, if we manage to keep the Crimea. The Council's proposal for Odessa's evacuation and moving troops to the Crimea has been accepted by General Headquarters. Our task now is to find the best way to fulfill its directive."

—"But isn't it too early to talk of our evacuation?" Rear Admiral Zhukov asked quietly.

"Evidently, if the Crimea is lost, it would be senseless to hold on to Odessa", Voronin argued.

"The danger of losing the Crimea is not yet its surrender", said Kolybanov, secretary of the Odessa Regional Party Committee and Military Council member. "Odessa has more than once been on the brink of falling, yet we are still fighting on. . . ."—

Indeed, it was a disappointment to withdraw from Odessa on the eve of a prepared offensive to be carried out by strong battle-wise troops that had proved their endurance. So much blood had been shed for that city. The people of Odessa lived in the hope that our army would soon put the invaders to flight. And now it had to be abandoned. That was very hard to accept.

Vice Admiral Azarov asked:

—"Is the situation in the Crimea so hopeless and its loss inevitable?"

—"It's very bad indeed. I've been at Perekop and in the Ishun area. I must tell you frankly that with our forces in the Crimea there is no hope of holding on to the Ishun line. The loss of the Crimea will entail the loss of Odessa. Our

sea lanes will be constantly under air attacks. The enemy air force will
promptly take advantage of the Crimean airfields. It's a tragedy that we have
no forces there to contain the enemy. . . . The 51st Army cannot do it. . . .

—I want to make it clear to you: the Front Military Council has already
reported to General Headquarters that the 51st Army is very hard pressed,
and its troops are retreating towards Ishun where no dependable fortifications are available. They can be reinforced only with troops from Odessa. I
think the decision of General Headquarters is the best under the circumstances.—"

Lieutenant General Sofronov was instructed to draw up a plan of troop
withdrawals from the defence sectors and gradual evacuation of Odessa. The
plan of evacuation was to be endorsed by the Military Council and the
evacuation was to start on October 1.

Nevertheless, the Maritime Army Commander resolved to deliver the
counterblow prepared in Petrov's sector. Now this attack pursued a different
purpose. Formerly it had been planned to drive the enemy troops off as far
south as possible to stop their bombardment of the city and harbour. Now
this strike was to keep them at bay and to cover the withdrawal of troops
from Odessa. It was to mislead the enemy and enable Soviet troops to be
pulled out from their positions for embarkation on ships.

The strength of the forces taking part in that counterblow was, of course,
smaller now. It had been decided to evacuate Tomilov's 157th division,
which was the best in fighting capability, in the first place and move it to the
Crimea where reinforcements were needed desperately. Only the 384th
regiment of Colonel Sotskov was left with General Petrov's troops.

The Army Commander issued his orders to Petrov to launch that risky
offensive at a difficult time for all Soviet defenders. The necessity to abandon
Odessa which had been defended so stubbornly and could be held much
longer was an ugly reality to which it was hard to adapt. The planned
counterblow was also a very risky venture, since attacking troops could be
bogged down in fighting and fail to break off for evacuation under the
pressure of enemy forces which outnumbered them many times over.

When Petrov arrived at the Army HQ, he heard more tragic news. General
Sofronov had just received a telegram informing him of the death of his eldest
son, who had been killed in action near Moscow. Sofronov took it with
courage. He even promised to come to Petrov's command post in the morning
when the attack was to begin. However, the misfortunes of that day proved
too much for him. At night he had several heart attacks which ended in a
thrombosis.

On the morning of October 2, after a 20-minute artillery preparation and
devastating salvoes of Katusha rocket launchers, the Chapayev division with
a regiment from the 157th division went onto the attack. They carried the
enemy before them. The tankmen were real dare devils. Senior Lieutenant
Yudin who was in command of a battalion of home-made tanks—armoured

tractors—led his machines in a fast forward thrust and pursued the fleeing enemy until they had left Soviet infantry far behind. It was too dangerous, of course, for such "tanks" to get too far from the infantry units supporting them. The tankmen turned back so as not to get into trouble. But they did not return empty-handed. Having dispersed enemy gun crews and infantry, they captured twenty-four guns of various calibres, and were now hauling them back to their lines as war trophies.

Petrov was happy and sad at the same time:

—"Drat, if we had not lessened the momentum of our strike, we could have driven them off from Odessa by some thirty kilometres. Too bad that many who were to take part in this attack had to withdraw at the last minute. But we have taught the enemy a lesson anyway!"—

The immediate task had been fulfilled and some gaps had formed between units—some were lagging behind, while others had burst too far ahead to prepare for another strike. The forces of the two sides, however, were unequal. In fact, the 25th division was fighting against overwhelming odds. Having recovered from the first stunning blow, the enemy put up a stiff resistance and later went over to active operations.

The Chapayev division, however, was now firmly entrenched and would not budge an inch under mounting enemy attacks.

A New Appointment

Now that Lieutenant General Sofronov was disabled by his heart failure, the Military Council took a decision to appoint Major General Petrov as Commander of the Maritime Army. On October 5, he took over his new duties. On that day he began his war record as a high-ranking military commander.

As Commander of the Maritime Army, General Petrov not only had all its troops under his command and wider operational control—he was now facing larger enemy forces and a higher-ranking opponent as his opposite number.

In the Soviet Union quite a few books are in print written by generals about the war or their own war records. Unfortunately, little was written about enemy generals, and whenever they came into the field of vision they were commonly described with contempt or even in a grotesque light. I believe this is wrong, because a serious discussion of the war requires a serious and objective attitude to the enemy and its generals.

In the area of Odessa the Rumanian 4th Army was deployed against Soviet forces. Its Commander Cepurke G. Nicolae was not always independent in planning combat operations. That was done by General Antonescu, since in 1941 the Odessa area was the main battlefield for the Rumanian Army.

What kind of man was Antonescu from the military point of view? He was not, of course, the light-minded, almost comical hero of an operetta, as he was depicted in wartime newspapers. In a fight the rivals may shout at each other and use insults and harsh language. A fight is a fight. A historical analysis, however, requires objectivity, a calm assessment of personalities and their actions.

Ion Antonescu was born in 1882, that is he was 59 during the Battle of Odessa. He was a typical military officer—strong and rather tall, with a proud bearing and impressive appearance, a steady gaze and grey temples. He was, of course, a man of strong willpower and had a flexible mind, those qualities that brought him to the top in the power structure of the state. Small wonder, therefore, that the kings, both the old and the young one, obeyed him, not without some trepidation.

Antonescu was born into a family where several generations of his ancestors had been career military officers. In 1902 he entered a cavalry school and in July 1904 he was commissioned as a junior Lieutenant. In 1907 he took part in punitive operations against peasant insurgents in Moldavia. In those punitive raids more than 11,000 peasants were shot dead and many villages burned down. As we can see, his life path became outlined early.

When World War I broke out, Antonescu was serving at the Rumanian Army Staff with the rank of Captain. In 1919 he took part in the military intervention against the Hungarian Soviet Republic. He was commandant of a military school for four years. He also wrote a few works on strategy and tactics based on the experience of the First World War. Antonescu served as military attaché in different countries at various times. In 1933 he was Chief of the General Staff. In 1937 he became Minister of National Defence. Antonescu was close to the fascist organization "The Iron Guard" and did not conceal it.

At the court trial of Codrianu, one of the leaders of the Rumanian fascists, the judge asked Antonescu, who was a witness: "Is it possible that Codrianu has committed high treason?"—Antonescu came up to the defendant, shook his hand and exclaimed: "I would never have shaken a traitor's hand!"

That theatrical gesture of "nobleness" showed how much Antonescu was confident of his strong position. King Mihai was young, and Antonescu wielded real power in the state; he was in control of the army and government and had, in fact, relegated the King to the background, handling the affairs of state on his own. The King obediently signed whatever decrees Antonescu drafted. In September 1940, for instance, King Mihai signed a decree abolishing the Constitution and dissolving Parliament. "General Ion Antonescu has been empowered to rule the state", the decree said.

That, of course, had been preceded by a tug-of-war between various parties and forces inside and outside Rumania. The decree summed up its results and, in effect, legalized the fascist dictatorship. The Führer of the Rumanian fascists of "The Iron Guard", Horia Sima, also entered the new cabinet. The relations between Antonescu, Sima and Hitler were far from simple. Just as in other countries of Europe, Hitler relied on his "fifth column" to install the local fascists in power. He planned to do that in Rumania as well, and the ring-leader of "The Iron Guard", Sima, was a faithful and dependable stooge of the Nazis.

In a letter to Sima of December 5, 1940, Himmler addressed him as follows: "Esteemed Parteigenosse Horia Sima: . . ." This expression of Nazi fellowship was followed by a discussion of business matters, that left no doubt about the identity of Sima's true masters.

I keep a photo of those years. Even an instant of the past retained in a picture for posterity has much to tell. Here it is.

Antonescu and Sima are standing side by side. They are dressed in stormtroopers' uniform— brown shirts without insignia, broad army waist and shoulder belts. Sima is short, with a sunken chest, his sleek black hair combed back neatly, which makes him look like Goebbels.

Antonescu has changed from his ornate attire of a General into a brown shirt: why not look tougher in a power struggle!

Huge figures of Hitler's Generals are seen towering behind their backs, a head taller than their Rumanian cronies. It's a symbolic scene. A more graphic illustration of Rumania's prewar position is hard to imagine.

Antonescu's face is averted from Sima's and he is looking away. This pose is also meaningful. Antonescu had joined up with the Iron Guard, it is true, but he would not think of surrendering his powers to them. He was eager to be a Führer himself. Hitler knew it all too well, but he badly needed Rumanian oil to keep his Panzer and Luftwaffe armadas on the move.

Hitler could wait for one of the rivals to knock the other one out. Moreover, a fight between them would cause a row between the parties backing them up, riots might flare up in the country at a time when Hitler had his forces poised for war.

Understanding Antonescu's intentions and his influence as a leader relying on the support of the military and unwilling to share his power with anybody, Hitler sacrificed his like-minded junior partner Sima and chose to collaborate with Antonescu. The "noble" General Antonescu suppressed those unwilling to obey him and became, in fact, the Führer of Rumania in his own right, as well as Hitler's faithful servant.

As for Sima, the Nazis brought him to Austria, where he was "interned" near the small town of Wiener Neustadt and kept him in reserve as a menace to Antonescu: whenever the latter showed disobedience, he was reminded of Sima, his stand-by double.

On November 23, 1940, Rumania officially acceded to the Berlin Pact of military alliance, which was known at the time as the Berlin-Rome-Tokyo Axis. Rumanian territory was used to prepare a spring-board for an attack on the Soviet Union: airfields were built, ports were re-equipped, and second railway tracks were laid. Hitler initiated Antonescu into his Barbarossa Plan of conquest of the USSR.

Here is another photo: Hitler and Antonescu are bending over a map, the

Führer enthusiastically explaining his strategic plans. On June 22, 1941, Antonescu unhesitatingly pronounced this fatal phrase: "I order my forces to cross the River Prut!" That order was published in all newspapers, and the sunrise on that morning was welcomed with the tolling of church bells and a divine service in honour of the coming victory.

That was the General who was opposing Petrov and the Command of the Odessa Defence District as a whole.

The Evacuation Plan

Late at night on October 6, Rear Admiral Zhukov assembled the divisional commanders and political commissars as well as the commanding officers of separate units to brief them on the evacuation plan.

This plan was a subject of debates not only when it was drawn up and endorsed but in the postwar period as well, both in literature and in conversation.

In fact, there were two different plans: the one drawn up by Sofronov before he became disabled and the other implemented by Petrov. The argument focused not only on which of the two was better, but also on who was the man who had carried out the evacuation so brilliantly.

It is a maxim current among military men that a decision that leads to victory is correct. Both evacuation plans were correct, each for its own situation, with sea-going transport on hand, which was of crucial importance. General Sofronov had been promised ships to carry his troops and he had expected to pull them out of Odessa gradually, 5 to 6 transports taking a load of men and equipment every night.

. . . Life is full of surprises. One of them awaited me when my manuscript was submitted to the Institute of Military History under the USSR Ministry of Defence. The person who was to examine it was Vancetti Sofronov, the son of General Georgy Sofronov, Commander of the Maritime Army in wartime.

Since he was most familiar with the events of the Battles of Odessa and Sevastopol he was requested to review my manuscript. He did that competently and supplied me with new material for this book: his father's published and unpublished reminiscences.

I take advantage of his courtesy to give here General Sofronov's own account of his work on the evacuation plan and its essential difference from General Petrov's plan:

—"Now let us size up our transportation facilities", Zhukov said and got down to making a list of transport that could be used for troop evacuation. Azarov helped him.

—They read and supplemented the list several times and then Zhukov handed it to me.

"—Here's a list of vessels for you to draft the evacuation plan."

—I withdrew to my office and set about planning a retreat to successive rear lines to allow our divisions to pull out of battle and evacuate by sea.

—Now four of our divisions were deployed along a frontline of 65 km. Two divisions left alone on this line were not enough to check the enemy, so it had to be shortened by retreating to the second line lying across Kryzhanovka, Usatovo, Tatarka, and the Sukhoi salt lake. That line was 40 km. long, of which 15 km. ran across salt lakes, a natural obstacle to attackers. Two infantry divisions could hold out there, however briefly.

—I considered several choices in my head before making up my mind: This was a new problem. I was not familiar with it even in theory.

—I proposed that we avoid a battle within city limits to spare civilians the horrors of street fighting. The enemy had a few hundred guns and mortars to keep the city under fire for a few days, long enough to reduce it to ruins. Explosions would start fires, and the whole city would soon be ablaze. Of its 300,000 residents tens of thousands might be killed or wounded or trapped under collapsed house walls.

—In my plan our last two divisions were to withdraw from the second line of defence and promptly embark on ships. There would be just enough space to accommodate the men, so the horses would have to be abandoned, and part of the motor vehicles and even artillery destroyed lest they fall into the enemy hands. That would cost us less than the city's destruction and civilian casualties. No breathing space is long enough before death, as the Russian saying goes, so it did not matter much if we abandoned Odessa three days later or three days earlier as long as we had resolved to surrender it.

—Zhukov remarked: "I have no objections to your plan, General. I hope we won't have to destroy our vehicles, not to speak of artillery, however. We'll petition with Admiral Oktyabrsky for more transport to carry them."

—I did not have to wrack my brains over the evacuation plan any more. Before long I suffered a thrombosis and was taken to Sevastopol on October 5.—

General Petrov was worried. The evacuation order might affect the morale of Soviet troops at a critical time when staunchness mattered most. Some might wonder why their company or battalion should hold on to their positions and fight to the last ditch when a general retreat was inevitable anyway. To make matters worse, the enemy launched another general offensive on October 9.

Prisoners captured on that day testified that new units had arrived to bolster enemy forces. They were under orders to make a determined effort to break into the city's suburbs.

Would our depleted units be capable of holding the front? It was more likely that the enemy would smash the first echelon, overtake the retreating troops and swoop down upon the embarkation sites.

In the new situation the initial plan of staged retreat was no good any more. General Petrov and his staff, therefore, came forward with a different plan: to pull out all forces at once, board the ships quickly and sail off before the enemy realized what was going on. That was a hazardous plan, of course, and required every move to be scheduled to the minute. The enemy was to be misled ingeniously lest our simultaneous retreat be discovered too early and end in catastrophe.

The new plan was opposed by Rear Admiral Zhukov, Commander of the Odessa Defence District. He was strongly in favour of Sofronov's plan, which, in addition, had been approved by the High Command.

Petrov argued that the evacuation could not be kept a secret for long, and information about it would soon leak to the enemy anyway. By an all-out attack the enemy would overrun the positions of the covering units and would soon be on the back of the embarking troops. The covering units had too few men to fight off the enemy's twenty divisions concentrated at Odessa. These would break towards the harbour and then the retreating troops would have to fight for their lives.

Petrov insisted on his plan and finally persuaded the Command of the Odessa Defence District to accept it. When it was reported to the Commander of the Black Sea Fleet, Vice Admiral Oktyabrsky, the latter raised strong objections to it and insisted on the initial plan.

General Petrov knew only too well that the Commander and Military Council of the Fleet had strong misgivings about reporting to General Headquarters that simultaneous evacuation was the best way of retreat under the circumstances, because their message radioed only two days ago had set out a different plan with a schedule and order of staged evacuation.

They might not yet be fully aware of the change in the situation, which was the chief motive for changing plans. Petrov hoped they would finally realize that. Thousands of lives were in danger after all, and troops were needed in the Crimea urgently. His plan would help to do just that.

Major General Krylov, already known to the reader, had a part to play in approving the new plan of evacuating Odessa. Here is the account he gave me in conversation:

—On the morning of October 10, I was summoned by Rear Admiral Zhukov to see him on a matter of urgency. As soon as I was in his office, he told me: "It's hard to prove that the new plan is realistic speaking over the radio. The Military Council requests you to go to Sevastopol at once and report all the details to Vice Admiral Oktyabrsky personally."

—Next morning I was on the Admiral's flagship and speaking to him. He listened to my arguments carefully but hesitated to take a decision. And small wonder. The price to be paid for an error in haste would be very dear.

—I believe it was by no means easy to revise the plans and schedules of troop movements, of loading and unloading numerous transports. "Discuss your proposals with the Fleet Chief of Staff", the Admiral said.

—I went to the Chief of Staff Yeliseyev and discussed the new plan with him and Kulakov, member of the Fleet Military Council. My arguments and calculations were accepted with understanding, though as staff officers they knew that would mean a lot of new hard work at a time when every minute counted.

—Then all three of us went back to Admiral Oktyabrsky. He listened to our arguments and then said to Kulakov: "You should go to Odessa yourself and find out the situation on the spot. Your report to the Military Council will be needed for the final decision. The Fleet Staff should work on the new plan without delay regardless of whether or not it will be implemented."

—That was the end of my mission, Khrenov concluded.—

On the next day Divisional Commissar Kulakov was in Odessa. In a matter of two or three hours he discussed the situation with quite a few officers and learned all the details. A man of decision and strong will-power, invariably cheerful and friendly, Kulakov was very popular among Odessa defenders, especially among Navy men. He was widely regarded, so people were frank with him. His judgement quickly changed in favour of the new plan. General Petrov and Rear Admiral Zhukov persuaded him completely.

Kulakov radioed a message to Admiral Oktyabrsky. After some time the Admiral radioed back his consent to troop withdrawal in one echelon and embarkation on the night of October 16.

The nasty weather seemed to have set the stage for the city's sad parting with its defenders. The sunny autumn with leaves rustling under the feet, which did not fall off by themselves in this season but were knocked down by numerous bomb and shell explosions, the blue sky with occasional fleecy clouds now gave way to a cold spell and the sky was overcast with an ominous leaden haze. A chilling wind was blowing and the streets were deserted.

Yet that stillness was deceptive. Odessa was preparing to carry on its fight against the invaders after all troops had been withdrawn. Partisan units and scout teams were being formed and weapons and ammunition were being stored in secret depots. Army engineers led by General Khrenov and Colonel Kedrinsky were busy preparing some big surprises for the conquerors once they had invaded the city. Those were some of the new radio-controlled mines used in the war.

General Petrov was involved in that operation, too. In January 1981 I visited Colonel General Khrenov and heard his story of that curious episode of the Battle of Odessa:

—The biggest charge was laid under a building on Marazlievskaya Street, which, as we expected, the invaders would choose for their headquarters, Khrenov told me.—The effect of the blast depended on its accurate timing. It was important not simply to destroy the enemy headquarters but to trap the highest-ranking officers assembled there. For that we needed an efficient agent left in the city, who would find out about some large gathering of enemy generals and promptly report it to us.

—In August I had reported to Moscow that we had no plans of the catacombs and that local executives could not find anybody familiar with them enough to help us. I desperately needed a plan for laying mines at the most vital spots.

—A few days later a young man in civilian clothes came to see me. He identified himself as Vladimir Badayev, Captain of the State Security Service. He had flown in from Moscow along with two Odessa natives who knew every corner in the catacombs under the city.

—I would later learn of his posthumous decoration with the Gold Star of Hero of the Soviet Union. His true name was Molodtsov.—

... On October 22, when Generals Petrov and Khrenov were already at Sevastopol, they received a radio message from Badayev about the time of a conference planned by the enemy top brass in the building on Marazlievskaya Street. At the right moment Khrenov ordered a coded signal to be radioed to set off the explosive device installed in the cellar under the building.

The explosion was so powerful that the building collapsed burying some 50 generals and high-ranking officers under its ruins.

Visiting Rumania in 1981, I met a Rumanian ex-pilot, George Coman. He was about 70 but still in good shape, lean and lively. He was an engineer in an organization doing some business with their Soviet counterparts and made occasional business trips to the USSR.

As he was telling me of his wartime experiences in the Battle of Odessa and the situation in the city after the withdrawal of Soviet troops, he suddenly exclaimed:

"Do you know of the great surprise your saboteurs sprang on our High Command? Our generals set up their headquarters in the biggest and finest building on Marazlievskaya Street. Seized with euphoria, they had neglected to have its cellars searched for mines, and paid for that with their lives."

"There was a tremendous explosion which shook the whole city."

"Did you see it?"

"I wouldn't have been standing and talking with you now if I had. I only heard a deafening bang. I ran to the headquarters and saw an enormous crater in its place with ruins and debris on all sides. A few dozen generals who were in conference had been killed."

October 15, 1941

By October 15, the transports *Chapayev, Kalinin, Vostok, Abkhazia, Armenia, Ukraina*, and a few others had cast anchor at Odessa harbour. A sham scene of disembarking reinforcements was played on the landing piers with convoys of vehicles covered with tarpaulin imitating their movements into the areas behind the units deployed on the front line. Radio stations were on the air, transmitting messages from non-existent fresh units.

Early in the morning when an artillery duel began as usual, Soviet gunners laid a devastating barrage on the enemy forward positions and then lifted fire to give it depth. The barrage was so effective that the enemy batteries fell silent for a time. During the day Soviet artillery kept firing at enemy batteries and infantry positions. Methodical fire was occasionally followed by a brief barrage to hold the enemy in trenches and in constant tension.

At 16:00 hours the Military Council of the Odessa Defence District came on board the cruiser *Chervona Ukraina* riding at anchor on the quayside. At 17:00 hours Petrov and Krylov with the operations group of the Army Staff arrived at the naval base headquarters. The Navy placed their communication facilities at his disposal and linked them to the army field lines, so the generals could control troop withdrawals from their battle positions into the harbour.

Despite intensive Soviet fire, the enemy command suspected that something was going wrong. The 31st regiment of the 25th division and the 161st regiment of the 95th division were suddenly attacked exactly when they had started to pull out. Their commanders immediately suspended the withdrawals and repelled the attack. The attackers suffered tangible losses and backed down, and the defenders resumed their retreat.

Enemy aircraft bombed the transports anchored in the harbour but, fortunately, missed all their targets but one, the motorship *Georgia* converted to a hospital ship. She was hit by a bomb and caught fire, but it was soon put out and 2,000 wounded men were transferred to other ships. The *Georgia* was later towed to Sevastopol.

When it grew dark, battle troops started arriving at the landing sites. Petrov looked at the men who had been fighting for Odessa so long and so tenaciously, and his eyes were sad. His heart went out to them. He loved these people and respected them. But he was worried and his nerves were at a breaking point. If the enemy attacked them now with all his enormous forces while they were in columns on the march a disaster would be inevitable. The enemy, however, was evidently unaware of the deadline for the Soviet retreat and was biding his time. It was not unlikely that the enemy command, who had by now learned their lesson when their large forces suffered ignominious defeats even at the hands of even scant and undermanned units of the Maritime Army, concluded that these movements looking like a retreat were intended to lead them into a trap.

As soon as the rearguard battalions got under way, Soviet artillery and coastal guns intensified fire. They were to unleash their full fire power the enemy and spend all ammunition, down to the last shell. Then the guns had to be blown up.

Soviet warships moored close by kept firing, too. It was about 2 hours after midnight when the rearguard troops started to embark on transports and warships. The trenches they had abandoned, however, were not empty. Reconnaissance and partisan units took over their positions and were firing at the enemy with all their machine-guns and rifles to create the impression of a full-scale battle going on.

Here is General Petrov's eyewitness account of the last hours of the Battle of Odessa.

TC—E

—On October 15, after sunset, the mass of the Soviet forces noiselessly pulled out of their positions, drew up ranks and headed for the harbour. Some two hours later the covering units left to maintain rifle, machine-gun and mortar fire along the front line also retreated quietly under the cover of night and marched towards the embarkation sites. Only groups of reconnaissance men were left in the trenches to imitate battle activity. After midnight, however, they also arrived at the harbour on vehicles left in hiding near their positions.

—On the night of October 16 the waterfront was a busy scene of troops streaming in from all neighbouring streets and lanes and boarding ships lying alongside the piers. Although complete silence had been ordered, the water-front was literally swarming with men so that noise and the hubbub of voices were unavoidable. The personnel of the naval base were a model of efficiency. There were a couple of funny accidents. Two awkward troopers fell into the water but were quickly rescued by seamen. Some stragglers were wandering over the piers in search of their units. For all that the embarkation was completed on time.—

The embarkation was coming to an end when German aircraft appeared over the harbour. At first two reconnaissance planes came and dropped a few bombs. A warehouse caught fire. Fires also flared up in two or three other spots. The blaze brightly lit the entire harbour zone. A group of six or eight enemy planes soon raided the harbour but failed to score many hits.

By 4 o'clock in the morning more than 40 ships had taken their full load of men and weapons and set sail for their destination in the Crimea. Warships riding at anchor on the quayside with the cruiser *Krasny Kavkaz* as their flagship provided air defence for the evacuating troops. They were prepared to support them with their long-range artillery if the enemy moved in closer.

When the ships carrying the main forces were ready to sail off General Petrov was offered the best submarine chaser and a high-speed launch for added security to take him and his staff officers away. He declined to leave until he knew that the last trooper was safely on his way. It was only after the last ships had put to sea that Petrov, Military Council member Kuznetsov and Chief of Staff Krylov accompanied by his operations group boarded their craft. She slowly sailed along off the coast as they watched sadly the blown-up piers and port facilities, equipment reduced to scrap iron, lonely horses abandoned for the shortage of space, and fires still going on here and there.

Petrov was standing near the deckhouse when enemy aircraft attacked their ship. A Junkers-87 dive-bomber swooped down accurately and low on its target, and he could see a black bomb sliding off its belly and speeding down relentlessly. By a deft manoeuvre, however, the captain steered the ship to avoid a hit at the last instant. The bomb missed the ship by a hair's-breadth and fell into the sea, splashing the deck with water. The plane came back and dived again and again but each time the captain proved too fast for its bombs.

It was not until they made sure that no stragglers had been left behind that they headed for the harbour exit and caught up with the other warships. Petrov went over on board the cruiser *Chervona Ukraina*. All day long the ships were on their way in the direction of the Crimea. Enemy aircraft attacked them several times but failed to cause much damage. The ship anti-aircraft fought back and held them at bay.

Once they had come ashore at the Sevastopol naval base, Petrov was met by Rear Admiral Zhukov. He congratulated the Army Commander on his successful operation. Petrov briefly described the last events on the high seas:

—Many ships came under air attack, but only one transport was lost. She was late and sailing empty. Her crew was rescued. The last few ships were now coming in. You can be sure the whole Maritime Army had made it. Now the Crimea's defenders would have a relief.—

But what was happening in Odessa now that it lay open to invasion. General Petrov left this account of the events that followed the Soviet withdrawal:

—Reconnaissance men picked from among sailors, infantry men and officers were left in the city to watch enemy movements. On their arrival in Sevastopol they reported that during the night of October 16 the enemy had made no active steps to cross the front line, although it was clear that Odessa was being evacuated.

—At 8 o'clock in the morning of October 16 individual enemy patrol groups timidly and hesitantly ventured beyond the former front line and towards 13:00 hours they were seen in the city's suburbs. During the day on October 16 the Rumanian army stayed in its positions, fearing to enter the city, and it was only on October 17, a day after the Soviet evacuation, that their forward units moved into Odessa.—

There was jubilation in Bucharest. Antonescu was awarded the rank of Marshal for "taking the fortress of Odessa". One familiar with the details of the battle for the city may be tempted to reword it: "for the invasion of the city of Odessa after its evacuation by the Red Army." In this way time makes its just corrections in the causes for the extravagant celebrations of that "victory", whose details were certainly concealed from the Rumanian people.

In his book of reminiscences "The Lost Victories" Field Marshal Manstein writes:

—On October 16 the Russians evacuated the fortress city of Odessa, which had been sieged without success by the Rumanian 4th Army and transferred the army which had defended it to the Crimea by sea. Although, as our air force command reported, Soviet ships with a total displacement of 32,000 tons had been sunk, the majority of transports from Odessa reached

Sevastopol and ports on the Western coast of the Crimea. First divisions of this army appeared at the front soon after the start of our offensive.—

The Field Marshal has greatly exaggerated the figure of casualties inflicted on the Soviet convoy but his reference to the failure of the siege is true to fact.

Nevertheless, the city was in enemy hands. That was an ugly reality. Yet it was also an occasion to recall King Pyrrhus of Epirus who had defeated the Romans in battle but so many of his warriors were killed that he exclaimed: "Another victory like that will leave me without my army!"

In their unsuccessful attempts to take the city the invaders lost 160,000 officers and men. The Maritime Army also suffered great casualties but, though heavily outnumbered, it preserved its fighting fitness and its weapons and equipment.

In the Battle of Borodino Napoleon failed to defeat the Russian Army, which withdrew under orders from Field Marshal Kutuzov. The army of the French Emperor, who was a talented and experienced general, suffered such enormous losses and was so shocked by the staunchness and heroism of the Russian troops that despite their retreat from the battlefield historians have awarded victory in that battle to Kutuzov and the Russian Army.

That was a Pyrrhic victory for Napoleon.

The Battle of Odessa had similar implications for the invaders, on a smaller scale of course, with regard to its impact on the outcome of the war. Skilful direction of combat operations at first by General Sofronov, and later by Rear Admiral Zhukov and General Petrov was crucial to Soviet success in that battle.

General Petrov coped with the tasks of directing the Soviet land forces in an area cut off from the rest of the country and the Soviet-German Front as a whole. Within a space of only 12 days, between August 5 and 15, acting jointly with the energetic Rear Admiral Zhukov, he carried out a manoeuvre unexpected to the enemy and highly advantageous to his own troops: a gradual withdrawal of military equipment, and material assets followed by a sudden retreat and transfer of his Army to another area of hostilities.

The scale of the evacuation is best illustrated by these figures: 15,000 civilians, 500 pieces of artillery, 1,158 motor vehicles, 163 tractors, 3,500 horses, 25,000 tons of factory equipment, 20,000 tons of ammunition and, finally, 86,000 troops. That was a classical example of efficient co-operation between the Army and Navy, because the enemy enjoyed an overwhelming superiority in numbers and all kinds of weapons and held the strategic initiative.

Similar battles were already on record in the Second World War by that time. But just as no two battles are absolutely identical, their results cannot be identical either. In the Dunkirk operation of 1940 the British, French and Belgian troops, a total of 43 divisions, defeated in earlier battles in France were taken off and landed in Britain within a period of ten days, from May 26 to June 4.

The retreating Allied forces were held in pincers by two German groups, which enjoyed supremacy in tanks and aircraft. A total of 693 British and 250 French naval and merchant vessels were used to lift Allied troops from the French coast. They were carried from shore to ship in launches and life-boats under a hail of bombs and bullets. German aircraft attacked them in armadas of up to 300 bombers and 500 fighters. More than 338,000 troops were rescued, 68,000 British and 40,000 French troops were taken prisoner.

Moreover, the Allies abandoned at Dunkirk all of their tanks, artillery and war material, as well as 63,000 motor vehicles. The Germans sank 224 British and 68 French warships and transports. That was a real massacre.

With their large land and naval forces the Allies could have organized a stiff defence and, narrowing the front gradually, withdrawn their troops and equipment. Or they could have delivered a counterblow to embarrass the enemy and withdraw all troops during one night; with their large land and naval forces that was feasible.

In short, good opportunities were missed, especially as the Germans had suspended their offensive for three days—from May 24 to 27—for reasons historians have yet to explain. At the time, however, the Allied forces and their command were so demoralized that the ten-day tragedy at Dunkirk looked more like a stampede than an organized retreat.

The German Lieutenant General B. Zimmerman gave this comment on the outcome of that operation:

"The German public viewed the taking of Dunkirk as a great victory. In fact, however, it was a setback, because the British had rescued their forces. . . ." These forces "(even if without equipment) were able to withdraw to Britain and make the backbone of the British Army."

Thus, the Allies lost about 300 ships and had 100,000 troops taken prisoner, as well as military equipment, and yet that operation is considered a success!

What laurels then have been deserved by the Commander and Staff of the Maritime Army, the commanding officers of units and ships who carried out the brilliant operation of withdrawing Soviet troops from Odessa without losing a single trooper and a single rifle to the enemy and who managed to sustain almost no casualties at sea.

In the hard days of 1941 when towns and cities were lost to the invaders, Odessa, cut off from the rest of the country by enemy troops and the sea, held its ground for 73 days. This is a fact this writer wants to emphasize without the slightest intention to belittle the part of the troops who fought heroically on other fronts.

In the gruelling early months of the war when the invaders were unable to muster enough strength for a decisive onslaught on Moscow and Leningrad, the Maritime Army with only 4 heavily depleted divisions and ships of the Black Sea Fleet held in check 20 enemy divisions and 7 brigades. That was an effective contribution to our eventual common victory.

The Battle of Sevastopol

The Crimea, October 17–24, 1941

When he set foot on Crimean soil, General Petrov heaved a sigh of relief. His throat was parched and he felt thirsty. A sailor brought him a full bucket of water from a nearby well. It was ice-cold and crystal clear. He drank it with pleasure and splashed it over his face and neck. Then he asked his faithful orderly Kucherenko:

"Anton, please fetch me a barber."

Troops of the Maritime Army were landing at different places and drawing in to their assembly points. They could not put themselves in order after their long battles, the sea journey and the hustle and bustle of disembarkation. The Army Commander could also afford a few minutes of rest.

Anton soon came back with a dishevelled strapping lad who looked anything but a barber. Aide-de-camp Kakharov asked sarcastically:

"A tonsorial artist? He looks fit to cut throats to me. Who will lead the Army then, you?"

Kucherenko was confused. He motioned to the barber and they both vanished. Finally, he brought along a girl he had found in some army unit. She was in uniform and carried a barber's case.

"Now, that's the right person for the job!" Kakharov exclaimed cheerfully.

On October 17, with the evacuation of Odessa over, the Maritime Army command assembled at the Navy headquarters. Everyone was in a cheerful mood: it was the first gathering of the Army's commanding officers after the trials of the two-month siege. Vice Admiral Oktyabrsky improvised a luncheon for his guests.

General Khrenov came up to Petrov:

"Well, where do we stand now, General?"

"We're still shaping up but once we get more weapons and equipment we'll be ready to move in and join the fight where it's hottest."

Petrov knew of the critical situation on other fronts from radio and press reports. The Germans were on the approaches to Moscow. Battle fronts now bore the names of towns lying on the routes leading to the capital: Naro-fominsk and Podolsk. The Nazis had succeeded in bursting open the Soviet defences and captured the towns of Kalinin, Mozhaisk and Maloyaroslavets.

Leningrad was under siege.

On the Southern Front the Nazis had besieged Rostov. They were determined to capture it at all costs, considering it the gate to the Caucasus and the Baku oil-fields. Earlier, on August 23, 1941, Hitler had sent a memo to the High Command of the German land forces, which said in particular:

—For political reasons it is a matter of urgency to move into Russia's oil-producing provinces in order to block her fuel supply, and primarily to give Iran hope for practical assistance from Germany in the near future in case of its opposition to threats from Russia and Britain.—

The German High Command attempted a penetration to the Caucasus through the Crimea as well. The shortest route from the Ukraine to the Caucasus lay across the Crimea. What is more, the Crimea was a highly convenient area for deployment of air forces. While it was under Soviet control the Soviet Air Force could bomb the rear of the enemy forces operating near Rostov and raid Rumania's oil-fields. If the invaders seized the Crimea, they could naturally turn it into a bridgehead for an offensive directed towards the Caucasus and an airfield protected by sea from which the Luftwaffe could make raids on the Caucasus.

The General Staff of the Wehrmacht moved Manstein's 11th Army and a Rumanian mountain corps to the Crimea. On October 18 they went on to the offensive. The German 11th Army was to deliver the main strike across the Perekop isthmus, while the Rumanian forces were to capture the Chongar bridge. In both sectors they were opposed by Colonel General Kuznetsov's 51st Separate Army.

The German 11th Army Commander Erich von Manstein, who was a Colonel General at the time, was an experienced strategist and, since he was General Petrov's constant opponent (just as of other Soviet Army and Navy commanders in the Battle of Sevastopol and later) it may be relevant to present his brief biography here.

Fritz Erich Lewinski (alias Manstein) was born in Berlin on November 24, 1887 into the family of Eduard von Lewinski, who was later to become an artillery general and Commander of the 6th Army Corps. Manstein took the surname of his uncle, General Georg von Manstein, by whom he was adopted. His ancestry on his father's and mother's sides was of Prussia's old officer families.

On finishing at cadet school he entered the 3rd Regiment of Foot Guards in Berlin. In 1913–1914 he was trained at a military academy. In World War I he served at first as aide-de-camp with the 2nd Reserve Regiment of the Foot Guards and saw action in Belgium, Eastern Prussia and Southern Poland. From May 1915, after recovering from a severe wound, he served as a staff officer in General von Halwitz's and General von Below's armies. He took part in the offensive in Northern Poland, the campaign in Serbia, and in the Battle of Verdun. From the autumn of 1917 he was Chief of Staff of the 4th Cavalry Division. In May 1918 he was appointed Chief of Staff of the 213th

Infantry Division operating on the Western Front. He participated in the offensive in the Reims area in May and July 1918 and later in defensive battles in the West until the end of the war.

Early in 1919 Manstein was a staff officer of the South border defence force in Breslau (Wroclaw). Following the war he held various staff and regimental appointments in the Reichswehr. From February 1934 he was Chief of Staff of the 3rd Military District (Berlin). From July 1935 he became chief of the operations branch of the General Staff of the Army.

In October 1936, he was appointed Chief Quartermaster, which made him first assistant and deputy to General Ludwig Beck, Chief of the General Staff.

In February 1938 Manstein was relieved of his staff appointment and given command of the 18th Infantry Division. He participated in the occupation of the Sudetenland as chief of staff of an Army. In 1939, he served as chief of staff to General von Rundstedt, Commander of Army Group South and took part in the invasion of Poland. Later he accompanied Rundstedt to the Western Front as Chief of Staff of Army Group A.

Before long he was relieved of that post and appointed to command an army corps. In that post he took part in the campaign in France in 1940 and was awarded a Knight's Cross.

In March 1941 he was appointed to command the 56th Panzer Corps and in June led its thrust on the Eastern Front from Eastern Prussia through Dvinsk (Daugavpils) as far as Lake Ilmen.

In September 1941 he was promoted to command the 11th Army.

Manstein arrived in the city of Nikolaev on September 17, 1941 to replace Colonel General von Schobert killed by a time bomb planted by partisans. The Soviet defences on the Perekop isthmus were not under attack by his whole Army but only by the 54th Infantry Corps, which was followed by the 30th Infantry Corps; the isthmus was too narrow for larger forces to be committed simultaneously. Manstein presents his own story of the battle:

—A surprise attack against the Russians was out of the question. They had prepared well-fortified defensive positions in advance and were expecting our offensive. Just as at Perekop encirclement or at least flanking fire were impossible, because the battle front lay between the Sivash salt-lake and the sea. There was no alternative to a frontal attack. . . .—

Further, Manstein lays it on thick, to put it mildly:

—The Russians outnumbered our forces. . . . The six divisions of the 11th Army were very soon opposed by eight Soviet infantry and four cavalry divisions, since on October 16 the Russians had transferred their Army which had been defending Odessa to the Crimea by sea.—

In reality, however, the Perekop positions were defended by the 156th Infantry Division alone.

A few words about the Nazi forces advancing on the Crimea will illustrate the actual balance between the belligerents.

Manstein's 11th Army included the 30th and 54th Corps, each consisting of three infantry divisions, the 49th Corps of three mountain divisions and two motorized SS divisions "Adolf Hitler" and "Viking". Manstein also had up to 40 regiments of artillery of different calibres. His Army was supported by 350 aircraft, 200 of which were bombers.

Petrov was ordered by the Commander of the 51st Army to check the enemy advance and go over to the offensive, relying on his own resources, and, by recapturing the Ishun positions, to restore the situation that had existed a week before. These positions had been lost to the Nazi forces which had broken through the Soviet defences and burst out with their panzer and mechanized columns into the vast Crimean steppe where no fortifications or troops were deployed to stop them.

Petrov's troops had no artillery or air support, and their reserves of ammunition were scanty. They had no tanks either. The Army Headquarters' demand was short: "Attack immediately or the enemy will seize the whole Crimea in two days!"

Defying all difficulties, the troops of the Maritime Army attacked the invaders doggedly and hurled them backwards. On October 25 the German divisions had to shift to the defensive. On October 26, however, having brought up reinforcements, Manstein moved seven infantry divisions into a narrow sector backed up by a large number of tanks and aircraft.

The Soviet defenders had only small arms to repel enemy infantry and no weapons to fight tanks. The enemy pressed the Soviet troops back at the left flank, sliced through the junction between the 9th Infantry Corps of the 51st Army and the Maritime Army and started encircling its positions.

The Soviet defenders were suffering great losses, and it was clear that a breakthrough by the invasion forces was inevitable. The Military Council of the Crimean defence forces ordered a retreat southwards to the intermediate lines in the depth of the peninsula.

After the receipt of that order communication with the Soviet Command in the Crimea was broken off.

Petrov was in a quandary. He had only his own judgement and foresight to rely upon in taking decisions in that critical situation where so much depended on him alone. He realized that the Maritime Army had been moved to the Ishun positions belatedly when the decisive fighting was over. Hence its failure to hold off the invading forces. The Army had to retreat, which was a sad fact to accept for all the exonerating objective circumstances, such as overwhelming enemy numbers and the unavailability of sufficient fire power and mechanized equipment.

Manstein's forces were swiftly rolling on across the steppes towards Feodosia and Kerch and in the heartland of the Crimea they were circling the Crimean mountains on their way to Yalta and Sevastopol.

On the night of October 31, the Military Council of the Maritime Army

assembled in conference in a clay house on the outskirts of the small village of
Sarabuz.

Petrov briefly outlined the situation and argued that it would be meaningless for the Maritime Army to retreat towards Kerch the ways to which were
still open, because that would leave Sevastopol, the main base of the Black Sea
Fleet, unprotected: the city had no land forces capable of defending it.
Therefore, the Army should retreat in the direction of Sevastopol, though that
would mean fighting its way through the lines of German units which had
already outflanked its left wing. The Council agreed with his plan.

That decision put thousands of lives at stake, and the Army Commander
alone was to assume the burden of responsibility. Therefore, Petrov called
another conference. He ordered his Chief of Staff to summon the commanders and political commissars of the divisions of the Maritime Army and
those placed under his command in the last few days to the village of Ekibash.
They were to assemble at 17:00 hours.

With fierce fighting going on it was hard for the commanders to leave their
units, even for a short time, but all of them arrived at Ekibash, anticipating a
serious change. The meeting was held at a local hospital. Petrov and Brigade
Commissar Kuznetsov, Military Council member, were seated on stools and
the unit commanders on benches set around a simple table.

Petrov looked at his old comrades, trying to read their minds from their
faces. Were they not too much upset by their first setbacks? They had put up a
good fight during the border battles of June when the invaders made their
surprise attack, and they had retreated according to their own timetables, not
to the enemy's dictate.

The conference was attended by Major General Vasily Vorobyov, commander of the 95th Infantry Division, Major General Trofim Kolomiyets,
commander of the 25th Chapayev division, Colonel Petr Novikov, commander of the 2nd Cavalry Division, Colonel Philip Kudyurov, commander of the
40th Cavalry Division, Colonel Ivan Laskin, commander of the 172nd
infantry division, which had recently been incorporated in the Maritime
Army. Some commanders of regiments deployed nearby were also present.

Petrov stood up, looked at the officers closely, and said, his head twitching
nervously:

"We have summoned you to discuss the situation and the Army's further
operations. The enemy has seized Jankoi and is in pursuit of units of the 51st
Army which are retreating towards the Kerch peninsula. The pressure on our
Army has eased slightly, because the enemy is trying to outflank us and trap us
in a pincer movement.

"We are undermanned and undergunned to prevent that. Our right flank is
in danger. German tanks were seen south of Simferopol today. The road to
Simferopol through Bakhchisarai is probably cut. We have no contact with
the Crimean headquarters and are outflanked on three sides. Checking the
enemy advance in the steppe is impossible.

"If we retreat into the mountains, the enemy will be left in full control of the flat terrain and the roads to Sevastopol and Kerch. We have to choose between them. The Kerch road is open and it will take us overnight to reach the Kerch peninsula where we can dig in.

"The 51st Army is retreating in that direction, also, and may set up defences on the Ak-Manai line. The Sevastopol road is blocked. Taking it means fighting hard. But Sevastopol is the citadel of the Black Sea Fleet and is crucially important for our control of the sea.

"It's no secret that Sevastopol is defenceless against an overland attack since no field forces are stationed there. If the Maritime Army fails to arrive there before a large enemy force, the fortress may fall. Now let's hear your opinions. Each will be heeded."

Petrov fell silent for a long moment to allow everyone to gather their thoughts. Then he turned to the Commander of the 161st Infantry Regiment of the 95th Division:

"Colonel Kapitokhin, go ahead!"

Kapitokhin was curt: "I opt for Sevastopol."

Major General Kolomiyets, Commander of the 25th Chapayev Division, its Commissar Stepanov, Colonel Kudyurov, Commander of the 40th Cavalry Division, and other officers were of the same mind.

Vorobyov, Commander of the 95th Division, its Commissar Melnikov, and Lieutenant Colonel Prasolov, its Chief of Staff, opted for Kerch. Vorobyov argued:

"The real situation in the Bakhchisarai area is unknown. The Germans may be there in force. With hostile forces on both flanks the Army may be trapped. We have too few guns to fight them off. In the mountains we'll lose what has remained of our logistics. The Kerch road is free and will let us keep the Army intact for further fighting. We can dig in and hold out at Kerch."

When all had spoken, Petrov summed up:

"Four are in favour of retreating to Kerch. The majority want a break-through to Sevastopol. This agrees with the Military Council decision of last night. So we go to help Sevastopol. The main forces will be pulled out of their lines after dark. You will see the routes of your units on my map."

Petrov instructed the officers to get their troops to the River Alma by morning. The conference had lasted for less than an hour, and the Commanders promptly returned to their units with new marching orders.

That critical decision showed Petrov's strategic foresight. Aware of the overriding necessity of wise action, he put his Army and himself at risk. He realized only too well that if Sevastopol were lost, enemy naval forces might have the Caucasian coast within easy reach for an invasion by a landing force. Holding the Black Sea naval base, Soviet troops would remain at the rear of the enemy and in control of part of the Crimean peninsula.

The defence of Sevastopol, just as the battle for Odessa, would enable the Maritime Army to hold a large number of enemy troops bogged down in fighting and deny them a part in any offensive against the Caucasus. Thus, direct access to the Caucasus which Hitler craved for so avidly would be blocked.

Reminiscences of Prewar Years

A person's action of any significance stems from his outlook on life, his convictions and character. Its sources can be traced to his biography, upbringing and life experiences.

Only four years before the conference at Ekibash Petrov had seen some plays of fortune that now prompted him to hold this counsel with his comrades-in-arms, which was rather unusual in military affairs, where the chain of command is law.

Petrov always trusted his comrades and was a dependable friend, and his comrades and friends repaid him in kind. Support from his Party comrades had once helped him in a dramatic situation. In the prewar years slanderers and informers had instigated a case against him. He was accused of off-duty association and drinking with a person already subjected to repression, and of concealing his own record of service as an officer in the White Army during the Civil War.

These charges look absurd today. In fact, he had never concealed his officer record, and even we cadets knew about it. He had never served in the White Army, not even for a day. That army was formed after the Revolution with the object of fighting it. Petrov had done his stint in the Russian Imperial Army, it is true, but he joined the Red Army when the Revolution came.

A certain Vasilyev, who was a member of the Party commission of enquiry, levied accusations on Petrov and his deputy for drill training, Colonel Filatov.

"Filatov is a very dangerous person. I move for his expulsion from the school and bringing the matter before the Military Council."

As the Commission records testify, though Petrov was on the verge of expulsion from the Party himself, he immediately took a stand in defence of Filatov, calling these charges unfair. Another member of the Commission, Maklashin, retorted:

"Your remark on Filatov's behalf shows your formal attitude. Filatov behaves as a wrecker and is disliked and feared by cadets. His hostility may result in practical harm."

I knew the climate at our school in those prewar years when it was under Petrov's command and I knew Colonel Filatov for many years. Thus I can safely say that all those accusations of wrecking and hostility were nonsense. The climate at our school was friendly, we were trained well, and we lived like one friendly family. We were raised as patriots dedicated to the country and Party. My school mates gave their lives for them—what can be better evidence? All my graduation class of 1941 was sent to serve in the Western border districts. Of the 100 Lieutenants of my school company only five survived the war. The allegations that we were afraid of Filatov were absurd. In fact, we loved him for his courtesy and tact, and he encouraged our sense of dignity. As for the charge of wrecking work, I must say that he reported to work earlier than anybody and left for home late after hours. He was devoted to us and never spared himself to help us. His war record is equally splendid: he was promoted to a General and given command of a division and was awarded many war medals for courage in battle. He was Petrov's life-long friend and visited him in hospital until his last days of life. Filatov is not with us any more, and he has left no reminiscences either.

The examination of Petrov's case by the Party commission ended favourably for him, in relative terms, by the standards of those times. He was not expelled from the Party and retained his position as school commandant, but could not avoid a severe Party reprimand.

Dark clouds, nevertheless, hovered over his head for a long time. In 1939 the charges were repeated.

Those years are usually recalled only for what was bad and often for actions that were dishonourable. In Petrov's case, however, a few persons displayed rare courage and honesty.

Looking through Petrov's personal file, I found some small sheets of grey paper. As I read them, I thought sadly of how such a small piece of paper could decide a person's fate. There were twelve carbon copies of an inquiry about Petrov's record as a Party member, which had been sent to various persons who knew him. It was explained in the inquiry that he would soon be held responsible for his "links with enemies of the people" and "anti-Party activities". The name and initials of the addressee were written in ink on every copy.

It is easy to imagine the reaction of recipients of these inquiries in those years. Their wording left no doubt about what Petrov was in for.

To the credit of the persons who wrote replies to that tendentious inquiry it should be stated that these remarkable communists, risking very much or rather risking everything, said the truth about Petrov. I feel the readers must know the names of these honourable and courageous people. I shall briefly quote their replies, which were called a "Party reference" (unfortunately, the positions and initials of their authors are not indicated in all letters).

"Chernukhin, member of the Communist Party since February 1919: . . . Petrov is a veteran Party member. I trust that he is dedicated to the Party of Lenin and Stalin."

"Regimental Commissar Evstafyev: I have known Petrov since 1933 as an experienced and disciplined commander dedicated to the Party of Lenin and Stalin."

"Chelmadinov, member of the Communist Party since July 1918: I have known Petrov since 1929. He is dependable politically and morally, and in his practical work is following our Party line and actively struggling for it."

"Kurbatkin, member of the Communist Party since 1920: . . . Petrov is indisputably dedicated to the Party of Lenin and Stalin. He deserves complete trust. In view of his competence and wide outlook he can be appointed to a more important position than he now holds."

"Patolichev, member of the Communist Party since 1927: ... I knew Petrov in the period 1922–24 as a staunch Bolshevik. In that period he was a regimental and brigade Commissar of the 11th Cavalry Division of the 1st Mounted Army. He is an exceptionally sensitive and tactful man, and was a general favourite of his regiment. He struggled mercilessly against distortions of and digressions from the Party line, especially in the period of struggle against the *basmach* gangs, when it was necessary to correctly pursue the Leninist-Stalinist policy on the national question.

"I repeatedly took part jointly with Petrov in battles against the *basmachs*, where he displayed courage, strong will power and presence of mind and invariably appeared at the most critical and dangerous spots."

Similar replies were sent in by Sergeyev, Party member since 1923: Bazhenov, Party member since 1919; Bochkarev, Head of Chair at the Frunze Military Academy, Party member since 1918; Vyrypayev, Party member since 1925; Filatov, Party member since 1938; Brilev, Party member since 1939.

I am recalling these dramatic events in Petrov's life without any intention to discuss the repressions of those years. The Party has long denounced whatever was perpetrated illegally at that time. But it seems to me that invisible threads extended from those years to the conference in the Crimea described above.

The honesty of Communists had saved Petrov at one time. The opinion of other people and their good advice had always meant much to him, but after those events his respect for his comrades and his reliance on their support in a critical situation became greater still.

The Retreat to Sevastopol, October 1941

Issuing his new orders and indicating avenues of retreat for different divisions, Petrov could not suspect that he would soon have to revise his plan of retreat. On the same night he received information about a breakthrough of the enemy strike forces along a coastal road to the river Alma, which was to be the next defence line of the retreating troops. He had to find immediately new routes of retreat and set new tasks to the divisions already on the march.

It was a formidable problem to turn the whole Army without dependable communication with units, under constant air attacks and the pressure of enemy land forces. All that had to be done during one night.

Petrov immediately went to see the Commander of the 95th Division, sent his Chief of Staff Krylov to the 172nd Division, and a few staff officers to other divisions and units. That was a simple and natural means of securing effective troop control by which Petrov and his staff, avoiding misunder-

standing and mistakes and casualties from unexpected encounters with
enemy troops, promptly turned the enormous mass of men and equipment
and directed them to the south-east around Simferopol, and further into the
mountains, because the steppe was already in the invaders' hands.

All heavy artillery and part of the logistics had been providently moved
along the highway to Alushta and Yalta and further to Sevastopol. Otherwise
five regiments of heavy artillery would have fallen into the enemy hands, since
their huge guns could not be hauled along steep and narrow mountain roads.

Petrov with his staff was controlling the course of the retreat and rearguard
battles and slowly moving southwards.

The further events are best described by Marshal Krylov, who was with
Petrov in those days.

—Petrov realized that he would have to organize the city's ground defences
at all events. He knew nothing of the state of fortifications and the situation
prevailing there in general, and that was a discomforting thought. He
wondered if he should hasten to Sevastopol with his field staff to be fully
prepared for the arrival of his main forces.

"That was a hard problem for the Army Commander, because he would
have to leave his main forces at a critical time. He went to Alushta to discuss it
with Vice Admiral Levchenko, Commander of the Crimean Forces.

—Levchenko, an old sea dog, was greatly worried about Sevastopol. He
was convinced that his rightful place was there and ordered Petrov to go to
Sevastopol at once. "You have generals who can lead your troops to their
destination. You now must be organizing a pliable defence together with the
naval command. . . .—

On November 2, Petrov and his field staff left for Sevastopol and arrived
there on the next day. He had delegated his duties to Major General
Kolomiyets, Commander of the 25th Division. He kept in touch with him by
radio and actually remained in control of the Army.

The First Assault on Sevastopol, November 1941

With the first news of the enemy breakthrough into the Crimea and the
danger to Sevastopol, the Military Council of the Black Sea Fleet declared a
state of siege.

Within a week of staying in Sevastopol, Petrov carried out enormous work
in organizing its defences, relying on his experience of the Civil War and the
Battle of Odessa. The naval and land forces and various special units which
had entrenched themselves on the approaches to the city repelled the attempt
of the German 11th Army to take Sevastopol with a rush. Moreover, the
invaders failed to prevent the retreat of the Maritime Army towards
Sevastopol. Now that it was here, the city's defences were competently
reorganized into an efficient system for repulsing an overland attack.

Defence has always been justly regarded as a passive way of waging war.

The attacker usually holds the initiative. Here, just as in chess, the White make the first move. In the conduct of combat operations the attacker makes the first move, and the defender reacts to it.

Let us see what Manstein writes in his memoirs about his intentions as the leader of the attacking side.

—Now the 11th Army was confronted by the task of taking by storm the last enemy stronghold in the Crimea—Sevastopol. The earlier this offensive was undertaken, the less time the enemy would have to organize defence and hence the greater the chances of success. . . . Before the attack it was necessary to bring up reinforcements. The four divisions deployed in front of the fortress were certainly not enough to assault it. Their strength was insufficient even for forming a continuous front. Moreover, it was found that the enemy . . . had managed to increase the strength of the defending forces to 9 divisions within a relatively brief space of time. This fact illustrated the urgent necessity of severing the Russian sea lanes.—

A few decades after those events Manstein has camouflaged the real situation at Sevastopol. He does not say a word about the failure of the first assault on Sevastopol by two German corps, which were opposed by scattered and hastily formed detachments of Marines and later by undermanned units of the Maritime Army that had come to their rescue. In his memoirs the Field Marshal often speaks of his affection and respect for the German soldiers. As we see, however, he has failed to remember the soldiers he sent to their death in that first attack on Sevastopol as well as his ill-conceived plans that suffered a fiasco.

Manstein describes the preparations for storming Sevastopol in the chapter entitled "The First Offensive on Sevastopol". I shall quote his assessment of the steps taken by the command of the defending forces which compelled respect even on the part of an enemy.

—The Soviet commander's vigorous measures checked the advance of the 54th Army Corps on the approaches to the fortress. Relying on their sea communications, the Russian forces even considered themselves strong enough to open an offensive with naval artillery support from the coast north of Sevastopol against the right wing of the 54th Army Corps. It had to be reinforced by moving in the 22nd Infantry Division of the 30th Army Corps. In that situation the Army Command had to give up its plan to take Sevastopol by a surprise attack. . . .—

However, the Germans went ahead with their offensive, delivering strikes in all directions. That put Petrov's forces in a very difficult situation. He had neither sufficient reserves nor large units at his disposal and was unable to secure significant superiority even in one decisive sector. For all that, the city's defences proved impregnable and the enemy was held at bay. The counter-blows of the 7th and 8th Marine brigades skilfully planned by Petrov were not very strong but they embarrassed Manstein. He took them for new reinforcements brought in by sea from the Caucasus and, fearing their further advance, moved a fresh division to oppose them. His hope for taking Sevastopol by storm was immediately dashed. Thus, in the opening stage of the battle the Sevastopol defenders, though undermanned and undergunned, won a clear victory.

The lull that had set in following that first contest allowed Petrov to take a look around, analyze the general tide of hostilities and the position of his Army.

It was a rainy autumn with unexpected spells of sunshine and cold night winds. The white stone city looked festive even in rough weather. The autumn leaves rustled on the trees and under foot. The first snow fell on November 27. Petrov visited the city and stood awhile on the Grafsky pier.

We don't know what he mused on, watching the sea but it would hardly be wrong to suppose that he who had but recently read lectures on the history of the art of warfare to students in Tashkent recalled the city's splendid past, Admirals Nakhimov and Kornilov, and compared the siege of Sevastopol in the Crimean War with its present defence.

—History repeated itself. Almost one hundred years ago the Russian Army retreated from the river Alma across the mountain and through Bakhchisarai to Sevastopol. The Maritime Army followed the same roads here. Its men hauled guns and carts by ropes loaded with ammunition and provisions. During the first siege the roads were probably worse. In 1854 the siege had begun in autumn, too. At first 7,000 and later 36,000 Russians were fighting off 67,000 British and French troops. There were no ground defences prepared in advance, and troops had to build them with their own hands.

Then, just as now, three defence lines and an advanced position were built. A combination of fire, trenches and dug-outs made it possible to sustain positional defence, the first in war history. Petrov might be thinking of ways to apply that experience to his own plans.

In his time Admiral Kornilov, on learning the date of impending assault, ordered the full fire power of his ground artillery and warships to be unleashed upon the invasion forces. That would bleed them before they attacked. Their casualties were staggering, and they were yet unable to rally for attack at the zero hour.

What useful lesson could be learned from that historical event? Admiral Nakhimov, who took over after Kornilov had been killed in that first assault, repelled many more attacks. The Sevastopol defenders held their ground for 349 days. How long could we endure? Now the invaders were better armed and relied on a greater potential. Their air power alone made them a formidable opponents. Yet we were not left to fight them on our own. The whole country was fighting along with us on a front extending from the Black Sea to the Arctic. The tide of the fighting seemed to be in the balance. Soviet forces had dealt the invaders telling blows at Smolensk and Yelnya. Leningrad was staunchly holding on. In the south Soviet forces had driven the enemy back beyond the river Mius and liberated Rostov.

That offensive of Soviet troops in an area close to the embattled Sevastopol inspired the defenders of the hero city.

In those days Hitler was compelled for the first time to announce a retreat of his "invincible" army. He relieved Field Marshal Rundstedt of command of Army Group South for the loss of Rostov and appointed Field Marshal Reichenau in his place.

After his initial setback in storming Sevastopol, Manstein began preparing another offensive in a thoroughgoing way. The 11th Army Headquarters were located in Simferopol. Manstein himself, with his Chief of Staff and a group of operations officers, settled down at the village of Sarabuz, the very same place where Petrov had recently held a conference with his commanders. Manstein lived in the building of a collective farm board and, as he writes, "we stayed in that modest apartment until August 1942, leaving it only twice in June when our headquarters were near Sevastopol to visit the command post in the Kerch sector."

As we can see, Manstein was not a very mobile commander in controlling his forces. He spent many days and nights in that apartment examining maps and searching for a way to take Sevastopol, the only stronghold of Soviet forces remaining in the Crimea. Hitler repeatedly insisted on faster action and rebuked Manstein for his sluggishness. He was eager to get rid of the Sevastopol pocket of resistance as early as possible, because it was a hindrance to the unobstructed advance of the Nazi forces towards the Caucasus.

Wartime documents that have come to light today allow us to know more than what was known to General Petrov at the time. To gain a clearer idea of the battle that was gathering momentum let us see what Manstein himself writes about his offensive plan and the direction of the main strike.

—To break the resistance of the Sevastopol fortress control of the port— the bay of Severnaya—was to be gained as speedily as possible. That was the key to success. As long as the fortress had access to the high seas through open lanes the Russians would have the advantage of superior weapons and numbers. Hence the main thrust was to be aimed from the north or north-east towards the Bay of Severnaya. That was not the way the Allies had dealt their blow in the Crimean War when they enjoyed supremacy on the high seas.

—For us it was not the city but the port that was the coveted goal. Only in the north, however, could our Army take advantage of its powerful artillery to support the attacking forces.

—Therefore, the Army Command resolved to deliver the main strike from the north or north-east. A secondary offensive was to be launched in the south with the chief object of holding and distracting enemy forces.

—The 54th Army Corps was to attack in the north with the forces of four divisions—the 22nd, 132nd and 50th Infantry Divisions and the 24th

Infantry Division recently brought in relying on the support of the greater part of our heavy artillery.

—The holding attack in the south was to be carried out by the 30th Army Corps which had on its strength the 17th Infantry Division in addition to the 72nd Infantry Division brought in from Kerch and a Rumanian mountain brigade. The 73rd Infantry Division moved in from the Kerch Peninsula was the reserve of the forces attacking from the north.—

Manstein had chosen November 27–28 as the days for attack. However, he proved unable to move his forces into action on the scheduled day. Amongst the reasons for that failure he listed Russian winter, poor roads and slow transport. It was not before December 17 that preparations for the offensive had finally been completed.

In fact, however, it was not these factors that forced Manstein to delay his attack. On November 26, which General Petrov had identified as the day of a possible German offensive, the Sevastopol defenders unleashed the full fire power of their artillery and their air power on the unsuspecting German troop concentrations.

On that day Petrov more than once thankfully recalled Admiral Kornilov of the Crimean War and his experience in organizing defence. All the artillery batteries of Sevastopol, including heavy coastal guns, opened up at once in a sweeping barrage of the enemy positions. The warships riding at anchor in Sevastopol harbour joined them. All aircraft available to the defenders made frequent sorties to unload their deadly cargoes on the invasion forces.

Those were crippling blows indeed and the German troops were heavily mutilated, like their predecessors had been in the distant days of the first defence of Sevastopol. Their attack had been thwarted.

On December 5, 1941 Soviet forces went over to the offensive in the Battle of Moscow. In record time they routed Army Group Centre and drove it far away from the Soviet capital. The German casualties were enormous.

The German defeat in that historic battle filled all hearts with joy. In those days, perhaps, Petrov was not yet fully aware of the ignominious fiasco of the Nazi blitzkrieg doctrine but he clearly saw a turning in the tide of the war. He eagerly desired to support this offensive in the north by a strike in the south but his forces were inadequate.

"We will keep Sevastopol and hold the powerful 11th Army. That is a great help, too. Perhaps this Army is just what the Germans needed most of all at Rostov and Moscow", he said excitedly.

The German High Command blamed all its setbacks on the severe Russian winter. In his directive of December 8, 1941 Hitler wrote:

—The unusually early onset of a cold winter on the Eastern Front and the resulting bottlenecks in supplies have forced us to stop all large-scale offensive operations immediately and go on the defensive. . . . Sevastopol must be taken as speedily as possible. . . .

In a conversation with his staff officers General Petrov said, as though in a rhetorical address to the German High Command:

"Didn't you, gentlemen, know of cold Russian winters before? Every German schoolboy knows that. Didn't you know of Russia's vast territory? But you have maps to learn from. Are the roads too few for you? But we move along the same roads, and the cold, snow and rain don't spare us. You are seeking objective factors to cover up your setbacks. You want to justify your dare-devil plans based on military charts, but it takes more than wishful thinking to fight a war. Your chief miscalculation is this: we are not what you imagined us to be."

Another Assault, December 1941

At dawn on December 17 when the darkness of night still veiled the belligerent sides, a hurricane of shells suddenly swept the Soviet positions all along the Sevastopol defensive front. Simultaneously, the German air forces bombed and strafed Soviet troops, the city and harbour.

After a 25-minute artillery preparation, the invasion forces mounted an all-out infantry and panzer attack.

There was a flood of telephone and radio messages and requests from different defence sectors and higher headquarters at General Petrov's command post.

—The 773rd Regiment is retreating. The 4th sector commander Vorobyov has moved in the 149th Cavalry Regiment and a few rearguard units to fill the gap.—

—All our counterattacks in the third sector have failed, despite your assistance with reinforcements from your reserve.—

—The 8th Marine Brigade has lost 1,700 officers and men. Only two undermanned battalions have remained on its strength.—

The Germans kept on their attacks until dark. Next day the fighting resumed. The defending forces counterattacked fiercely but ground lost in the third and fourth defence sectors was firmly kept by the entrenched enemy infantry. The Soviet casualties were severe: 3,500 dead and wounded in two days.

Towards the end of the third day of the assault, the Germans had driven a wedge between the third and fourth sectors near the Mackenzie Mountain station. Neither the Soviet Army Commander nor the divisional commanders had any reserves left to dislodge the attackers from their new positions.

Rear Admiral Zhukov, acting Commander of the Sevastopol Defence District, sent an urgent message to General Headquarters:

—Stalin, Kuznetsov, Oktyabrsky, Rogov. Large enemy troop concentrations with fresh reinforcements supported by tanks and artillery have been fiercely storming the Sevastopol defences for three days. Ignoring their enormous losses in manpower and equipment the Germans are constantly feeding new troops into battle. Our troops are beating off attacks and holding their ground. Our great losses in equipment, machine-guns and mortars have forced troops to retreat to the second line of defence. . . .

—With the Germans advancing at their present rate the Sevastopol garrison will not hold out for more than three days.

—We urgently need reinforcements: one infantry division, aircraft, ammunition and draft battalions. Zhukov, Kulakov. 19.12.1942.—

General Headquarters responded promptly with a directive to the Command of the Transcaucasian Front and the Black Sea Fleet:

1.   The Transcaucasian Front Command. Take over control of the Sevastopol Defence District immediately.
2.   Admiral Oktyabrsky. Leave for Sevastopol immediately.
3.   The Transcaucasian Front Commander. Appoint a competent general to control overland operations at Sevastopol immediately.
4.   Move one infantry division or two infantry brigades to Sevastopol.
5.   Detail aircraft to Sevastopol to deliver air strikes.
6.   Bring 3,000 draft reinforcements and ammunition of the right calibres to Sevastopol immediately.

The third point of this direction shows that General Headquarters were uninformed or misinformed about the direction of overland fighting at Sevastopol. Anyone familiar with the events of that time will agree with this. Incidentally, Petrov would later be in trouble, quite unfairly, because of this directive.

. . . The sunrise on December 21 was cloudy and the sea was hardly visible under a blanket of fog. Warships were sailing towards Sevastopol carrying the 79th Marine Brigade, ten draft companies and ammunition under orders from General Headquarters.

Petrov was waiting for them at the pier. He was impatient. Every minute counted in that critical situation, and he intended to commit the arriving brigade to action at once to bolster up the crumbling defences.

In the meantime fierce fighting was going on near the Mackenzie Mountain station. Wounded Soviet defenders stayed on at their posts, because there was no relief to take over from them. All men fought to the death.

As soon as the 79th brigade landed, General Petrov ordered its commander, Colonel Potapov, to join battle at the fastest speed.

German tanks had burst through Soviet defence lines at the junction between two cavalry regiments. One of them had about eighty and the other, about one hundred survivors at the most. German tanks came close to Colonel Kudyurov's divisional command post and all staff officers joined the fight. There were a few antitank guns that held the tanks at bay, and when their crews were killed, Colonel Kudyurov himself manned a gun until he was cut down by a shell splinter.

A few survivors had managed to fight off the attacking Germans until they were joined by a reconnaissance battalion of the 95th Division and an engineer battalion which had come to their rescue. The defence line was stabilized for a time.

At dawn on December 22, after a short artillery preparation jointly carried out by batteries on land and naval ships the 79th Brigade and its neighbours on both flanks went into attack.

The opposing German forces went into attack at the same time. A fierce head-on battle ensued. The 79th Brigade proved a staunch opponent. It hurled the Germans backwards and forged its way along the highway towards Belbek. The 287th Regiment of the Chapayev Division kept apace with it at the right flank. Towards evening Potapov's brigade advanced as far as the heights in front of the Kamyshlovy ravine and almost completely stabilized the frontline in that sector. Captain Dyakonchuk's regiment was rescued from a German encirclement.

General Petrov learned of the Germans' advance towards Lyubimovka situated on the sea coast. That threatened the Soviet troops beyond Belbek with encirclement. The Army Commander had no forces strong enough to cut off the German wedge and reported that to Vice Admiral Oktyabrsky. The latter allowed General Vorobyov to withdraw his left-flank units towards Belbek to escape a trap, which made the front line shorter and enabled the fourth defence sector command to hold and defend a narrower sector more effectively.

What was the German view of the situation at the time? Field Marshal Manstein writes:

—I won't go into details in my story of this offensive because of limited space. The brave 22nd Lower Saxony Infantry Division led by its remarkable commander Lieutenant General Wolf bore the brunt of the fighting and its success was critically important. It cleared the supply zone of enemy troops between the rivers Kacha and Belbek and joined forces with the 132nd Infantry Division advancing more southerly in storming the heights on the southern banks of the Belbek river valley and burst out into the zone of fortifications south of the valley. The offensive wedge, however, steadily grew narrower, because the 50th Infantry Division and the 24th Infantry Division which were advancing from the east in the direction of the Bay of Severnaya had made very slight headway across the mountainous terrain, overgrown with almost impassable bush forests. Our troops suffered severe casualties in attacking fortifications stubbornly defended by the Russians. The onset of a severe cold demanded an extreme exertion of their strength. . . . If we had had fresh troops our breakthrough towards the Bay of Severnaya would have been a success. However, we had no such troops. . . .

Thus, the Field Marshal blamed his setbacks on cold weather and inadequate forces again. Even in this short quotation, he mentions four infantry divisions brought up to full complement before the offensive. And now these enormous forces concentrated in a narrow sector and delivering a blow at the junction between the fourth and third sectors proved unable to break through the Soviet lines defended by undermanned units exhausted by

venth day of the assault but Sevastopol was not
..n's order to his forces to take it on the fourth day,
.ces had not yet burst through the defence front in any
, of course, a total failure.
..nen the fighting was in the balance that could tip to one side or
..r one of the two commanders of the belligerent armies placed a
..r weight on his scale, the unexpected happened on the Soviet side. For
..rov personally that was an affront he accepted with dignity. The first to
learn the big news in the Army was Major Kovtun, Chief of Operations at the
Army Headquarters. This is his story:

—At about six hours in the morning, a Lieutenant General with a Gold Star
of a Hero of the Soviet Union on his chest stepped into my office where I was
on duty, studying maps and sorting out reports on the numbers of remaining
battalions, guns, tanks, aircraft and ammunition.

—I stood to attention. He asked my name and identified himself: "The
name's Chernyak. I'm your new Army Commander. What are you doing
here?"

—He examined the papers on my desk carefully. "Were you trained at an
Academy?"

—"No sir".

—"I can see that. The way you work was good in Napoleon's and
Kutuzov's time. You should compare the numbers of divisions, not battalions." I was silent.

—He reread my report. "You have so many divisions yet you cannot hold
your defence line. Your fighting spirit must have waned. But I will galvanize
you into action!"

—I ventured an objection: "But it's unfair to compare our divisions with
the German ones. Half of our regiments have only two battalions, and even
these are undermanned, while they have three full-sized battalions in every
regiment. . . ."

—He cut me short: "Make a report on the state of the Army for me. It's an
order!"—

The appointment of a new man to lead the Army was just as unexpected
news as his decision to start preparations for an offensive immediately, which
literally stunned his new subordinates. Not much was known about General
Chernyak in the Army. A few veterans of the Winter War with Finland
remembered him as a divisional commander who had distinguished himself
in breaking through the Mannerheim Line, for which he was awarded his
Gold Star.

The offensive order was not, of course, a manifestation of wilfulness or
incompetence on the part of the new Army Commander. That was indisputably a plan initiated at the Headquarters of the Transcaucasian Front in
Tbilisi, Georgia, where they had not yet gained a clear idea of the situation in
Sevastopol.

Petrov, appointed deputy to the new Army Commander, did not comment on his demotion. He was preoccupied with thoughts about the dangers awaiting the defending forces. He realized that the fate of Sevastopol was hanging by a thread.

One can only wonder what he felt about his demotion which was unfair and even insulting. In fact, there was no reasonable justification for that. He had proved his competence and skill in the Battle of Odessa. He had organized the defence of Sevastopol even before the breakthrough of the Maritime Army towards the city, which was defended only by scattered sailors' units and local draft battalions. He had been the mastermind behind the repulsion of the first German assault on Sevastopol. Another well-prepared German assault had actually been thwarted by December 21 under Petrov's direction.

The top naval commanders who had been by his side during those earlier battles raised their voices on his behalf, which was a bold action under the circumstances. Rear Admiral Zhukov repeatedly requested Vice Admiral Oktyabrsky to protect Petrov and finally the latter and Military Council member Kulakov sent the following message to Moscow:

—Comrade Stalin. Urgent. For reasons unknown to us and ignoring our opinion, the Transcaucasian Front Commander has relieved General Petrov of his duties as Maritime Army Commander. Petrov is a competent and dedicated commander who has not deserved a demotion. The Fleet Military Council has witnessed Petrov's excellent work in the Battles of Odessa and Sevastopol and now requests you, Comrade Stalin, to promote him to Lieutenant General, which he has certainly deserved, and leave him in the post of Commander of the Maritime Army. We are awaiting your orders.—

There was a prompt reply: —Oktyabrsky. Sevastopol. Petrov to be left in the post of Maritime Army Commander. Chernyak appointed your deputy for land forces. Instructions of Chief of the General Staff of the Red Army Shaposhnikov. Krasnodar. 25.12.1941. Kozlov. Shamanin.—

In the meantime, fierce fighting on the approaches to Sevastopol continued unabated.

The Chief of Reconnaissance reported to Petrov about Manstein's new deadline for taking Sevastopol—December 28.

"He evidently wants to make a Christmas present to Hitler", Major Potapov joked.

"Okay, we'll make him a good present, too," Petrov smiled sarcastically.

. . . Setting a new deadline for taking Sevastopol, Manstein hoped to compensate for his earlier setbacks in storming the city. Against Upon the background of the German defeat in the Battle of Moscow, that would enhance his prestige as a strategist. The stakes were high, and Manstein would stop at nothing to achieve his coveted goal. He was driving his bleeding divisions into battle, seeking to break his way towards Severnaya Bay.

On December 26, Soviet troops started to land on the Kerch Peninsula. That was not yet known in Sevastopol. More than 100 small ships of the Azov

Naval Flotilla under Rear Admiral Gorshkov's command, defying the rough seas, had landed a force of brave commandos who entrenched themselves on Capes Zyuk, Khroni and Tarkhan. Another force came ashore in the areas of Kamysh-Burun and Eltigen.

A strong gale delayed further landing and transportation of troops. On the night of December 29, a fleet under the command of Captain First Rank Basisty approached Feodosian and unleashed their full fire power on the port. That was a complete surprise to the Germans who were celebrating Christmas.

Soviet landing parties stormed the piers and carried the fight to the city streets. German artillery fought back ferociously. A shell hit a turret on the cruiser *Krasny Kavkaz* and wreaked havoc inside. The ship could blow up any moment because the explosion had caused a fire in the ammunition depot. The gunners Pokutny, Pushkarev and Pilipenko displayed great presence of mind and promptly put the fire out. Their excellent peacetime training now came in good stead.

The cruiser, *Krasny Krym* was damaged by a number of direct hits and lost many men killed. The landing operation, however, was successful and won commendation in a special order of the Supreme Commander in Chief.

The landing of Soviet forces at Kerch and Feodosia took Manstein by surprise. Here is his own testimony.

—That was a mortal danger to the Army at a time when all its forces except one German division and two Rumanian brigades were besieging Sevastopol.—

The Battle of Sevastopol seemed to have reached its climax. The invisible thread by which the Soviet defences were held had been stretched to breaking point. On December 30 German troops more than once burst their way to the Mackenzie Mountain station and were invariably driven back by its defenders. Hand-to-hand fighting flared up here and there. Towards evening, however, the Germans had taken the station. On the same night a message came from Admiral Oktyabrsky:

—The troops of the Transcaucasian Front and ships of the Black Sea Fleet have taken the towns of Kerch and Feodosia. The fighting continues. . . . Our units are moving into the rear of the enemy troops besieging Sevastopol.—

That was joyful news indeed. Those were the landing operations which had long been expected. The troops had patiently endured shortages of ammunition and reinforcements because they knew that they were needed for a build-up to make such an operation possible. It was a reality at last.

General Petrov, however, was experienced enough not to lapse into euphoria. He saw in his mind's eye Manstein seized with impotent fury at his headquarters now that his radiant hopes for a Christmas present to the Führer and for fame on the battleground of the German defeat at Moscow had been dashed. The Soviet landing forces which could be stopped only by forces withdrawn from Sevastopol meant catastrophe to him. He could be saved only by taking Sevastopol or at least the Bay of Severnaya from where his artillery could level the city to the ground.

Petrov realized that only too well and he did not allow himself and his subordinates to relax for even a moment. He was not mistaken, which is proved by Manstein's later admission:

—It was clear as daylight that reinforcements should be urgently moved from Sevastopol to the threatened areas. Any delay would be disastrous. However, that would take a decision to give up plans of storming and taking Sevastopol at a time when one final effort seemed to be enough to gain control at least of the Bay of Severnaya.—

Manstein made up his mind to take this high risk. He writes further:

—. . . The Army Command resolved, after the Russians had landed their troops at Feodosia, to take the risk of delaying an all-out attack and withdrawing troops from Sevastopol, which was increasing with every passing hour. . . . By agreement with the commander of the 54th Army Corps and the divisional commanders another final attempt to effect a break-through towards the Bay of Severnaya was to be undertaken.—

That was a desperate assault. Everything was put at stake. General Petrov had foreseen the possibility of such a desperate step. He was a man of perspicacity and accurately guessed the possible moves and even the most hazardous venture of his German opponent.

To guess the enemy's intentions, however, was not enough. He needed forces to counter that final blow.

General Petrov called an emergency conference of the commanding officers of units and formations not at his headquarters but at his observation post, right on the battlefield.

His voice was quiet but firm:

"In the fourth sector we have abandoned very important positions, which has allowed the Germans to advance further to the Bay of Severnaya, the key to all our defences. We have suffered great casualties and are short of ammunition.

"Our troops, however, are fighting heroically and their staunchness is admirable. The Nazis are almost played out, their losses are enormous, but, I am sure, they will make another desperate attempt to overrun our defence lines. They have pledged too much to win this battle and have to justify their losses at whatever cost .

"Our strength is waning, it is true. But we must hold our ground and hurl them backwards. The city must be defended!" He raised his voice: "This is an order of the Motherland, the people, and the Party! It is our sacred duty to defend Sevastopol and its fate depends on your courage and staunchness. This is the crucial hour in the defence of Sevastopol. Here is my order: not a step backwards! There is no way of retreat: behind us is the sea!"

At dawn all Soviet artillery opened fire on the German attack positions. It had taken the German troops two hours to recover from that stunning blow before they finally mounted an offensive in the very same direction—from the Mackenzie Mountain station towards the Bay of Severnaya.

Fierce battles lasted for two hours, often with bayonet charges and point blank fire and the Germans were finally driven back. They mustered all forces available and charged again. That attack was also repulsed. The Germans had regrouped and brought up all their reserves for another assault, this time with panzer support. The Soviet troops counterattacked and wiped out attackers in close combat and finally broke the back of the German offensive. The enemy beat a retreat.

The Sevastopol defenders did not yield an inch of their ground in that bloody battle. Manstein admits that:

—. . . Our attempt to take the fortress of Sevastopol by storm failed again. We only retained the advantage of more solid encirclement of the Russians. . . . We also captured convenient attack positions for a later offensive. That, however, was a poor consolation in view of our great casualties.—

His admission is true only in respect of German casualties. In fact, as soon as Manstein had started bringing up reinforcements from Sevastopol to fight the Soviet landing force at Kerch, General Petrov immediately took advantage of the enemy's withdrawals and by vigorous attacking moves regained much of the ground lost in recent fighting. I will not describe these difficult counterattacks of exhausted Soviet units. Their success largely depended on their enthusiasm and confidence in their righteous cause. As a result of these battles the "convenient attack positions for a later offensive" allegedly captured by Manstein's forces remained on paper, but his enormous casualties were real.

That was another splendid victory for the commanders and the rank-and-file of the forces defending Sevastopol. Not only had they held the city but by keeping the main forces of Manstein's 11th Army in check, they secured the success of the Soviet landing operations at Kerch and Feodosia. That was, indeed, a very good New Year present from the Sevastopol defenders to the country and people.

Bracing Up for a New Fight

The Maritime Army was constantly at work improving its defence fortifications and their engineering standards. That work was done by the hands of the same soldiers and sailors who were invincible in battle. They dug about 350 kilometres of trenches all along the length of the 36-kilometre battle front which consisted of three defence lines up to 12 kilometres in depth.

The Sevastopol defenders expected another decisive assault on the city. General Petrov pinned great hopes on artillery, which he regarded as the most formidable weapon of war. There were 14 to 15 guns in position along every kilometre of the front line. His Chief of Artillery Ryzhy knew all about his business, and with his superior skill in fire manoeuvre he could concentrate as many as 300 guns to achieve a devastating effect where necessary. All artillery, including the heaviest-calibre guns were prepared to fight enemy tanks over open sights. Stores of ammunition brought by submarines were providently arranged in the safest places. Soldiers stocked themselves with home-made mines, hand-grenades and Molotov cocktails.

A Sudden Blow

To show the character of the hero, the writer of an ordinary novel usually depicts him in a series of events and difficult situations which illustrate his image. The main difficulties at war are caused by the enemy, of course. There are also other difficulties not directly related to enemy action: in the Battle of Sevastopol, for instance, they were isolated from the main forces of the Red Army and its logistic rear, bottlenecks in supplies and ammunition shortages, the difficulties involved in medical aid to the wounded and many others.

Yet the enemy forces and their commander mattered more than any other factor. Indeed, every enemy general was a man with his own biography, habits and character traits. These were not irrelevant to the battles in which they took part. German generals knew their business and many of them were men of talent. All the greater, therefore were the merits of the Soviet generals who defeated these strong and skilful enemies.

I wish to illustrate my general statements on this subject with some concrete facts. I have outlined in the foregoing the biography of General Petrov's main adversary—von Manstein. We have also seen him in action suffering repeated defeats at Petrov's hands. It would be relevant and fair, therefore, to show the abilities and character of this adversary by a graphic example especially as there is a good occasion for that.

Manstein had suffered a defeat in his first assault in November and in the decisive attack on Sevastopol in December. Petrov parried his blows and inflicted enormous casualties on his troops. At the time of these setbacks Manstein learned of the Soviet landing operations at Kerch and Feodosia. That was followed by Soviet troop landings at Evpatoria and Sudak. Manstein found himself in an unenviable position, to put it mildly. Hitler was driven to a frenzy by the surrender of the Kerch Peninsula. Count Schponek, Commander of the 42nd Corps which had been routed here was dismissed, recalled to Berlin and brought before a court martial, presided over by Goering.

The hearing was short and looked more like a travesty of justice. Count Schponek was found guilty and condemned to death. It is true, the death penalty was later commuted to life imprisonment.

These events were certainly a good cause for Manstein to worry about his own setbacks. He saw the main dangers and complications, however, in future events. These were not just landing parties operating in the Crimea but large forces which had opened a new front.

In that critical situation Manstein displayed his foresight as an experienced strategist. His assessment of his position was objective and correct.

—In the early days of January the Russian forces landed at Feodosia and moving from Kerch had actually opened an avenue of approach to the vital artery of the 11th Army—the Jankmoi-Simferopol railway. . . . The Russians had attempted to interfere with withdrawals of troops from the Sevastopol front and attacked our new positions which were not yet well fortified.—

That attack was undertaken by General Petrov. In a few days he had done whatever was possible and more to repulse the attacking German divisions but now he mounted an attack with his scant forces to hold back the German units pulled out of their positions at Sevastopol and force them to return.

If the Command of the newly-formed Crimean Front had acted with the same determination as the Sevastopol defenders, its success would have been complete. For unknown reasons, however, it was incredibly sluggish and failed to mount a decisive offensive. Even Manstein was puzzled by that.

—If the Russians had taken advantage of the situation prevailing and pursued the 46th Infantry Division retreating from Kerch, rapidly as well as delivering a determined strike at the Rumanians retreating from Feodosia, the situation would have become hopeless and not only in this new sector of the Eastern Front held by the 11th Army. The fate of the whole 11th Army would have been at stake. . . . The enemy, however, failed to seize that opportunity. The Russian Command had either misunderstood its advantages in that situation or had not dared to capitalize on them immediately.—

Manstein, therefore, regained the initiative. At first, he managed to set up a defensive front and check the advance of Soviet forces and then, witnessing the inaction of the opposing commanders, took prompt and effective action, scoring much success.

The following is Manstein's story of those events.

"The Russians continued to keep their 44th and 51st Armies on the Kerch Front. At the end of April their total strength was 17 infantry divisions, 3 infantry brigades, 2 cavalry divisions and 4 tank brigades, that is, a total of 26 large formations.

—The Army Command could oppose these forces with no more than 5 German infantry divisions and one panzer division. . . . Since the Rumanian formations (up to 3 divisions. V.K.) were fit for offensive operations only symbolically, the actual balance of forces in the operation planned under the code name *Bustard Hunt* was even less favourable. Moreover, the offensive on the Parpach Isthmus could be effected only by a frontal attack. The two seas ruled out any possibility of a flanking manoeuvre. In addition, the Russians had built a defence line deeply echeloned in depth. Was it indeed possible to defeat two Russian armies in that situation with a 2 to 1 balance of strength in their favour?"

To be fair, a correction would be relevant here. There were not two but three Soviet armies here. The third one was the 44th Army commanded by

Lieutenant General Chernyak, the very same man who had come to Sevastopol to replace Petrov. Here he was in command of the 44th Army during the whole operation—from February to May, 1942. The 51st Army was commanded by Lieutenant General Lvov. In February 1942 the 47th Army of Major General Kolganov concentrated on the Kerch Peninsula and joined the troops on the Kerch Front.

Manstein realized that in the narrow and long extended isthmus between the Black Sea and the Sea of Azov he would achieve nothing by a frontal attack against a large mass of opposing troops. Proficiency in the art of warfare, an imaginative approach, reliance on some objective factors conducive to success were needed now. And he had them at his disposal.

First, the factor of surprise. Confident of its superior strength, the Command of the Crimean Front did not believe in the possibility of attack on the part of the Germans who had much smaller forces here. Second, Manstein delivered a distracting blow in the south of the isthmus, along the Black Sea coast and by his main thrust using an armoured division against the advanced positions of one of the Soviet armies in the centre, along the front line, in fact, he ruptured the entire system of Soviet defences as far as the Sea of Azov. Third, Manstein took advantage not only of the surprise factor but also of the manoeuvrability of his troops and their efficient control. During ten days, from May 8 to 18, Manstein cleared the Kerch Peninsula; in the Adjimushkai quarries Soviet officers and soldiers waged a heroic fight from May 16 to October 31, 1942.

In his memoirs "The General Staff in War Time", General of the Army Shtemenko writes about those tragic days:

—As far back as late January General Headquarters sent their representative L. Z. Mekhlis to the Crimea. The General Staff assigned Major General Vechny to accompany him. They were expected to help the Front Command to organize an operation for forcing the Germans to lift the blockade of Sevastopol. As was his custom, Mekhlis limited his aid to reshuffling commanding officers. First of all, he replaced Chief of Staff Tolbukhin with Major General Vechny.

—Between February and April, the Crimean Army Group, supported by the Black Sea Fleet, made three attempts to pierce the German defences but invariably failed. The Soviet forces had to go over to the defensive.

—In the meantime, the Germans were preparing for an offensive. They intended to dislodge the Soviet forces from the Kerch Peninsula and then to pounce in force upon the heroic defenders of Sevastopol. The German Command unmistakably identified a weak spot at the coastal flank of our 44th Army and moved large panzer and air forces there to be supported by a landing force from the sea. After breaking the Soviet defences here and developing their offensive northwards and north-eastwards, the Germans would take in the rear of the armies of the Crimean Front.

—The Germans attacked on May 8, burst through our positions and advanced rapidly into the hinterland. The defences of the Crimean Front with no reserves behind the lines were disorganized and troop control was lost. After twelve days of heroic fighting the Crimean Army Group suffered a severe defeat.—

One of those guilty of that catastrophe was Mekhlis as can be surmised from Shtemenko's evidence and, since Petrov was to co-operate with him later, a few words about his style of work would be relevant.

Two surviving documents eloquently illustrate it. One of them is Mekhlis' message to the Supreme Commander-in-Chief of May 8, 1942.

—Now is not the right time for complaints but it is my duty to report information about the Front Commander to General Headquarters. On May 7, that is on the eve of the German offensive, Kozlov had called a Military Council meeting to discuss the plan of a future operation to take Koi-Asan. I recommended him to shelve this plan and issue immediate instructions to the armies in view of an impending German offensive. In his order the Front Commander emphasized that the offensive was expected between May 10 and 15 and suggested a defence plan of the Army Group to be drawn up before May 10 and submitted to all commanding officers and headquarters. The entire situation on that day, however, showed that the Germans would attack in the morning. On my insistence the mistakes in dates were corrected. Kozlov also opposed a plan to bring reinforcements to the sector of the 44th Army.—

The supreme Commander-in-Chief was not taken in by that attempt to evade responsibility for the Crimean debâcle and he radioed back a reply:

—You have taken a strange stance as an onlooker who is not responsible for the affairs on the Crimean Front. This is a convenient stand but thoroughly rotten. You are not an onlooker on the Crimean Front but a plenipotentiary representative of General Headquarters answerable for all successes and setbacks of the Front Command and obliged to remedy its mistakes on the spot. You along with the Front Command are to blame for the weakness of the left flank. If the situation showed that the Germans would attack in the morning and you took no steps to organize a rebuff but satisfied yourself with passive criticism, so much the worse for you. This means you have not yet realized that you were sent to the Crimean Front not as the chief executive of the State Control Committee but as a responsible representative of General Headquarters.

—You request us to replace Kozlov with somebody like Hindenburg. But you certainly know that we have no Hindenburgs in reserve. Your duties in the Crimea are not very complex and you could have coped with them on your own. If you had used attack planes not against secondary targets but against enemy tanks and manpower, the Germans would not have burst open our defences and their tanks would have been stopped. One need not be a Hindenburg to understand this simple thing after two months on the Crimean Front.—

Following the Kerch catastrophe, Mekhlis was dismissed from his post of Deputy Commissar for Defence and Chief of the Central Political Department of the Red Army and demoted to the rank of corps commissar. Front Commander Lieutenant General Kozlov and divisional commissar Shamanin were dismissed from their posts and demoted by one rank. The Front Chief of Staff Major General Vechny was dismissed. Lieutenant General Chernyak, Major General Kolganov, Major General of the Air Force Nikolayenko, the Front Air Commander, were demoted to colonels.

The Third Assault on Sevastopol

Now that Manstein had his hands free in the other areas of the Crimea, there was no doubt that he would concentrate all his forces against Sevastopol. Sevastopol was a thorn in the side for the whole German Army. Manstein and Hitler himself were eager to get rid of this nagging pain. Hitler summoned Manstein to his headquarters to hear his report on the progress of the siege, and endorsed his plan of the next assault. Now it was Hitler's own decision.

On coming back to the Crimea, Manstein ordered all the forces of the 11th Army to be brought up immediately to the Sevastopol area. To protect the coast he had left only the 46th Infantry Division on the Kerch Peninsula, and some Rumanian units in other sectors.

The Nazis liked to give exotic names to their operations. Their next decisive assault on Sevastopol was codenamed *Sturgeon Catch*. Now the Germans enjoyed absolute air supremacy in that area, preventing troop reinforcements and supplies to be brought by sea to Sevastopol. Only submarines could reach the besieged city but they could not bring much. The German Air Force kept Soviet warships off the harbour which deprived the land forces of their artillery support.

A few figures will illustrate the balance of forces before the next German offensive. The defenders had 38 tanks against the German 450 (a ratio of 1 to 12), 116 aircraft against 600 (1 to 5), 600 pieces of artillery of various calibres against more than 1,300. Moreover, Manstein had received huge 600 mm. siege guns under Hitler's special orders. Manstein himself assessed his fire power as follows:

—In the history of the Second World War the Germans never massed as much artillery as in their offensive on Sevastopol.—

This statement requires no comment.

Manstein realized this next assault on the city was his last chance. In the event of a setback he would be finally discredited in the eyes of the army and Hitler. Therefore, he went out of his way to secure whatever was necessary for a successful assault.

Now that he had massed enormous forces, Manstein acted with confidence. To clear the way for his attacking troops he intended to make a breach in the Soviet defences by a devastating artillery and air attack.

At dawn on June 2, 1942 German artillery and air forces delivered their first strike of tremendous power. For a full day the ground was shaking and fountains of earth were thrown up by innumerable shells. The city and port were ablaze. Smoke and soot veiled everything. Daylight turned into dusk. The Soviet defenders were expecting a German attack any moment but, hour after hour, the Germans bombed and strafed their positions without going into attack.

That was a full day of continuous ferocious bombardment. The nervous strain on the Soviet troops was exhausting. They were ready to fight but the Germans withheld their attack. The next morning the Germans resumed their fierce air and artillery strikes at the city and its defences.

Here is an eyewitness account of that hell, by Lieutenant General Laskin now living in Minsk.

—About 2,000 guns and mortars kept firing at our positions without a moment's interval. Shells whined overhead and exploded on all sides. The thunder of guns merged into a deafening roar, splitting our eardrums. Bombers in groups of twenty to thirty attacked us without caring for their targets but coming in wave after wave and literally ploughing up the earth throughout our defence area.

German aircraft were in the air above our positions all day long. We could not hear their engines in the continuous thunder of guns and shell explosions. Groups of bombers following in rapid succession looked like countless flocks of fantastic black birds. A whirlwind of fire was raging at all our positions. The sky was clouded by smoke from explosions of thousands of bombs and shells. Yet planes kept coming in wave after wave and showered us with a hail of bombs. Enormous clods of earth and uprooted trees flew into the air. More than 1,000 guns and mortars were firing simultaneously at our narrow fourth defence sector and about 100 bombers were raining bombs upon us. An enormous dark grey cloud of smoke and dust rose higher and higher and finally eclipsed the sun. In my sector, where the Germans were making their main thrust, they outnumbered us one to nine in manpower and one to ten in artillery, not to speak of the tanks, because we had none. Add to that the complete German air supremacy. . . .—

Sevastopol was reduced to a heap of smouldering ruins. Only a few clusters of houses on the outskirts were not demolished.

The intensity of German artillery fire and bombing raids in different sectors gave General Petrov the clue to identifying the direction of the main German thrust. He realized that it would be undertaken in the fourth sector defended by Laskin's division and Potapov's brigade, while the secondary strike would be dealt along the Yalta highway in the south.

Soviet artillery counterattacked at 2:55 on the next day. As German prisoners of war testified later, the German artillery preparation was to start at 0300 hours and the assault at 0400 hours in the morning, so General

Petrov had forestalled it by only five minutes. That, however, was of critical importance. Unfortunately, the Soviet artillery was short of ammunition and could keep firing for only twenty minutes. Nevertheless, the German infantry had already moved into attack positions and suffered severe casualties, communications were disrupted and the German troops were stunned for some time. To launch an organized attack, the German Command was compelled to bring up forces from the second echelon and open the offensive not at 0400 hours as planned but after 0700 hours.

As though to avenge their losses, the Germans again unleashed their artillery and air power on the Soviet positions even more ferociously than before.

Finally, the Germans went into the assault. The defenders met them with dense and accurate fire. The attack bogged down, and Manstein ordered all his artillery and air forces into action again to soften up the Soviet defences. There were more and more air raids and squalls of bomb and shell explosions.

But let us go back to Laskin's story.

—My command post was within a mile of the first line of trenches and I saw clearly a multitude of infantry and tanks emerging from the cover of the Belbek valley. More than fifty tanks were advancing on the positions of Colonel Shashlo's 747th Infantry Regiment and the left flank of Colonel Potapov's 79th Brigade. The tanks were rolling along under cover of a dense artillery barrage. Our artillery knocked out a few tanks and our machine-guns were taking a heavy toll of lives but the tanks and infantry were doggedly forging ahead. Our observation post was showered with artillery and mortar shells and bombs. Dug-outs were caving in and trenches filled with earth.

—The terrain in our defence zone was disfigured beyond recognition, the earth was blackened and pockmarked with shell craters. We groped our way through the debris in the trenches, stepping over dead bodies. . . .

—Enemy attacks followed one after another. There was a screen of dust and smoke in front of the Soviet Lines, and one could see nothing beyond fifty metres.

—At last evening came and the fighting ceased as darkness thickened. Isolated shots and explosions and short bursts of automatic fire were still heard now and then. Officers were counting survivors in their units. Faces were black with dust and soot, and almost everyone became hoarse.—

None of the Soviet commanders had a wink of sleep on that night. The soldiers in the trenches did not sleep either. They were repairing their trenches and preparing for tomorrow's fight. Signalmen were restoring communications and engineers were patching up mine fields. Logistic men were bringing in food and ammunition.

Petrov phoned to Potapov and ordered him to mount a counterattack with the full strength of his 79th Brigade at dawn on June 8 and restore the defences on its left flank.

A counterattack against superior enemy forces was, of course, dangerous and almost hopeless. The Soviet defenders could muster no more than two battalions and a few tanks of obsolescent models for that desperate action. Faithful to his tactics of active defence, however, Petrov ventured to take that hazardous step to give whatever help he could to the troops confronting the Germans in the sector of their main thrust. The 79th Brigade attacked in the morning with artillery support but was hurled backwards. The Army Commander had no other reserves, nor had the commanders of the defence sectors any either.

Having repulsed the counterattack, the Germans again swamped the Soviet positions with artillery fire as their aircraft rained bombs upon them. The artillery barrage was followed by German tanks and infantry. The Soviet defenders had almost nothing left to hold them off as they had run out of ammunition and more and more lives were snuffed out by enemy fire. Nevertheless, the first attack in the main direction was repulsed by the 172nd Infantry Division. That, however, was followed by another, even more vehement attack. Tanks and infantry were moving ahead relentlessly while aircraft cleared the way for them by bombing strikes.

On the afternoon of June 8 Laskin reported to General Petrov:

"The Germans are steadily wedging themselves into the divisional defences. I have no reserves left. I request more artillery support. Ryzhy is helping well but the coastal guns hit targets too far from the front line."

"Can your division hold the main defence line until dark?"

"It will."

"This should be done at all costs. At night the 345th Division will come to your rescue," Petrov assured him.

It had been a very hard day, especially in the sector of the main German thrust. Many Soviet commanders were killed. The Soviet troops were heavily depleted. Petrov was dead tired after the second day of the German assault but he felt satisfied. He realized that in that desperate situation the Soviet defenders were again frustrating the plan of the Germans to pierce the defences and take the city by a single thrust after so many days of continuous artillery and air bombardment.

The Germans, however, had only gained a foothold at the front edge of the Soviet defences. That was definitely a success for the defending side and Petrov was clearly aware of that.

But what was Manstein's assessment of the progress of the battle? Here is an excerpt from his memoirs.

—All along the perimeter of the fortress front flashes of gunfire were seen at night, and in the daytime clouds of dust and rock fragments, stirred by explosions of shells and bombs rose skyward. That was, indeed, a fantastic decor for a grandiose spectacle! Yet the spirit and self-sacrifice of the soldiers fighting for victory here were stronger than the nature of this "iron land", than all the weapons used by the attackers and defenders. . . . Here the spirit of the German soldier, his courage, initiative and self-sacrifice were opposed by the desperate resistance of the enemy, whose strength derived from the familiar terrain, the endurance and incredible staunchness of the Russian soldier. . . .

These lines, tinged with a romantic euphoria, which Manstein wrote after the war, are not consistent with his mood in the days of that fighting. On June 9, the German offensive petered out and came to a halt. Chief of Reconnaissance Potapov reported to General Petrov that, as testified by German prisoners of war, the German 132nd and 50th Divisions had sustained forbidding casualties and were unable to advance. The German 24th Division had lost more than one third of its strength. The total German losses during two days of fighting amounted to 20,000 officers and men.

The defence of Sevastopol could be likened to a rubber ball. It was depressed at places by the attackers but was not punctured in any spot. In the main direction of attack in the sector defended by Laskin's division the Germans had failed to advance by more than three kilometres.

Petrov had no forces left strong enough to counterattack and, to make matters worse, they had run out of ammunition and could not sustain effective fire. Every attack ended in hand-to-hand fighting. Though utterly exhausted, the Sevastopol defenders invariably found strength for a traditional Russian bayonet charge. The Germans were no match for them in close combat and, as a rule, took to their heels.

There was a new problem that plagued the defenders. Numerous German corpses abandoned in no man's land started to decompose under the scorching sun. The wind carried the nauseating stench to the Soviet trenches. There was no escape from it. The hungry men could not force themselves to eat. Even the sight of food was revolting to them.

On June 17 the Germans fiercely attacked the fourth defence sector and burst their way towards the sea coast, cutting off what remained of Kapitokhin's units and encircled coastal battery No. 30.

The battery was blocked on all sides. About 200 men were trapped in its casements. They kept firing until they had spent their last shell. The crew led by the battery commander Alexander and commissar Solovyov refused to surrender, and took shelter in underground bunkers. At night they even ventured to make sallies, killing German troops.

A German infantry regiment, two engineer battalions, tanks and artillery were moved in to capture the battery. The gunners fought them off, firing through the gun-ports. The Germans plugged all air chutes to block the access of fresh air into the bunkers, and the battery Diesel engines stalled through lack of air, leaving the trapped crew in complete darkness. The infuriated Nazis tried to smoke them out with poison gas. Wounded men were the first to die.

When their reserves of water and food had been used up, a group of men resolved to escape into the mountains where they could join the Partisans. They managed to climb out through sewerage pipes and attempted to fight their way through the German cordons. In a fierce clash many were killed and the others were taken prisoner, Alexander among them. He was brought to Simferopol and thrown into prison. The Nazis long persuaded him to go over to their side, all to no avail. He was brutally beaten up and finally murdered.

Commissar Solovyov, who was wounded, was unable to walk and had opted to stay at the battery. He shot himself at the last minute to avoid capture when all hope was lost.

A few wounded crewmen trapped underground were still fighting back. The Germans drilled a hole in the heavy steel door and pumped poison gas into their shelter. They finally captured the battery when all of its defenders were dead. According to their own evidence, the Germans had lost up to 1,000 men killed and wounded during their siege of the battery.

In spite of the enormous difficulties of the early period of the war the mainland gave effective aid to the Sevastopol defenders. Between June 13 and 17 the 138th Infantry Division and over 6,000 draft reinforcements were brought here. A dear price had to be paid for that aid: the *Abkhazia* was sunk in Sevastopol harbour. That luxury liner converted to transport had made sixteen sailings to Sevastopol, bringing hundreds of tons of ammunition and carrying thousands of wounded on her way back. The destroyer *Svobodny* was sunk by a direct bomb hit. The beautiful liner *Georgia* was within a few miles of the Sevastopol piers when a group of Junkers planes which had pierced her fighter cover sunk her in full view of the crowds expecting her on the shore. The soldiers and sailors who were on board swam ashore but her cargo of 500 tons of shells went to the sea bottom.

The seamen never relaxed their efforts to organize a sealift to the besieged city. The cruiser *Molotov* which arrived on June 16 brought the remnants of the 138th Brigade and 600 tons of shells. Work was going on at a feverish pace all night as her cargo was unloaded and wounded were carried onto her decks. With 2,000 wounded and 1,000 women and children on board the cruiser weighed anchor at dawn and sailed off escorted by the destroyer *Bezuprechny*.

The last transport to make port at Sevastopol was the *Belostok*. She had arrived on June 18, 1942 and on her way back, the next day, was sunk by German torpedo boats.

The "SCH-214" submarine which had been making shuttle sailings to carry men and supplies to Sevastopol was sunk on June 20. A regiment of Douglas cargo planes was assigned to maintain an airlift to the Sevastopol Defence District on June 21. Until July 1 its airmen had made 117 flights, bringing 185 tons of ammunition and carrying back a total of 1,471 wounded servicemen and 336 civilians.

On June 26 the destroyers *Bezuprechny* and *Tashkent* set sail from Novorossiisk for Sevastopol. At about 19 hours the *Bezuprechny* was attacked and sunk by German dive bombers. The *Tashkent* repelled air attacks, bringing down two planes, evaded an attack by torpedo boats and safely reached Sevastopol harbour. She was the last warship to have fought her way to the besieged fortress.

On the night of June 27, having taken on board more than 2,000 wounded and refugees, the *Tashkent* left Sevastopol harbour. During four hours she repulsed 86 massive German air attacks. She was literally showered with bombs. Her gunners brought down two planes and her captain steered her skilfully to avoid direct hits but close explosions severely damaged her hull. Rescue ships sailed out of Novorossiisk, fought off the attacking aircraft and towed her to port.

There was a great dearth of ammunition in Sevastopol. Resourceful port divers offered to retrieve shells from the sunken *Georgia*. Defying artillery fire and air attacks—a few hundred bombs were dropped upon it on June 18 alone—they brought up 38 tons of ammunition which was immediately carried to the front line.

The casualties suffered by Soviet troops in the last few days were severe: more than 7,000 officers and men killed and over 14,000 wounded. The 172nd and 95th Infantry Divisions retained, in effect, only their numbers. There were few survivors in the trenches and no more than twenty shells was left for each gun.

On June 20 the soviet defences in the city's northern quarter were limited to a few isolated strongholds.

Manstein's headquarters were relatively far from the scene of the fighting but he sensed its ferocity.

—It was hardest to drive the Russians out of their last fortified defences on the northern shore of the bay. The Soviets had hewed out in precipitous rocks deep galleries with armoured gates where they had stored ammunition and supplies. Their garrisons refused to surrender. When our engineer troops approached the first of these caves there was a tremendous explosion inside, a large part of the rocky coast collapsed, burying the defenders and our soldiers.—

Fighting continued in the other galleries for ten days, and the Germans lost a few hundred officers and men.

At sunrise on June 25 the Germans mounted their strongest attacks in the third defence sector. There were endless air and artillery attacks again. Soviet artillery was now practically silent; its stocks of ammunition had been completely exhausted. During the day German aircraft dropped 3,000 bombs on the Soviet defenders in that sector alone.

On June 27 German tanks overran the positions of the 25th Infantry Division, cutting down its men at point blank range. Towards evening the Germans had ruptured the defences of the 8th Marine Brigade and captured a position of advantage on the Sakharnaya Golovka hill. When they had run out of ammunition the Marines fought the attackers with stones. The remnants of the 25th Infantry Division and the 3rd Marine Regiment retreated towards the Inkerman station.

On the night of June 28 under cover of a smoke-screen the Germans started to cross the Bay of Severnaya in rowing-boats and launches. Troops of the 79th Brigade and the survivors of the crew of the *Zheleznaykov* armoured train tried to stop them with rifle and machine-gun fire but without much success. No artillery was now available to fight off the landing force.

In the meantime German aircraft were literally raging over the battlefield, bombing and strafing machine-gun nests and wiping out the last pockets of resistance. Towards noon units of the German 24th Infantry Division had finally crossed the Bay of Severnaya. Simultaneously, the Germans supported by intensive artillery fire and bombers mounted an offensive in the direction of the Fedyukhin heights and Mt. Sapun-Gora.

At 6 a.m. in the morning the Germans overran the positions of the 386th Infantry Division. Its men engaged them in fierce hand-to-hand fighting. Soviet defenders were fighting heroically in their trenches, and would rather die than retreat.

To help the defenders in this sector Petrov threw into battle the remnants of the 25th Infantry Division, the 9th Marine Brigade, and the 142nd Infantry Brigade to delay the German advance in this area. These troops, however, were utterly exhausted and proved unable to turn the tide of the fighting. In a neighbouring sector the 8th Brigade was almost totally wiped out and its commander Colonel Gorpishchenko was severely wounded. The survivors of the 386th Division retreated to the village of Dergachi where their commander Colonel Skutelnik attempted to organize defence.

During the latter half of June 29 the German Air Force made repeated bombing attacks against the last pockets of resistance in Sevastopol, dropping more than 10,000 bombs.

On the morning of June 30 the Germans resumed their air strikes and advanced all along the front, now pressing their attack mainly along the Yalta and Balaklava highways. Manstein expected that Petrov would send all those still capable of bearing arms to defend the Bay of Severnaya; therefore, the German thrust in a new direction from the south would be unexpected and irresistible, since the defenders had no strength left to repulse it. The Soviet units here were still fighting back and their retreat never turned into a stampede.

The front before the Soviet troops had narrowed, and German artillery now scored more hits with the same number of guns.

It would seem that nobody could survive on the scorched battleground scarred by shell and bomb craters. On the approaches to the city, however, its defenders were still holding their ground. Exhausted, bleeding and burnt officers and soldiers who had had no sleep, rest or food for days were holding on and fighting to the last ditch.

Major General Novikov's 109th Infantry Division and units of Colonel Blagoveshchensky's 9th Marine Brigade were still resisting the Germans at the right flank. They retreated slowly, fighting back fiercely and inflicting heavy casualties on the Germans.

At the left flank, two German divisions—the 50th and 132nd—were keeping up pressure against the mutilated Soviet units. Another two German divisions—the 24th and 22nd—were advancing towards the Malakhov Hill from the coast of the Bay of Severnaya. They were resisted by the remnants of the 79th Infantry Brigade, artillery and logistic units.

The Soviet positions on the Malakhov Hill were under constant artillery and mortar fire and air strikes. Lieutenant Commander Matyukhin, commander of the 701st coastal battery, positioned here, was manning the only remaining gun, firing over its sights. Finally, this gun also fell silent. On the next day, however, a handful of defenders of the Malakhov Hill were still holding on.

Having suppressed this last stronghold, the Germans advanced close to the city itself. Sevastopol was in flames and veiled in black smoke rising from its ruins. It has been ruthlessly bombarded during the last few days.

In his "History of the Second World War", the French general L. Chassin writes:

—In the last 25 days of the siege of Sevastopol German artillery fired 30,000 tons of shells into the city, while Richthofen's air forces which supported Manstein made 25,000 sorties and dropped 125,000 heavy bombs, almost as much as Britain's RAF had dropped by that time on Germany since the beginning of the war.

The Last Days

No army leader, however talented or skilful, can plan and carry out what has no prerequisites in the material, technological and spiritual potentials of a nation's army and economy. Therefore, speaking of General Petrov's illustrious record, I am not overlooking the fact that he would have been unable to implement his most brilliant decisions without a high commanding post in the Red Army. It is true, in the Battle of Sevastopol the Soviet industrial potential could not be brought into full play, because the city was cut off from the rest of the country, but Petrov relied on the high morale and patriotism of his officers and men. The final battles for Sevastopol provide a good example of that.

The Maritime Army had not retreated from Sevastopol. Many of its men, from those who counterattacked Zigler's group in the early days of the siege to those who had reserved the last cartridge for themselves on the last, 250th day of the battle, rest in peace in the sacred earth of Sevastopol.

Few defenders survived the battle. But the struggle continued on other fronts, where their experience and courage were a great help. The Supreme Commander praised the Sevastopol defenders in a special order: "Their selfless struggle is an example of heroism to the entire Red Army and the Soviet people."

On July 1, at a joint meeting of the Military Councils of the Black Sea Fleet and the Maritime Army Vice Admiral Oktyabrsky read out a message from Moscow ordering the evacuation of Sevastopol in view of the futility of its further defence. The message ordered a few hundred commanding officers to be taken out of the city. General Novikov was to stay on to direct the rearguard battles.

Having come back to his headquarters, Petrov asked his Chief of Staff Krylov.

"Please call in all commanding officers of the divisions and regiments. We evacuate."

Krylov looked at him in disbelief. Petrov added:

"I'll give the details at the conference. We are under orders to leave Sevastapol. You will come with me."

Krylov was still hesitant. "What happened?"

"We are military men and have to obey orders. It's not for us to decide where we are needed most now. Send Bezginov into me. I'll dictate my final instructions to him."

This writer met Colonel Bezginov and heard his story of the last few hours in Sevastopol.

—Krylov called me in the afternoon: "The General wants to see you." I came into Petrov's room. He looked sad and concerned, and jerked his head nervously.

—"Sit down and write", he told me. "The enemy has taken Sevastopol. I order Major General Novikov, Commander of the 109th Infantry Division, to take command of the remaining units and fight on as long as possible and then retreat into the mountains to join forces with the partisans."

—After a long silence, he added: "That's all. Type this for the divisional commanders."

—The order was signed by Petrov, Military Council member Chukhnov, and Chief of Staff Krylov. Special passes were issued to commanding officers ordered to leave by plane or submarine. They were not many, because only a few planes were available, and the naval command deemed it useless to send in ships in view of the total German air supremacy.—

After giving his last order Petrov withdrew into his compartment. After a little while Chukhnov became worried. His instinct told him that something was wrong. He opened the door and looked in. Petrov prostrate on his couch, his face turned to the wall, was opening his holster. Chukhnov rushed to him and seized his hand. The two men were silent for a long time. Then Chukhnov spoke up: "So you have decided to help the Nazis to get rid of you. But who will come back to liberate Sevastopol? You haven't thought about it yet, have you? It must be your duty in the first place."

Petrov sat up. His eyes were roving. He searched for his pince-nez, stood up and buttoned up his holster.

Late at night Petrov with Military Council members Chukhnov and Kuznetsov, Chief of Staff Krylov, his deputy Morgunov and other staff officers of his Army went to the pier where a submarine was awaiting them. The clear night sky was studded with stars and the bright moon threw a golden trail on the tranquil sea. But the city was blazing with numerous fires and spewing up clouds of black smoke. They heard rifle and automatic fire far away; that was Novikov's division fighting on the last line.

Officers and privates stood on the pier in silence. They slowly stepped aside to make way for their commanders. Petrov's head jerked and he looked down, probably to avoid seeing familiar faces. He did not speak to anybody, feeling as though he was walking on burning coals. Their stare seemed more deadly than the guns of a firing squad.

He would later say that he was leaving Sevastopol, hoping to organize the rescue of survivors. He could help them only from the outside and that hope suppressed his impulsive desire to stay with his fighting men. Sixty-three staff and commanding officers boarded the submarine, and she sailed for Novorossiisk.

German planes and gunboats chased the "SCH-209" submarine relentlessly for three days, and she executed intricate manoeuvres to escape her pursuers, now dodging and coming to a halt, now diving into deeper waters and changing her course. Finally, she dropped anchor at Novorossiisk harbour on July 4.

That had been a gruelling experience for the crew, but for Petrov it was harder to endure because of his older age and the after-effects of a shell shock. Yet not once did he betray how badly he felt to anybody.

During those long hours of enemy pursuit when the crew was choking on the hot air poisoned with diesel exhausts and the acid vapours from storage batteries, the General felt more depressed by an awareness of the tragic fate of his officers and men trapped in Sevastopol. Though he had left them in the besieged city under orders from the High Command, the realization that he was now in safety while they were fighting for their lives still hung over him. Whatever was done to save the defenders of Sevastopol had not been enough to effect their rescue. That sad memory would pain him as long as he lived.

At Novorossiisk the new arrivals were met by officers from the Black Sea Fleet headquarters and a group of their comrades who had arrived there earlier. Some even carried bunches of flowers. The newcomers, however, were certainly in bad shape for that ceremony, their faces grimed and unshaven, clothes soiled and crumpled. They were utterly exhausted by their arduous sailing and battle fatigue.

Right from the pier the passengers and crew went to a steam bath-house, from which all of them—Generals, officers and men—emerged dressed in identical crisp-new cotton uniforms of privates. On the next day, however, the Generals were supplied with uniforms fitting their high ranks.

The danger of captivity and death was past, but Petrov did not feel happy at all. In one of his conversations with Vice Admiral Oktyabrsky he frankly said many bitter words straight in the face of the Admiral. Petrov was confident that with more efficient organization the heroic defenders of Sevastopol who were still alive could have been rescued from their doom.

His words were not taken lightly. Petrov's name would drop out of the Admiral's later articles and speeches about the heroic defence of Sevastopol.

There is a disagreement as to whether it was possible to evacuate the defenders of Sevastopol from Cape Khersones.

According to one view, naval vessels, if sent to help out the defenders of Sevastopol, might have been lost. A long war was yet to be fought. The Black Sea Fleet, which had already suffered heavy casualties, had to defend the sea lanes, and the coast of the Caucasus. Another reason was the German air supremacy. Now that the Luftwaffe had air bases in the Crimea with the sea coast a short way off, refuelling and taking on a new bomb load was a matter of minutes. Even a small number of planes flying frequent sorties could effectively influence the course of battles.

And still, for all its sparing attitude to ships the command of the Black Sea Fleet could have remembered about the relative safety of night and providently taken steps to bring to Sevastopol's harbour as many lifeboats as possible, even the simplest ones. Under the cover of night, hundreds of such boats could have escaped from Cape Khersones, as is proved by those survivors who had escaped on self-made rafts, barrels, inflated tyre tubes, and other makeshift facilities.

In his article "The Sea Transport in the Battle of the Caucasus", Doctor of History Basov writes:

—On August 4 (i.e., twenty to twenty-five days after the tragedy on Cape Khersones, a long enough period for a rescue operation. V.K.) groups of transports and auxiliary craft escorted by naval launches began breaking through the Kerch Strait under enemy fire.—

Another testimony is to be found in "The Black Sea Fleet", a book by a group of Navy veterans:—Over fifty small transports, 325 fishing trawlers and more than 2,570 lifeboats were scuttled or destroyed in the ports of the Sea of Azov, since it was impossible to take them to the Black Sea.—

At the end of June all these vessels or at least part of them could have been brought from the Sea of Azov without obstruction. There were many such vessels in the Black Sea harbours, also. If each of the 325 fishing trawlers had taken 100 passengers, more than 30,000 Sevastopol defenders could have been saved.

I have been asked in hundreds of letters to describe in greater detail the final battles on Cape Khersones. This, however, is a different story which lies outside the subject of this narrative. I will quote only one eyewitness account. What one man saw gives a general idea of the heroic resistance and tragic events of those days. It is a letter from Victor Gurin, a sergeant second class and a former scout, who lives in Taganrog today.

"General Novikov set up his command post at the site of the 35th battery. All were expecting rescue ships but they never arrived to our great disappointment. All officers and political instructors who were still alive were summoned to the new command post for a briefing.

"New units were formed out of scattered groups of officers and men of savaged marine brigades and infantry divisions.

"To strengthen our defences we reinforced the old earthen ramparts, assembled their surviving defenders and assigned them to their stations.

"Men climbed to their firing nests over the precipitous slopes of coastal cliffs. General Novikov ordered a roll-call of officers and men and inspected their stocks of weapons and ammunition. The defence line was organized anew. At dawn on July 1, 1942 the first German aircraft attacked our positions. Coming from the side of the sea wave after wave, they bombed and strafed the shore defences and the cliffs where our men were entrenched and dropped leaflets demanding our surrender.

"Our casualties were severe. Our vehicles left at the edge of the sea were sprayed with a rain of incendiary bombs and many of them were hit. The choking black smoke rising from burning vehicles soon enveloped our positions in a thick smokescreen.

"I was in command of a platoon of submachine-gunners and antitank riflemen at the defence line of the 35th battery. Now tanks with lines of drunken Nazis following them attacked us. When they came near our positions, we counterattacked them. That fighting, the last in my life, went on for three hours. Dead and wounded men could be seen strewn on the ground on all sides.

"The Nazis were thrown back to the Yukharina Ravine and the place called Maximov Dacha. In the total confusion of the battle Nazi airmen bombed friend and foe. The enemy lost thousands. At night German funeral squads picked up and carted away only German corpses, leaving Rumanian and Tartar dead to rot where they were. We were emaciated with thirst and hunger and had no strength left to bury our dead.

"On July 1 we repulsed eight German attacks. They could not dislodge us from our positions; we were determined to die rather than give up. On the night of July 1 a few Soviet motor launches entered the Bay of Kazachya, and one of them started mooring at the pier.

That was rescue at last! Crowds of men rushed to the pier, and it collapsed under their weight. The launches had to keep their distance. Many swam to them and were taken on board, but they could not take all, and hundreds who could not make it back to the shore were drowned. The launches sailed off and were soon out of sight. We realized that all hope for rescue by sea was now lost.

"A decision was taken to pierce the German lines by a few surprise attacks.

"Before sunrise on July 2 Novikov informed us of the breakthrough plan. Frankly speaking, not much hope was pinned on it in view of the open terrain. To the signal of a green flare we attacked the Germans in several spots, taking them by surprise. Fierce fighting lasted until dawn. Only a few of our men were fortunate to have fought their way through the Germans' lethal fire and three defence lines.

Many of our men were killed in that attack, we were forced to retreat to our positions and take up a circular defence. There were thousands of corpses lying on the shore and in the water. The stench was unbearable. German aircraft attacking from the side of the sea were bombing and strafing our men on the steep coastal cliffs and rock terraces. German snipers had sneaked to a position of advantage near our burnt lorries and were killing off our officers by accurate shots.

"The sector between the 35th battery and the Bay of Kazachya had been pierced by German tanks and infantry by the end of the day and they reached the sea shore. We had nowhere to escape and were fighting to the last ditch. The Germans steadily pressed us and our defences were crumbling everywhere. Nevertheless, during July 2 we were still clinging to the narrow strip of the shore and fighting on.

"We beat off ten attacks on that day. A group of soldiers climbed down the coastal cliffs to the sea shore by ropes and made makeshift rafts of boards of lorry platforms. They decided to sail on them towards Cape Violent where they could climb precipitous cliffs and escape into the mountains to join the Crimean guerrillas. . . ."

On the day when General Petrov and other Soviet commanders were leaving Sevastopol German radio announced the taking of the fortress. Martial music and praises of the valiant German Army were broadcast all day long. In the evening Hitler, in a special message, expressed his thanks to Manstein and promoted him to the rank of Field Marshal.

What price had been paid for it? During the eight months of the siege the invaders lost up to 300,000 officers and men killed and wounded. During the last 25 days of the storm the number of dead topped 60,000. That was a mountain of corpses. Every killed German soldier had a father, a mother, a wife or a sweetheart, children, brothers or sisters. Each of them is entitled to ask what Manstein gave them in exchange for his Marshal's baton.

In April 1944, two years after these events, there was a second Battle of Sevastopol, but this time the invaders were on the defensive, while the Maritime Army, the 2nd Guards Army and the 51st Army were the attacking side. The Maritime Army was now under the command of General Melnik. In August 1944 Petrov was appointed to command the Fourth Ukrainian Front which incorporated the Maritime Army.

Before that storming of Sevastopol, in June 1943, the German High Command had made a statement to foreign correspondents:

—Sevastopol is taking on its former appearance. A formidable fortress is rising from its ruins. The German High Command has done whatever was necessary to turn Sevastopol into a stronghold no enemy would venture to approach. If the Russians decided to attack Sevastopol, any attempt on their part would be foiled. There is not an inch of ground in Sevastopol without fortifications or a heavy gun.—

That statement of the German High Command was not simply a propaganda bogey intended to intimidate the opponent. At one time Soviet troops had built a formidable defence line at Sevastopol which had withstood a siege of 250 days, and the Germans now had added to it defence works and weapons built and installed during the two years of occupation.

And now that the Crimea had been liberated, Soviet forces came up to the defence lines girdling the city. The assault was started on May 5, 1944. The fighting was fierce but it took the attackers only five days to break the German resistance and take the city.

. . . The Soviet defence of Sevastopol has gone down in the history of the art of warfare as a classical example of defensive combat in which land and naval forces displayed superior skill.

The Battle of the Caucasus

A New Appointment

Petrov certainly deserved a rest after the ordeals of the Battle of Sevastopol and his narrow escape by submarine. Yet a rest was too much to afford for a general when fierce fighting was at its climax on all fronts. In the middle of July 1942 Petrov left Novorossiisk and arrived at the Front Headquarters in Krasnodar. Here he learned of his summons to Moscow. Next morning he boarded a plane and was on his way.

He came back with a new appointment: Commander of the 44th Army. The reasons for that appointment and the role the 44th Army was to play in the impending battles on the southern wing of the Soviet–German front would be made clear by an outline of the general situation on the theatres of war.

By July 1942 quite a few large and small battles had been fought out, and the belligerent sides had inflicted staggering casualties on one another. The balance of military success had so far been tipping in favour of the German armies. They had seized a large part of Soviet territory and were still close to Moscow and besieging Leningrad. They were poised for a thrust towards the Volga and the Caucasus. Their superior numbers and weapons were an advantage that was yet to be countered.

The Caucasus is an enormous chain of mountains between the Black Sea and the Caspian. People of many different races and nations live in its Republics and autonomous regions—Azerbaijan, Armenia, Georgia, Daghestan, Checheno-Ingushetia, Northern Ossetia, Kabardino-Balkaria, the Stavropol and Krasnodar territories. The Main Caucasian Range divides the area between two seas and extends from Novorossiisk on the Black Sea coast to Baku on the Caspian coast, a distance of over 1,000 kilometres.

Most of this area is difficult for travel by any means of conveyance, and in the mountains only horses can be used to haul cargoes along their steep and rocky roads, while higher up even horses are helpless and people have to rely on their own strength and stamina to negotiate the rugged terrain. The northern part of this area is flat, rolling on to the Stavropol and Salsky steppes and the narrow strip along the Black Sea coast. All these were the scenes of hostilities that went down in history as the Battle of the Caucasus.

Soviet troops in the Transcaucasian area were on the alert round the clock to ward off a possible attack from the territory of neighbouring Turkey or Iran or from the Black Sea.

Turkey was openly preparing for war against the USSR. She was nurturing ambitious plans of conquest in addition to her aim of assistance to the Axis powers. A Turkish magazine wrote in February 1942:

—The day is not far off when we, like Tamerlane, will march from Anatolia to India, ascend the Himalayas and found a union of Daghestan, the Crimea, Kazan and Iran. All of Turkey's foes will be vanquished.—

The immediate aim was to seize the Baku oil fields. A mobilization plan had already been carried out, and 26 combat-ready Turkish divisions were deployed for attack across the border. The invasion was to commence in November 1942 after Berlin's announcement of the fall of Stalingrad.

As the danger to the Caucasus was drawing closer from the Don basin and neighbouring areas, the Soviet High Command redeployed part of the Transcaucasian forces to deal with this new menace. The sector was named the Transcaucasian Front.

The Commander of the Transcaucasian Military District appointed in January 1942 was General of the Army Ivan Tyulenev, a knowledgeable and experienced man thoroughly familiar with the local conditions. He was a veteran of the February and October Revolutions of 1917 and had a record of frontline service in two wars. In the First World War he was a master sergeant in the Kargopol 5th Dragoon Regiment and was awarded four St. George's Crosses for valour.

His record in the Revolution was quite illustrious: a delegate of the first Petrograd Soviet of Workers' and Soldiers' Deputies, a Communist Party member since 1918, Chief of Reconnaissance in Budenny's 1st Cavalry Army and Brigade Commander in the 4th Cavalry Division. He had taken part in fighting Denikin's and Wrangel's White Guards, the forces of bourgeois Poland, Petlyura's Ukrainian nationalists, the anarchist bands of Makhno and Antonov. In 1920 he fought the White Guards in the North Caucasus, and in March 1921 he led the 137th Infantry Regiment in the assault on the fortress of Kronstadt seized by mutinous navymen. For his courage and valour displayed in battle, he was decorated with three Orders of the Red Banner, a distinction few officers could boast at the time.

The Transcaucasian Front Headquarters worked out a plan of defence of Transcaucasia from the north. On July 16 General Tyulenev submitted it to the General Staff. In this plan the 44th Army was to defend the Soviet Union's main oil-producing regions of Baku and Grozny.

General Petrov assumed command of the 44th Army on August 2, 1942, at a time when the Germans were advancing swiftly from the Don. The army was digging in, preparing for a fight. A few lines of fortification were built on the northern approaches to Baku. Troops were aided by local civilians organized by the Central Committee of the Communist Party of Azerbaijan. The rivers Terek and Urukh were the backbone of the new defence line to protect the Baku and Grozny oil-fields and the approaches to Makhachkala which were the most probable targets of the German offensive.

Operation Edelweiss

Whenever a military debacle was suffered by Nazi Germany, Hitler invariably searched for a scapegoat who was not, as a rule, the chief culprit but a convenient person to be punished. The Nazi defeat at the walls of Moscow infuriated him. On December 19, 1941 he summoned Field Marshal Brauchitsch, Commander-in-Chief of the Land Forces, to his headquarters and berated him for two hours. Brauchitsch was forced to resign. Hitler had taken the debacle at Moscow as a personal insult. Goebbels quotes him in his diary:

—If Brauchitsch had done what he had been expected and obliged to do, our situation in the East would have been different. The Führer had not had the slightest intention of advancing in the direction of Moscow. He had been planning to invade the Caucasus and thus hit the Soviets in their most vulnerable spot. Brauchitsch and the General Staff, however, believed that plan to be wrong. Brauchitsch had strongly insisted on an offensive against Moscow. He wanted success for the sake of prestige, not real success.—

Indeed, at the time of taking the final decision to attack the Soviet Union there had been a debate among the Nazi chiefs. Some top-ranking generals argued in favour of a strike at Moscow and Leningrad, which, as they believed, would bring the Soviet Union to its knees.

Hitler and another group of generals preferred a thrust in the south to seize the Soviet Union's major industrial centres. In the days of working out the Barbarossa plan of invasion of the USSR Hitler announced:

—The aim of this operation is to wipe out Russia's armed forces, capture her main economic centres and destroy her other industrial areas, primarily in the region of Ekaterinburg (Sverdlovsk today); moreover, it is necessary to take the Baku area.—

Thus, Hitler had advocated the southern variant from the outset. He believed that the Soviet armed forces should be undermined economically in the first place, by depriving them of their fuel resources and then whatever had not been destroyed would come to a halt by itself.

Brauchitsch and Chief of the General Staff Halder argued for a thrust in the direction of Moscow. Therefore, when Germany had attacked the USSR, the Wehrmacht moved its main forces against Moscow, although its offensive operations on other fronts were just as active.

In August 1941, however, when it became clear to all, to Hitler himself first and foremost, that the blitzkrieg had flopped, and that the German forces had been bogged down in a protracted war, the Führer became nervous and attempted to implement his original plan of a southward thrust in the direction of the Caucasus. In a special directive issued on August 21, 1941,

Hitler proclaimed:

—The plans of the High Command of the Land Forces regarding the further conduct of the war in the East are discordant with my own plans.

—I order as follows:

—1. The chief task to be accomplished before the onset of winter shall not be the taking of Moscow but capturing the Crimea, the industrial and coal-mining regions on the Donets River and disrupting Russian oil supplies from the Caucasus; in the north—encirclement of Leningrad and joining forces with the Finns. . . .—

I refrain from pronouncing judgement on the advantages or disadvantages of each of these two plans of conquest, especially as war historians are in agreement that neither of them was sound militarily, because the entire strategy of the Nazi High Command was one of adventurism where victory was impossible.

But let us attempt, without analyzing the enormous mechanism of war, the large and small controls by which this mechanism is operated, to apply logic to Hitler's plan, renouncing the derogatory subriquet "lance corporal" by which he was lampooned in wartime.

Towards the Forties Hitler had gained a lot of experience in building up armed forces, boosting war industries and directing large-scale military operations. Suffice it to recall the conquest of Poland, France, and other European countries. In the light of all these events, Hitler's intention to seize the oil sources and to deprive the Red Army of its fuel supply does not look like a hair-brained scheme at all.

In the last war the internal combustion engine was the chief factor of combat. It was omnipresent: on land—in tanks and motor vehicles, in the air—in aircraft; at sea—in warships and submarines. All this weaponry could be made useless by a disruption of fuel supplies. The main Soviet oil sources were in the Caucasus, which accounted for 86 per cent of the total production at the time. Many of the biggest oil fields of Siberia and the Volga area of today had not yet been prospected let alone developed.

Let us imagine for a brief moment what could have happened if the Germans had indeed succeeded in capturing our oil fields in the Caucasus, however absurd this may now seem. It will be recalled, for instance, that a German advance to the banks of the Volga also seemed absurd in 1939.

Hitler was certainly informed of the courage and remarkable staunchness of the Soviet soldiers and realized that their stiffening resistance could not be overcome unless the tide of hostilities was drastically turned in his favour. In conversations with members of his staff he argued: why contest Soviet tankmen and airmen in battle and risk losing the war to these formidable fighters? When they run out of fuel their tanks and planes can be collected like empty cans. Their crews will be helpless without their machines.

In short, Hitler determined to take the affairs of war into his own hands. He no longer trusted his generals and declared that openly. After the fiasco of the offensive on Moscow he carried out a reshuffle in the top echelon of the Wehrmacht, dismissing the Commander of Army Group Centre Field Marshal von Bock, together with Guderian, Weichs and Leeb—a total of 35 top-ranking generals.

The Führer issued an order announcing his takeover of command of the land forces. On June 1, 1942, he arrived at the headquarters of Army Group South in Poltava in the Ukraine. From that day on he was to direct personally all operations on the Eastern Front, particularly on its southern flank, to achieve his coveted goal of capturing the oil-fields of the Caucasus. He pinned great hopes on the forthcoming operations, as is evidenced by his statement at a conference: "Unless I get the oil of Maikop and Grozny, I must stop this war."

In the latter half of July 1942 the German forces took the city of Rostov and approached the Don. By that time a new operation, codenamed Edelweiss, had been planned under Hitler's personal instructions. He signed it on July 23, 1942. In accordance with his directive, the immediate task of Army Group A was to encircle and wipe out the Soviet forces which had retreated beyond the Don, after which it was to build up a powerful group of panzer and motorized infantry units and deliver a strike in the direction of Grozny and Baku.

Army Group B was to launch a thrust in the direction of Stalingrad to safeguard the flank of Army Group A and secure its operations, to occupy the area between the Don and the Volga, to disrupt Soviet shipping on the Volga and, after taking Stalingrad, to press its offensive along the Volga.

Chief of the General Staff Halder took exception to that plan. He argued with Hitler that it was impossible to accomplish both these tasks with the forces available and advised him to concentrate all forces for a thrust towards Stalingrad in the first place. That new attempt to delay the seizure of the oil fields infuriated the Führer, and though he did not dismiss Halder as Chief of the General Staff immediately, he ignored him for a long time.

On September 24, Hitler officially dismissed Halder and appointed Colonel General Zeitzler in his place.

To carry out Operation Edelweiss the German High Command concentrated a formidable force: the thrust into the Caucasus was to be launched by Army Group A under the command of Field Marshal Wilhelm List, the 1st Panzer Army under Colonel General Ewald von Kleist, the 4th Panzer Army under Colonel General Richard Ruoff, and the Rumanian 3rd Army under General Petre Dumitrescu.

Army Group A had a total of 40 divisions: 18 infantry, 3 panzer, 4 motorized infantry, 6 mountain, 3 light infantry, 4 cavalry and 2 security divisions. All of them had been brought up to strength, very well armed and provided with a large number of motor vehicles, tug lorries and armoured personnel carriers.

The German High Command planned to pursue the offensive across open terrain, as well as to deliver a series of strikes across mountain passes of the Main Caucasian Range. For that purpose, Army Group A had on its strength one of Hitler's most favourite formations: the highly trained 49th Mountain Corps of General Rudolph Konrad. The Corps included four crack Alpine divisions: the 1st and 4th Mountain Rifles, the 97th and 101st Chasseurs.

The 1st Division of Mountain Rifles named Edelweiss was commanded by Lieutenant General Hubert Lanz. He was an experienced mountain climber with a record of ascents in the Alps, the Caucasus and the Himalayas.

Mountain climbers of the Edelweiss Division were favourites of the Wehrmacht Command and the Nazi élite. They enjoyed a comfortable living and were trained in the Swiss mountains and in the French Alps. Photos of these "snow leopards", as they were lovingly called by their admirers, were often printed on the covers of fashionable magazines.

These Alpine climbers, who were supplied with a full outfit and weapons for waging mountain combat, were under orders to seize the mountain passes and descend to the Black Sea coast where they would assist the German troops advancing from Novorossiisk in the Taman Peninsula along the sea coast.

Now that he had assumed command of the land forces and direction of this decisive operation, Hitler was contemplating far-reaching plans which were not limited to capturing Grozny and Baku. That was evidenced by the concentration of the special corps "F" in the rear of Army Group A. The corps was so code-named after its commander, General Helmut Felmi. The corps was indeed highly specialized in its composition, training and tasks. It was to be committed to action after Army Group A had taken the Georgian capital of Tbilisi. The corps "F" was to launch an offensive towards Iran, Iraq, the Persian Gulf and India.

Twenty-six Turkish divisions ready for combat were deployed along the Soviet–Turkish border, and Rommel's forces were advancing on Alexandria in Africa, so in that situation the German plan did not look fantastic.

Corps "F" was armed to the teeth to be able to cope with its tasks. It included highly mobile motorized battalions with up to a thousand officers and men in each. The first and second battalions were crack troops of the Wehrmacht, while all the officers and men of the third battalion were Arabs—Iraqis, Syrians, Libyans, and others.

Every battalion was equivalent to an infantry regiment in its combat efficiency. There was also a separate panzer unit of 25 tanks and an air force unit of 25 aircraft. The corps was equipped with field and anti-aircraft artillery, motor vehicles, and had logistic services with a bakery, a medical unit and various repair teams.

In addition, the corps had an arsenal of weapons sufficient to equip a complete division of volunteers and defectors the corps command expected to enlist on its way.

The corps was under orders to follow in the wake of Army Group A and, depending on where its offensive on Baku would be more successful, to take advantage of that success immediately and move into Iran.

Army Group A was supported by the 4th Air Force Fleet under the command of General Richthofen, "German's No. 1 Ace", as he was called. He was one of Hitler's favourites.

This air armada consisted of more than 1,000 aircraft of the latest designs flown by the best German pilots. Since the airfields were close to the battlefields, Richthofen could very quickly manoeuvre his formations and win air supremacy, relying on the vast number of his planes.

To secure the success of Army Group A by staving off the blows of Soviet forces, its left flank was protected by Army Group B under the command of von Bock. In November 1942, Army Group Don was formed and placed under the command of Field Marshal von Manstein to burst the ring of encirclement around the 6th Army of von Paulus.

On the right flank, the German forces considered themselves protected by the Main Caucasian Range.

Preliminary Considerations

Hitler, who had appointed himself Commander-in-Chief of the Land Forces, arrived at his headquarters near Vinnitsa, to be closer to the theatre of operations that would decide the outcome of the war and his grandiloquent plans of conquest of East and West.

Before the story of the German strike, let us see what was going on on the Soviet side. What was the Soviet High Command's view of the situation? What steps was it contemplating to thwart that powerful and resolute German thrust towards the Caucasus?

Of course, the Soviet Supreme Commander Joseph Stalin had not overlooked the trend of the fighting on the Don and the advance of German forces towards the Caucasus. However, he did not attach to that direction the significance it had assumed in view of Hitler's plans. The fighting on the Southern Front that was in progress or might develop in the summer of 1942 was, in his view, which was law at the General Headquarters, of secondary significance, like that on all other secondary fronts. Stalin believed that the German Army was planning another general offensive against Moscow.

Here is the opinion of Marshal Grechko:

—Estimating the German intentions for the summer campaign of 1943, the General Headquarters believed that the enemy would deliver his main strike in the direction of Moscow.—

General Shtemenko writes:

—The Soviet strategic command headed by Stalin was convinced that sooner or later the Germans would again unleash their power on Moscow. The reason for that belief was not only the danger of German strikes from the Rzhev area. Intelligence reports from abroad indicated that the German High

Command had not yet abandoned its plan to capture the Soviet capital. . . .
Other members of the General Headquarters, the General Staff and most
Front Commanders shared that opinion. . . .

—As it transpired later, the forecast of General Headquarters and the
General Staff was mistaken. The German High Command assigned this task
to its armed forces: to stabilize the situation on the central front, to take
Leningrad and link up with the Finnish forces on the northern front and to
break through towards the Caucasus on the southern front.—

Finally, Marshal Zhukov has this to say:

—Stalin feared for the Moscow direction most of all. The General
Headquarters and the General Staff arrived at the conclusion that the Orel–
Tula and Kursk–Voronezh sectors were the area of greatest danger from
where the Germans could strike out towards Moscow, outflanking it from the
south-west. Therefore, a considerable part of the reserves of the General
Headquarters was concentrated on the Bryansk Front to protect Moscow
from this side at the end of the summer.—

Thus, Hitler was planning to defeat the Red Army by one powerful blow in
the Caucasus, to carry the war into Iran, Iraq and India and step up
operations in Africa. The Soviet High Command, however, was expecting a
German thrust towards Moscow. That miscalculation was not due to any
misinformation about enemy intentions. There were reliable intelligence
reports about German troop concentrations for a thrust in the Caucasus.

"A History of the Second World War" presents a scheme of deployment of
forces which graphically shows the miscalculation of the Soviet High
Command.

It shows the percentages of Soviet forces and armaments on various
strategic fronts as of July 1, 1942.

Fronts and sectors	Infantry Armies	Divisions	Guns and mortars	Tanks	Warplanes	Strength (numerical)
Northern sector (Karelian Front)	7.3	5.3	5.4	2.5	9.3	5.4
North-western sector (Leningrad, Volkhov, North-western fronts)	27.3	29.7	27.6	16.0	14.2	23.8
Western sector (Kalinin, Western	32.7	31.3	31.6	40.3	32.7	33.2

Fronts) South-western sector (Bryansk, South-Western, Southern Fronts)	25.4	28.3	29.6	38.3	29.2	31.2
Caucasian sector (North-Caucasian Front, 44th Army of Trans-caucasian Front)	7.3	5.4	5.8	2.9	14.6	6.5

The Kalinin and Bryansk Fronts in the Western sector were in direct proximity to Moscow, and the forces deployed on them constituted about one half of the total strength of the Red Army. In the Caucasus, however, only 5.4 per cent of all Soviet divisions and a mere 2.9 per cent of the tanks, the decisive strike weapon of modern warfare, were to resist vastly superior German power.

What motivated the General Headquarters to keep such large forces at Moscow? As it seems to this writer, the motives were psychological as well as strategic. All in the General Headquarters had suffered a great shock when the Wehrmacht had invaded almost half of the country's European part and threatened to storm the Soviet capital.

In the spring of 1942, therefore, when fighting was still going on not far from the capital, General Headquarters would not risk to lessen the protection of Moscow and move its reserves to the south when the enemy forces were so near and could undertake another attack on the capital. As for intelligence reports about the danger in the south, such reports had more than once proved inaccurate, exaggerated or simply false. They might, after all, have been provoked by the enemy with the intention of drawing Soviet forces away from Moscow. The south was far away but the German tanks were near.

Whatever the reasons for all those mistakes, in 1942 the Germans managed to concentrate enormous forces and effect a devastating thrust towards the Caucasus. The miscalculation on the Soviet side resulted in great casualties for the forces defending the approaches to the Caucasus. It was the unprecedented heroism of Soviet troops and the superhuman efforts of the Soviet Command in the Caucasus that checked the advance of the attacking forces despite their vastly superior numbers and weapons.

That was a critical time, indeed. Briefing his envoy Wendell Lewis before sending him to Moscow, President Roosevelt told him frankly:

—It may happen that you will get to Cairo at the time of its fall and you may find yourself in Russia at the time of her collapse.—(*Retranslated from the Russian*).

Roosevelt had in mind Cairo's possible capture by Rommel and a possible invasion of the Baku area by German forces.

In August 1942, at the time of fierce fighting in the foothills of the Caucasus, Prime Minister Winston Churchill flew to Moscow. He reminisced about those days:

—I was musing over my mission to that grim, sinister Bolshevik state I had at one time tried so hard to strangle in its cradle and regarded as a mortal enemy of civilized freedom until Hitler's rise. What was I to tell them now? General Wavell, who had a flair for poetry, summed up all that in a verse he had shown me last night. The last line of each quatrain ended thus: "No Second Front in 1942". That was like bringing a large block of ice to the North Pole.—(*Retranslated from the Russian.*)

It was in those days of August, when fighting flared up on the last line of the way to Baku—the line of the Terek River, where General Petrov's 44th Army was resisting the attackers—that talks were in progress in Moscow where the Allies frankly declared that a second front would not be opened in 1942.

The 44th Army

On August 8 the General Headquarters issued a directive to form the Northern Army Group of the Transcaucasian Front. It consisted of the 44th and 9th Armies, the 11th Infantry Corps and, later, the 37th Army. Lieutenant General Maslennikov was appointed its commander.

By that time Army Group A had pushed the Soviet forces back to the foothills of the Main Caucasian Range and the Terek River. Field Marshal List sent Hitler the following reassuring message:

—The Army Group Command is confident that this resistance can be overcome by hard pressure. The strong enemy forces in the area of the Terek bend can only put up a short fight against a German attack. . . . It seems that the enemy has deployed all his available forces in the forward positions, so that once this line is broken through all Russian resistance will end.—

Hitler was overjoyed: the long coveted Baku oil was near at hand. The Red Army would soon be paralyzed by a fuel shortage, and the Wehrmacht, all its fuel tanks full, would swiftly advance into Iran, Iraq and India along the routes charted by him. Indeed, he would prove to his arrogant generals that he knew more about strategy and could fight a war better than they did.

Glad news was coming from Africa as well: at the end of June Rommel had taken Tobruk. The British commander, General Clopper, with 33,000 officers and men had surrendered, though the fortress had enormous stocks of ammunition and food. The war trophies were large enough to last

Rommel's Afrika Korps for a few months before it could link up with the troops completing the conquest of the Caucasus.

On August 23, two panzer and two infantry divisions of the 1st Panzer Army commanded by Kleist struck out in the direction of Mozdok. They were opposed by a small Soviet force of one detachment under Major Korneyev, the cadets of the Rostov artillery school, and scattered units of the 26th reserve infantry brigade. For three days they held off vastly superior German forces. They fought heroically but it was an unequal battle. The Germans finally captured Mozdok.

When the German forces had advanced to the line of the Terek and Uruzh Rivers, they were engaged by General Petrov's 44th Army.

How strong was that army? Two of its divisions were Azerbaijanian, one Armenian, and one Georgian; they were newly formed and lacked regular training. Their men enlisted from Azerbaijanian, Armenian and Georgian villages were, of course, dependable, but they had no practice at handling weapons, and most of them did not know Russian, which naturally caused difficulties in training and direction of combat.

There were also two other factors in which the Germans enjoyed obvious superiority that could not yet be offset by any advantage for the Soviet side. First, the Germans had unchallenged air supremacy: their aircraft were in the air almost continually, bombing and strafing retreating Soviet troops and their new positions. Second, the Germans had a large number of tanks; true, the terrain was advantageous for fighting them, but Soviet anti-tank guns were few and far between.

The 44th Army had experienced defeat, when Manstein's forces drove the Soviet armies from the Crimean Peninsula. The Army had been involved in the landing operation at Kerch at the end of December 1941.

The Germans were advancing swiftly with enormous forces and had already gained 600 kilometres of ground. The oil fields of Grozny and Baku were now in real danger.

Watching the retreat of Soviet units, Petrov thought of the demoralizing effect that the spectacle of tired, sunburnt and famished soldiers must have on his own troops. He knew, however, that most of the retreating troops were well-trained and battle-wise regular soldiers. They were not to blame for their disaster; they had been simply overpowered by a superior force. They had no artillery and ammunition, no air and armoured support to help them withstand the blows of superior German weapons. Yet they could very well make the core of his own units of young and inexperienced soldiers.

Petrov ordered kitchens, canteens and make-shift bath-houses to be set up in the rear of his Army. Soldiers of retreating units could now take a rest, have a meal, shave themselves and change into clean clothes. They were ready for battle again. They knew that the General who had come to their aid had defended Sevastopol for 250 days and were proud to serve under his command.

These new reinforcements of Byelorussians, Ukrainians, Russians, Tatars and Caucasian natives cemented his weak and unstable Army into a fighting-fit force capable of breaking the back of the German offensive.

The battle front was drawing closer to the defence line on the Terek River, and fighting was already going on in the area of the resort towns of Pyatigorsk, Zheleznovodsk, Yessentuki and Kislovodsk. The 37th Army was stubbornly resisting the German advance there. It had managed to break off from the enemy, and towards August 16 it had retreated to the line of the 44th Army and set up positions at the Baksan and Gundelen Rivers.

Order 227

Those critical and tragic days, when the country's fate was at stake, are described in Soviet historical literature and memoirs. That was the case during the Battles of Moscow and Stalingrad. In the Battle of the Caucasus, however, the danger was equally great. The front of Soviet resistance was virtually crumbling and Soviet troops were being rolled back partly to Stalingrad and partly to the Caucasian Mountains. The German Army Group A was steamrollering relentlessly over the Krasnodar and Stavropol plains. The Soviet forces, which accounted for a mere seven per cent of the total strength of the Red Army, were, of course, unable to check the advance of that powerful group.

The situation at the Caucasian Front was going from bad to worse. The breakthrough of German panzer and motorized forces into the steppe areas beyond the Don and the Krasnodar plains threatened a German invasion of the Caucasus as an immediate probability. The Soviet High Command finally realized the full implications of that danger. An immediate counterblow at the German armies, however, was impossible, because Army Group B advancing on Stalingrad, forging ahead towards Baku had practically secured its forces against Soviet flanking attacks.

On July 28, 1942, Stalin issued Order No. 227 known to all war veterans as "Not a Step Backwards!" That order was without precedent in the course of the war. It was not only a bitter accusation of the Soviet officers and men in the line but also a final warning which sounded this note: to be or not to be!

Here are a few excerpts from that order:

—The enemy is feeding more and more forces into battle and, ignoring his enormous casualties, is fighting his way forward, invading new areas, devastating and ruining our towns and villages, raping, looting and killing peaceful civilians.—

—Some stupid men at the front are lulling themselves with the idea that we can retreat further to the east because we have a vast territory, a lot of land, a large population, and more bread than we need. . . . This idea is thoroughly false and plays into the enemy's hands.

—Every officer and man and political instructor must realize that our resources are not unlimited. The territory of the Soviet state is not a vast desert, and its people—workers, peasants, members of the intelligentsia—are our fathers, mothers, wives, children. ... After the loss of the Ukraine, Byelorussia, the Baltic area, the Donets basin and other regions we now have much less territory, a smaller population, less bread and metal, fewer factories and plants. We have lost areas with over 70 million people, which produced more than 800 million poods (16 kg) of grain and more than 10 million tons of metal a year. Now we have no superiority over the Germans either in manpower or in grain reserves. A further retreat would be suicidal to the people and the country.—

—From now on there will be no further retreat. Not a step backwards!

—It is the duty of every serviceman to defend his position to the last, not to surrender an inch of Soviet territory, to fight for it to the last ditch.—

—Can we withstand the blow and hurl the enemy backwards? Yes, we can. Our factories and plants are now working excellently, and our fighting forces are getting growing numbers of warplanes, tanks, artillery and mortars.—

—What else do we need then?

—We need more order and discipline in the companies, battalions, regiments, divisions, tank units and air squadrons. We must enforce the most stringent order and iron discipline in our army, if we are to save the situation and defend our motherland.—

That order prescribed dismissal of commanders of armies, corps and divisions guilty of a retreat without authorization. The same penalties were to be applied to commanders and commissars of regiments and battalions whose men had abandoned their positions without an order.

Order 227 introduced penal companies and battalions, which, incidentally, had a direct relation to myself. What is more, whereas for others that order meant a prohibition to fall back, for me it was a change to take a step forward.

I shall quote my reminiscences published in the book "Soviet Writers at the Fronts of the Great Patriotic War" in 1966, that is, long before I conceived this novel. This refers to a problem long settled at the 20th Congress of the Soviet Communist Party. I have no intention to stir old memories or make complaints. This is simply a fact of my biography, and facts are stubborn things, as the saying goes.

—When the war broke out, I knew nothing about it. It may seem strange that such an event that reverberated throughout the world could have missed someone's ear. Yet it had missed mine. I had no idea of the outbreak of the war either on June 22, 1941, or after a week or after a month. How could that happen one may wonder. In those days I was in prison, in solitary confinement.

—How had I landed there? It was very easy in those days. One only had to say a couple of wrong words. ... But this is not the subject of my reminiscences. Much has been written about those times. ... I have no intention to generalize and will limit my story to my own experiences.

—I lived with my parents in Tashkent, Uzbekistan. In 1939, on graduating at secondary school, I entered the Tashkent officer school. In May 1941 I was to be commissioned as a lieutenant.

—Shortly before graduation, however, I was arrested. The reason was as follows:

—Once, preparing for a seminar, I was reading a pamphlet about Lenin's article "What Is to Be Done?" I want to make it clear that I was not in any way a conscious opponent of the Stalin cult. I simply admired Lenin and resented the fact that his name was often overlooked.

—So, on that evening, reading the pamphlet, I underlined Lenin's name with a red pencil—it was mentioned sixty times, and Stalin's name with a blue pencil—it was mentioned eighty times. Then I addressed my neighbour, also a cadet, seated next to me:

—"What the hell? When Lenin was writing 'What Is to Be Done?' he had no idea of Stalin's existence. Why then should Lenin be overshadowed by Stalin? Why credit Stalin with what he has never done?"

—I showed the cadet my count of the names. That was enough. I was arrested. At 19 years of age I was pronounced "an enemy of the people". The first question I heard from my interrogator was: "Who has instructed you to discredit the great leader Joseph Stalin?"

—That was an ominous question in those days. I had no answer to it.

—After a few months I was transferred to a common cell. Naturally, I started asking my prison mates about the latest news. One of the inmates, an elderly, emaciated man, said sadly: "Bad news, young man, our troops have surrendered Kiev."

—I thought he was mad and moved away from him. Then I spoke to another and another. They looked at me strangely, as if I was out of my mind. What else, indeed, could they think of a man who knew nothing about the war that had been raging over the country for several months?

—That was how I first learned of the war. Further developments in my case were routine: an unfair trial, a transit camp, a long travel by rail in freezing cold to a labour camp in the far north.—

As I have said, I was jailed before the war, in the period when dark clouds had thickened over Petrov, accused of association with "enemies of the poeople". At that time the "Petrov affair" had ended favourably for him, if a "severe reprimand with a warning and registration in a personal file" can be qualified as an acquittal. Honest communists had defended him. However, his ill-wishers probably felt dissatisfied.

To a question as to who had instructed me to discredit Stalin I could say nothing, of course, except that it was absurd. My interrogator suggested: "You are only 18, so it was certainly not your idea. Name the one who gave it to you." The interrogator went on insinuatingly: "You often visited the Petrovs even before entering your officer school. Was it not Petrov who compared Lenin and Stalin in some way?"

Later my interrogator more than once came back to his question, and I realized what he was driving at. In my solitary cell I had more than enough time to understand what was what. I knew that a cadet and budding poet was not of much interest to the people handling my case. They were looking for a chance to play it up into a big "affair" implicating high-ranking military officers.

It would be enough for me to recall some trivial phrase dropped by Petrov or the editor of the army newspaper which had published my first poems—I was questioned about him as well—and their fate would be sealed. They would be incriminated immediately on framed-up charges of conspiracy and court martialled.

Now I knew what I would say to outsmart my interrogator. To his next question about Petrov I exclaimed with feigned irritation:

"Nonsense! He would never talk with a cadet. He is a martinet. A salute, clicking the heels and standing to attention: 'Yes, sir!' is all he expects one to do."

I beg forgiveness before my thankful memories of Petrov. Nothing could be further from the truth. But he had really never talked politics with me.

I was just as nasty in my comments about the editor of the newspaper "Frunzenets", an intelligent and friendly man, who had given me many useful hints on penmanship.

In short, I was doing my best to frustrate any plan to frame these honest people. Neither of them was jailed in those troubled days, which proves that my ruse worked.

My own case, however, had no happy ending. I pleaded guilty to avoid a harsher punishment and was trundled in a cattle wagon to the far-away Tavdinlag timbering camp. That is where I was serving time when the Battle of the Caucasus began.

I wrote letters to Mikhail Kalinin, President of the Presidium of the Supreme Soviet of the USSR, asking for permission to serve in the firing lines. I had an officer training and was eager to prove my fighting fitness and dedication to the country. I never got an answer. My letters probably never reached him.

Strange as it may seem, the factor that helped me to regain my freedom was oil. When the oil-fields in the Caucasus were threatened with German invasion, and the prospect of losing the oil sources badly needed for the war effort became real, the State Defence Committee or some other high government body resolved to collect oil reserves in the Urals. Oil reservoirs were to be built in the area of Sverdlovsk.

In the summer of 1942 convicts who were younger and stronger were selected in my camp. I was lucky to be among them. We were quickly brought in a train of brick-red freight wagons to a building site on the outskirts of Sverdlovsk. We were to dig enormous pits, using only spades and carts. Rail tracks were laid to their edges, and oil was simply poured out of cisterns into these reservoirs. We dug many such pits, and other oil storages like these were probably made in other industrial areas.

There was a big city not far away, and I took advantage of that. I asked a technician who was not a convict to mail my next letter to Kalinin. That letter did reach the addressee, because at the end of 1942 I, as well as many other convicts as I would learn later, received an answer. My request was granted and I was to be enlisted in a penal battalion and sent to the front where I could expiate my guilt and, should I fail to do that, I was to complete my term in a labour camp after the war.

Incidentally, Order 227 of July 28, 1942 was issued on my birthday, and that stringent decree gave me a new lease of life.

For all the severity and even cruelty, as it may seem today, of the statute on penal battalions, for many it was a chance to reinstate themselves. It may happen in war that a serviceman cannot meet the challenge of combat and fails to do his duty for reasons beyond his control. He may be too frightened or confused or he may be a brave and skilful fighter himself but unable to influence the outcome of fighting when failed by his comrades or subordinates. Is it wise to bring him before a firing squad?

So penal battalions were justice done the hard way. I was one of their first members. It was very hard, of course, for one who had been so close to becoming an officer to begin his combat service not even as a rank-and-file soldier but as a rightless convict despised by many.

I learned the skill of fighting battle after battle, relying on my training to which Petrov had contributed so much, and I rose from the ranks to become a Colonel decorated with all the war medals a soldier and a trench officer can deserve. My highest award is the title of Hero of the Soviet Union.

Beyond the Front Line

Hitler was absolutely confident of success in his planned offensive and had no intention of sharing the laurels of his anticipated victory with anyone. He was staying at his headquarters in Vinnitsa to be closer to the theatre of operations.

His headquarters, disguised as a holiday home for officers of the Wehrmacht, had been built by army engineers in a few months. The building site was encircled with barbed wire entanglements and heavily guarded. A few thousand POWs working there, and German craftsmen doing finishing work, suspected that the purpose of construction was not what had been explained officially. After the completion of the work all who had taken part in it had been killed by SS men to prevent leakage of information.

To secure the main task of capturing the Caucasus and covering the left flank of Army Group A, the Germans made a thrust in the direction of the Volga and Stalingrad. On July 12, the German forces invaded the Stalingrad region.

In his Directive No. 44 of July 21 Hitler declared:

—The unexpectedly quick success of the operation . . . warrants our hope that the Soviet Union will soon be cut off from the Caucasus and hence from its main oil sources. The British and American war supplies will be seriously deranged. This and the loss of all industry in the Donets basin will deal the Soviet Union a blow that will have far-reaching consequences.—

Hitler was so convinced of the success of his troops in the areas of the Volga and Stalingrad that he withdrew the 4th Panzer Army from Army Group B and transferred it to Army Group A to lend greater momentum to its advance in the direction of Grozny and Baku.

On July 17 the vanguard forces of the German 6th Army engaged the forward-based units of the 62nd and 64th Armies of the Stalingrad Front on the line of the Chir and Tsymla Rivers in the bend of the Don.

That was the beginning of the great Battle of Stalingrad. The forward Soviet units stubbornly fought the advancing German 6th Army of Paulus for six days and forced its main forces to fall back. Hitler realized that his plans of a walkover towards Stalingrad were unrealistic. The group of Soviet forces was poised for a thrust towards Baku, so the outcome of the Battle of Stalingrad was crucial to the implementation of all his plans of the summer campaign, primarily the capture of the Caucasus. The threat from the north made the position of German forces in all sectors of the Caucasian front insecure.

Hitler longed to take Stalingrad before the opening of an offensive in the North Caucasus but that was easier said than done. On July 22 the German 6th Army reached the main line of defence of the Stalingrad Front 120 kilometres from the city.

Hitler was impatient to carry out his plan as soon as possible, and he knew that the Soviet armies opposing him in the Caucasus were tired and heavily depleted and unable to get reinforcements or supplies from the central areas of the country. Hitler was impatient, and therefore Army Group A went into the assault in the Caucasus on July 25. In the early days the progress of the German offensive was so swift that on July 27 General Heusinger, Chief of Operations of the General Staff of the Land Forces, transmitted this message to General Greiffenberg, Chief of Staff of Army Group A:

—Ease your pressure from the Rostov positions in the southerly direction lest the Russians retreat before they are encircled by the advancing left wing of your Army Group.—

Hitler was so satisfied that he allowed the 4th Panzer Army to be moved to the Stalingrad sector, because all attempts to take the city had so far failed. That transfer was a miscalculation which would cost Hitler and his General Staff dearly, because the blow the Germans were now delivering in the Caucasus was not a blow with a fist but with a flat hand, that is to say.

All that, however, would become obvious later but for the time being Field Marshal List's forces were steamrollering towards the Caucasus, bypassing

Soviet pockets of resistance. The 17th Army took Krasnodar on August 9. The 1st Panzer Army struck across Armavir in the direction of the Maikop oil fields and further towards Tuapse on the Black Sea coast where it would trap the Soviet forces as General Heusinger had planned. Armavir was taken on August 7 and Maikop on August 10.

Hitler and his retinue were seized with joyful excitement: Maikop meant their first capture of oil they craved so frantically.

Inspired by his success in the south of the Russian theatre, Hitler was eagerly looking forward to the entry of new Axis allies into the war; they would back up his efforts from their positions of advantage further south. "Are the Turks ready to join?" he enquired and got this answer in August:

—The Turkish Prime Minister Sarajoglu has declared to the German Ambassador: "As a Turk I desire Russia's destruction passionately. . . . Germany can settle the Russian problem, if at least half of the Russians living in Russia are killed."—

The Führer was also gladdened by the rising activity of Nazi sympathizers in Iran. Indeed, they were gloating over the Soviet setbacks in the North Caucasus and the loss of many Soviet towns to the Germans. Some of them even hoisted flags emblazoned with the Nazi swastika. Nazi agents were spurring them on and circulating rumours about the inevitable conquest of the Caucasus by German arms and invasion of Iran.

In the Far East Japan was openly preparing for war against the USSR. It was quite recently that Colonel General Ruhoff, pointing his finger at the sight of the blazing town of Bataisk, had proudly declared to the Japanese military attaché visiting the area of German operations:

—The door to the Caucasus is open. The hour is coming when the German Army and the Imperial Army of Japan will link up in India.—

Victory seemed near at hand. Festive flags were hung out all over Germany. Martial music and warlike speeches filled the radio waves. The reason for the jubilation was quite spectacular: flags with the Nazi swastika had been hoisted on the peak of Mt. Elbrus, the symbol of the Caucasus.

The Berlin press announced under banner headlines: The conquest of Mt. Elbrus crowns the conquest of the Caucasus. Illustrated magazines and newsreels were extolling the exploits of Captain Grott and his mountain rifles. Hitler decorated Captain Grott with the supreme award of the Nazi Reich—the Cross of Knighthood—and his soldiers with Iron Crosses. Radio Berlin was singing praises to these "national heroes".

These broadcasts were heard in Moscow and must have caused Stalin's resentment. Marshal Grechko testifies:

—The arrival of Lavrenty Beria at Sukhumi on August 23 entailed difficulties for the Front Command and the Staff of the 46th Army which were preoccupied with the problems of reinforcing the defences of the Main Caucasian Range. As a member of the State Defence Committee, Beria was supposed to give concrete aid to them. Instead he reshuffled the top echelon of the Front and Army Command and dismissed Major General Segatskov from command of the 46th Army.

—It was not those drastic measures, however, but the painstaking efforts of the Front and Army staff officers that enabled Major General Leselidze, the new commander of the 46th Army, to handle the levers of troop control effectively. The German mountain troops who had infiltrated the areas beyond the mountain passes were eventually wiped out.—

Troops of General Petrov's 44th Army carried out mopping-up operations to make the mountain passes safe again.

The Soviet High Command was worried about these possible routes of German invasion. In a directive signed on August 20, 1942 Stalin pointed out thiŝ danger and ordered special measures to reinforce the defences of the Georgian, Ossetian and Sukhumi roads crossing the Main Caucasian Range.

German Alpine troops, however, hoisted their flags on Mt. Elbrus on August 21. Comparison of these two dates speaks for itself. As evidenced by the Soviet war historian Ibragimbeili, a great expert on mountain warfare, the Command of the Transcaucasian Front had underestimated the importance of fortified defences in mountain combat, relying on what they thought were inaccessible summits and high-altitude passes that would forbid enemy infiltration.

They had also misjudged the fitness of the German mountain troops of the 49th Alpine Rifle Corps under the command of General Konrad, a knowledgeable specialist of mountain warfare.

So the Caucasian Mountains had no engineering defence works, whereas the Alpine rifles of the Edelweiss Division has reconnoitred these passes long before the war and were now confidently leading the assault on them. As it would be known later, many officers of the attacking forces had visited the Caucasus way back in the thirties, ascending its summits and high-altitude passes and exploring its deep gorges. It was familiar terrain to them, and they were leading their troops with the competence of Alpine guides.

Operation Edelweiss was nearing completion. More than two thirds of the territory to be captured under this plan was now under the German heel: almost the whole of the North Caucasus, the vast expanses of the Kuban valley and the Salsky steppes, the Maikop oil fields, the passes across the Main Caucasian Range, and Mt. Elbrus.

There was only one line of resistance to be overcome by the invaders in their advance on Baku. It was defended by the last forces of the Red Army in the Caucasus: three field armies, one of which was General Petrov's 44th Army.

A Fight to the Death

August 1942 was a time of sweltering heat in the North Caucasus, and the parched earth cracked under the scorching sun and the heavy wheels of

German combat vehicles.

General Petrov's army entrenched on the bank of the Terek where it branched out in streams to fall into the Caspian formed the right wing of the Northern Army Group, while the latter's left wing rested on the Main Caucasian Range. The city of Ordzhonikidze was the starting point of the Georgian Military Road winding its way along narrow gorges with precipitous rocks on both sides.

This is a place surrounded with legends. Roman historians called it the Daryal gate to the Caucasus, and numerous people migrated through it from Asia to Europe and from Europe to Asia in antiquity. There is hardly another place on earth where so much blood was shed in the past ages. The Polovtsy took Daryal from the Georgians, the Georgians from the Ossetians, the Greeks from the Persians, the Turks from the Greeks, the Arabs from the Turks, and the Georgians again from the Khazars. In the early 13th century the Mongol hordes fought their way through Daryal and invaded the Polovtsky steppe lands. Tamerlane twice led his army through the Caucasian gate. Fierce battles raged in this narrow passage in every century.

Now another army of aspirants to world supremacy had come up to this historical line. Never before had invaders massed such enormous forces as those Hitler had brought here.

The main German forces repeatedly assaulted the Soviet positions with rabid ferocity, all to no avail. Petrov's 44th Army was covering Grozny, the road to Baku and the Caspian coast. The 1st Panzer Army Commander Kleist concentrated two panzer and two infantry divisions in a narrow sector and shifted his thrust to Mozdok, which fell on August 25. That was another direction of the German offensive on Grozny. The Soviet 9th Army was in retreat unable to hold off the great mass of panzer and motorized infantry.

On August 31 Hitler gave this directive to Field Marshal List summoned to his headquarters:

—The key task of the 1st Panzer Army is to knock out Russian resistance in the bend of the Terek and pursue the offensive with all available forces, mobile forces leading the way, in the direction of Grozny to capture the oil fields at the earliest date.—

On September 2 the 1st Panzer Army with tank-borne infantry undertook a crossing of the Terek. The troops of General Petrov on the far bank put up a ferocious resistance. Petrov moved part of his forces across the river and dealt a flanking blow at the attackers. The 11th Corps of the Guards attacked the Germans from the other flank simultaneously. The German crossing was thwarted.

Thus General Petrov crossed swords with Colonel General Kleist. Ewald von Kleist hailed from an aristocratic Prussian family which had supplied a few generations of German generals. In the First World War he was a squadron commander and in 1929 he rose to the rank of Colonel. Even before Hitler's coming to power he had been a Major General in command of a cavalry division. His initial skeptical attitude to the Nazis changed to enthusiasm when he had learned of their imperial ambitions. In 1936 he was promoted to Lieutenant General and at the outbreak of the Second World War he was in command of the 1st Panzer Corps, winning applause of the Nazi chieftains by his rapid manoeuvres in the conquest of Poland. Along with Guderian he was a champion of tank warfare and took part in the conquest of the Netherlands, Belgium, France, Yugoslavia, and Greece.

From the first day of the invasion of the USSR he had been fighting with great persistence and ferocity. In the first phase of Operation Edelweiss Kleist's 1st Panzer Army had advanced more than 600 kilometres from the Don to the Terek. Now he was confronted by the Army of General Petrov and other armies of the Northern Army Group he was under orders to wipe out before taking Baku.

Having brought up reinforcements, Kleist ordered his army into another attack and on September 4 his forces cleaved through the positions of the 9th Army neighbouring Petrov's sector, and advanced by ten kilometres.

Here a force of over 100 tanks and assault troops were ramming the Soviet defences. Convergent Soviet ground and air strikes prevented their breakthrough towards Grozny and Ordzhonikidze.

General Maslennikov's three armies repeatedly counterattacked to hurl the invaders backwards to the left bank of the Terek and stabilize the front line.

At the time of this fighting General Petrov's army included four Azerbaijanian, two Armenian, and one Georgian infantry divisions, one Kalmyk infantry division, cavalry divisions and infantry brigades of Don and Kuban cossacks, natives of Daghestan, Ossetians and other ethnic minorities. In short, it was a really international force of fighting men.

The lists of officers and men decorated for their exemplary courage in those battles had many names of Caucasian natives who had changed into army uniforms but recently; yet their staunchness could do credit to any battle-wise troops.

German prisoners of war testified that their companies and battalions had been heavily mutilated. A few dozen survivors remaining in each unit were demoralized and unable to carry on the fight.

Thus, Hitler's order to wipe out Soviet resistance at the bend of the Terek remained unfulfilled. Army Group A had become bogged down. Now a scapegoat was needed as usual, because Hitler's virtues as a strategist were above scandal and he would never take the blame for the failure of Operation Edelweiss.

Hitler raged and raved, flinging accusations at the General Staff and the High Command of the Wehrmacht (OKW). He commissioned General Alfred Jodl, Chief of the OKW Operations Office, to investigate the reasons for the petering out of the German offensive in the Caucasus.

After a conference with Field Marshal List, Commander of Army Group A, and General Konrad, Commander of the 49th Mountain Corps, who had but recently been the pride and glory of the Wehrmacht, Jodl reported to the Führer the dim prospects of the Battle of the Caucasus. Hitler was infuriated. It was insolent insubordination on the part of Field Marshal List to have requested a calling off of Operation Edelweiss and the plan to break through the Caucasian mountains to the Black Sea coast.

On September 10, 1942 Field Marshal List was dismissed from command of Army Group A. To demonstrate his iron will, Hitler appointed himself to direct its operations from his headquarters at Vinnitsa. After a month of vain attempts to reverse the fortunes of war, however, he handed over this post to Colonel General Kleist.

On September 25, 1942 a thankful Kleist declared that he would drink a toast to the Führer's wisdom in Baku. As a man of action he added weight to his pledge by vigorous steps to turn the tide of hostilities. He aimed his main thrust at the so-called Elkhotov Gate, a valley between mountain ridges extending as far as Grozny and Ordzhonikidze. About 300 tanks were concentrated in that narrow sector. A swift panzer thrust was his famous tactic which had never failed him until the Terek line. Hitler allowed his favourite to strengthen his strike force with one of the crack motorized divisions of the SS—"Viking"—withdrawn from the Tuapse direction.

In the meantime, the Soviet General Headquarters, evidently unaware of this new danger, as can be surmised from its failure to order the Army Group in the North Caucasus to assume a rigid defence, issued this directive:

—The immediate and key task of the northern group of the Transcaucasian Front is to attack and wipe out the German troops on the southern bank of the Terek and restore the initial defence line of the 9th and 37th Armies. . . .—

An order is an order and has to be obeyed, of course. It is law in an embattled army and is not to be challenged if a war is to be waged and won. However, now, over forty years since those events, it is not binding on us and it seems reasonable to ponder on its relevance.

This was an offensive order worded in categorical terms to battle-weary troops who had been in retreat over a few hundred miles, who had neither tanks nor strong artillery nor any other weapons and equipment needed for a large-scale offensive. Worse still, they were confronted by a powerful enemy concentration in which the tanks alone numbered 300. What are indeed the chances of an offensive against a vastly superior enemy force holding positions of advantage and poised for attack?

The directive did not mention Petrov's 44th Army. It was entrenched in its initial positions and had even seized a bridgehead on the northern bank of the Terek from where the 10th Corps of the Guards was to go into the assault ordered by the General Headquarters.

Besides German frontal attacks General Petrov's troops had had to repulse a few assaults from an open flank where no Soviet forces were deployed in the steppe and hills over a distance of 200 kilometres, right up to the mouth of the

Volga. Those were the attempts of the special corps F of General Felmi to break through the battle positions of the 44th Army. That much vaunted corps had failed to live up to the Führer's expectations; it had suffered an ignominious defeat at the hands of Petrov's troops in the first line of defence and never made its way either to Iran or India. Later it would be chased and trapped by the 4th Kuban Cossack Corps of Cavalry Guards under Lieutenant General Kirichenko.

Thus, the Soviet forces had not yet prepared to carry out the latest directive of the General Headquarters when Kleist made his first thrust towards the Elkhotov Gate. German bombers coming in wave after wave literally ploughed up the entire valley and then German artillery unleashed its full fire power upon its scorched earth where no living thing could have survived. In that narrow passage between steep mountains every bomb and every shell seemed to hit its target.

When the valley had turned into a charred and smoking moonscape, Kleist threw into it a swarm of tanks and infantry with automatic weapons. The valley was too narrow for so many machines and men, so the tanks rolled on in a long, dense column. The ground was shaking under the heavy run of the steel caterpillars, the mountains echoed the roar of the engines, and smoke and dust turned daylight to dusk. It seemed nothing could stop this ruthless force. There were survivors in that hell on earth, however. They climbed out of their ruined shelters, checked their weapons and took their firing posts in the trenches. They knew they had to stop that mass of fire-spitting steel advancing on them. It was incredible but they did stop it.

Soviet artillery and mines were knocking out German tanks as they advanced, and antitank riflemen and soldiers armed with hand-grenades and Molotov cocktails were fighting them at close range from both sides. Soviet attack planes were zeroing in on their targets in this mess of men and machines. The columns of tanks seemed to be endless, and the gigantic battle lasted all day long. At nightfall the valley was a terrible sight of countless corpses and smoking crippled metal. The attackers had gained a few miles of ground but their plan of a breakthrough towards Grozny and Ordzhonikidze had been foiled.

Watching that scene, Kleist could not believe his eyes. He had never seen a battle of such ferocity, so staggering casualties and such a waste of effort. He shuddered at the thought of what he would have to report to the Führer. What would happen to him now? His choices were limited. Hoping for the best and knowing that the strength of the Soviet defenders was not infinite, he resolved to drive his divisions forward again. He had nothing to lose, after all.

During the next few days fierce battles continued. Major General Koroteyev's 9th Army bore the brunt of the fighting. In the early days of October Army Group A had finally exhausted its momentum. The German advance on Grozny and Baku ceased. The danger of losing the oil fields with innumerable implications for the Soviet war effort had been averted.

Incidentally, in planning the conquest of the Caucasus the German High Command had taken steps to form so-called volunteer national units of defectors and counter-revolutionaries of every description. That pursued a political aim: to create a semblance of hostility allegedly felt by the peoples of the USSR for the Soviet system and their willingness to wage armed struggle against it.

In the Nazi-occupied regions of the North Caucasus, German staff officers were detailed to recruit volunteers for national units to fight on the side of the Wehrmacht. Moreover, White Guard Generals, such as Krasnov and Shkuro, were brought here to raise support for the Nazi cause among Don and Kuban cossacks.

These generals, like others headed by Vlasov, would be captured in 1945, and Petrov would be directly involved in those events, which will be described in my later story.

Though the Nazis employed White Guard generals in their service, they were allowed only to form cossack units, which were placed under the command of the German General von Pannwitz. All these Nazi plans in the Caucasus, both military and political, were based on wishful thinking and had slim chances of success. Their failure, therefore, was inevitable.

The Tuapse Operation

It was October 1942, less than a month before the Red Army would launch its gigantic offensive at Stalingrad. Soviet reserve armies were concentrating for a decisive strike. Thousands of tanks and aircraft and combat vehicles had their fuel tanks full and fuel reserves for continuous combat were coming in from the Caucasus where Soviet troops had defended the oil fields and were now holding enormous German forces in check.

Hitler was still harbouring his ambitious plans of conquest in Asia, which hinged on his conquest of the Caucasus and he was now pinning his last hope on the Tuapse operation.

His reserves, however, had been used up. The adventuristic designs of the General Staff of the Wehrmacht and Hitler himself were now boomeranging against their masterminds. Iran, Iraq and India were now more distant than ever before. Even the last 100 kilometres on the way to Baku had proved rough going.

Hitler's grandiose plans were going round in his head in search of an answer and he finally found one. Of course, he must shift his hardest blows from the Baku sector to Tuapse, and attack the Soviet forces on the Black Sea coast. His own forces would cross the spurs of the Main Caucasian Range and cut off the Soviet 1st Army from all its supply sources in the hinterland.

Other Soviet forces would be staved off and the Soviet Black Sea Fleet driven out of its bases. The German forces on this battle front would strike out along the narrow strip of the coastline, swiftly advance on Kutaisi and

Tbilisi and, once these cities were taken, the road to Baku across Transcaucasus would be open.

Now another German build-up for a thrust in this new direction got under way. Eighteen of the twenty-six German divisions deployed on the Transcaucasian front were moved to the Tuapse sector to fight the Black Sea grouping of Soviet troops.

In a discussion with Keitel, Chief of the OKW, on September 18, 1942, Hitler declared:

—The crucial step to be taken now is a breakthrough towards Tuapse, the blocking of the Georgian Military Road and a thrust towards the Caspian Sea across Transcaucasia.—

From a military standpoint that plan was fairly shrewd; after invading the Black Sea coast and wiping out the trapped Soviet troops there, the Wehrmacht could shorten the front line roughly by 200 kilometres and relieve about ten divisions that would be moved towards the long coveted oil fields of the Caspian.

The German High Command concentrated the most battleworthy troops and an armada of tanks for that new thrust, so that they outnumbered the soviet defenders almost two to one.

Hitler entrusted the operation to Colonel General Ruoff's 17th Army. A devotee of the Prussian school of warfare, Ruoff resolved to deliver two strikes in convergent directions and take the Soviet troops in pincers. The Soviet 18th Army would be trapped and further German advance towards the Black Sea and Tuapse would be a walkover.

The Soviet Command had foreseen a German thrust towards Tuapse and had intelligence confirming such apprehensions. The defences in the Tuapse sector were strengthened and reinforcements were brought up here.

On September 27 Ruoff's Alpine rifles under the command of Lanz attacked the centre of the battle order of the 18th Army and pierced the Soviet defences. Units of the German 46th Infantry Division also captured ground. Within a week the Germans advanced into the river valleys leading to the sea coast.

Stalin reacted to these developments with a strongly worded message ordering immediate action to check the German advance. The breakthrough in the sector of the 18th Army was threatening the rear and flank of that Army defending the road to Tuapse. The command of the Black Sea group, therefore, resolved to restore the central battle front by a strong counterblow which was scheduled for October 2. The Germans forestalled this attack by their own blow in this sector on October 1 and pushed the Soviet troops back in other areas as well. As Marshal Grechko reminisced, the Soviet counterblow had been poorly organized and belated. Undertaken on October 7, it had petered out towards the end of the day.

Vigorous steps were taken to bring the situation under control. The Supreme Commander relieved Colonel General Chervichenko of command of the Black Sea group and appointed Major General Petrov as his successor. His splendid record in defending Odessa, Sevastopol and Baku must have been the reason for that unusual decision which placed him in command of an Army Group defending a broad front of crucial significance for the outcome of the Battle of the Caucasus. Now a Major General was to defeat a top-ranking opponent in the midstream of developments that promised the latter a near victory.

For all his talent and skill Petrov was unable to turn the tide of hostilities immediately. He needed time, at least a brief pause, to redeploy the forces under his command and, more important, sufficient strength to fight off the attackers. The Germans were still on the offensive and were capturing key points one after another. Their goal was near at hand and their pincers were about to close around the Soviet forces. The Commander of the German 17th Army was confident of victory. On October 16 he sent a message to the Commander of Army Group A:

—Russian resistance at Tuapse has weakened in the last few days following our constant attacks and air strikes.—

In that critical situation Petrov preserved his presence of mind and self-control. He was biding his time and issued no immediate instructions, which was a surprise to many. He would not act unless the situation was absolutely clear to him, as was his custom, and so his first move was a visit with a group of staff officers to the sector of the hardest-pressed 18th Army to get first-hand information on the spot.

I have no intention to offend its former command let alone its officers and men in the trenches and will quote Marshal Grechko:

—Inspection of the fighting fitness of troops and the state of defences revealed that the Commander of the 18th Army and his staff were uninformed of the actual situation on the front. They had lost contact with the troops on the Army's left flank. The Army Command were even unaware of the German capture of the town of Shaumian. They had ignored the specific features of the terrain and sought to establish a continuous front, feeding reserves into battle piecemeal, which scattered their forces, rather than concentrate them for delivering counterblows at the most critical points.—

The Front Military Council dismissed the Commander of the 18th Army, Lieutenant General Kamkov. Its new Commander was Major General Grechko, who had been in command of the 47th Army in the Novorossiisk sector. Grechko, however, had no time left to dislodge the Germans from Shaumian, as he had planned. On October 19 the Germans attacked and pressed the 18th Army back in the face of fierce resistance. The key Elisabethpol Pass fell into German hands. On October 21 the Germans attacked in three different directions. The battles were so ferocious that even Soviet regimental and divisional staff occasionally took part in hand-to-hand fighting. Nevertheless, the Germans were forging ahead, because their forces outnumbered the Soviet defences many times over.

Petrov was gleaning information about the German troops opposing him, exploring the terrain and patiently searching for a way to reverse the tide of the battle. Poor roads and the resulting ammunition shortages were partly to blame for the setbacks suffered by the Black Sea group. What could he do in the brief time he could afford to deal with this problem?

Torrential rains had reduced roads to streams of mud flowing from mountain slopes. Shallow rivulets had turned into violent torrents that were formidable obstacles to infantry and horses, not to speak of motor vehicles which, in addition, were very few.

Lieutenant General Shiyan, who was Captain in the Black Sea group at the time of those events, testifies:

—Autumn showers had made roads and trails impassable. In the trench lines ammunition was so scarce that troops sometimes had nothing but knives and bayonets to fight the Germans. Fighting units, undermanned as they were, had to detail men who would line up in a chain to pass over food and ammunition boxes from hand to hand.—

So it was ammunition and food that mattered most now. Indeed, the chain is no stronger than its weakest link, as the saying goes.

Petrov invited a group of logistic supply officers to his command post in a deep crevice. He briefly described the disastrous shortages of whatever the troops needed to carry on the fight.

"I've called you here because you know best how to deal with this problem. We are desperate. If you fail to find a way out, nobody will. We can't afford to lose this battle. We rely on you. Go to the mountains, look for suitable trails, ask old-timers for help. I give you three days. The troops will be having a hell of a time, fighting almost with their bare hands but they will know that aid is coming soon. And remember: our lives are at stake."

Petrov realized that the Germans' superior numbers and weapons gave them an advantage that could not be offset by logistics alone. He decided to ease the pressure of their frontal attacks by harassing action. Commando groups were formed in divisions and regiments to be sent behind German lines. Taking advantages of the mountainous terrain where enemy troops were operating in relative isolation commando groups attacked German headquarters and supply bases, disrupted communications, blew up bridges, sabotaged equipment and wiped out small German units.

The German casualties caused by these raids added up to an impressive total eventually. But, what mattered most, the Germans felt nervous and insecure and their fighting spirit waned.

Finally, the momentum of the German offensive had expired, the German troops were tired and demoralized, and the plan of taking Tuapse was called off.

The German 17th Army and the 49th Mountain Corps got stuck up on the passes of the Main Caucasian Range and on the approaches to Tuapse.

Winter was coming. A conference at the headquarters of Ruoff's 17th

Army had only one question on the agenda: What next? Opinions sharply differed. Some insisted that the Soviet forces had no strength left for a counterattack let alone a large-scale offensive, so the German offensive should be resumed and Tuapse taken before winter.

The 17th Army's Chief of Staff, however, had no illusions about the situation and the offensive potentials of the Russians in the Tuapse and Novorossiisk sectors. He transmitted his opinion to the Command of Army Group A. His caution was understood.

The Command of Army Group A resolved to give their troops a rest, bring up reinforcements, and fortify the positions captured before November. In the spring of 1943 they would be launched into another offensive, which would crush Russian resistance on their way to the oil fields of Baku and Iran.

Now that he had a respite Petrov was also thinking of his next step. The group under his command was building up strength. The General Headquarters reinforced it with two infantry, one cavalry, and one mountain division, six infantry brigades and four antitank artillery regiments. Would he sit on his hands when he could fight the Germans effectively even with smaller forces? He was now in firm control of the situation in all of his subordinate armies. So what next?

The weather was nasty with intermittent snowfalls and cold rains. Mountain roads and trails were slippery with ice so that troop movements and haulage of heavy guns along them were something the Germans would never suspect. Was it not the right time for an all-out attack?

Petrov's forces went into the assault. That was a complete surprise to the Germans. They fled in panic, abandoning weapons, vehicles and ammunition, everything they had stored for the winter. The German strike force that was to take Tuapse and seize the Black Sea coast was finally hurled back.

There was other good news. On November 9, 1942 the troops of the South Western and Don Fronts passed to the offensive at Stalingrad. On the next day the troops of the Stalingrad Front attacked the Germans from the opposite side to close the ring of encirclement.

Petrov was not under orders to pursue his offensive further. As soon as he had stabilized the front line, the 11th and 12th Cavalry Divisions were withdrawn from his group and moved to the Stalingrad area. It was realized that his troops were tired, heavily depleted, and lacked sufficient supplies for effective combat. Holding the Germans in check in his sector would be enough for the time being.

As a man of strategic foresight, however, he knew that any unit the Germans could now move to Stalingrad from his sector might influence the outcome of the great battle there. His group, therefore, continued bearing down on the opposing forces. His divisions were fighting their way forward in the face of fierce resistance throughout November and December. His troops were wading through mud and torrential streams at one flank and groping their way in snow blizzards sweeping the mountain ridges at the other.

In the meantime the Soviet Fronts at Stalingrad had linked up. The 6th Army of Field Marshal Paulus was trapped in the half-ruined city.

Operation Mountains and Operation Sea

In early January 1943 the situation in the southern area of the Soviet theatre of war was in rough outline as follows: the Soviet forces were battering the crumbling defences of the 6th Army of Field Marshal Paulus at Stalingrad and, while tightening the ring of encirclement around it, were striking out in the direction of Rostov and the Donets basin. The Soviet North Caucasian group was pressing the Germans back from the Terek, and the troops of General Petrov's Black Sea group were entrenching themselves along the Main Caucasian Range, from Mt. Elbrus to Novorossiisk, and preparing for an offensive.

The Soviet Supreme Commander ordered General Tyulenov, Commander of the Transcaucasian Front, to mount an offensive in the direction of Krasnodar and saddle the railway in the Tikhoretsk region to prevent a retreat of the very same German group that had but recently been at pains to make a breakthrough to the Caspian. It was to be trapped by Petrov's Black Sea group striking from the other side.

The offensive plan for the Krasnodar direction was made up of two parts codenamed Operation Mountains and Operation Sea.

In Operation Mountains the Soviet forces were to rip through the German defences in the Goryachy Klyuch area and liberate Krasnodar. That city in the Kuban valley, however, was not the eventual goal of the offensive. The Soviet forces were to cut off the Caucasian group of German forces from the route to Rostov.

Operation Sea provided for a swift advance of the 47th Army towards the mountain passes of Markotkh and Neberdzha. The Black Sea group was to carry out a seaborne assault close to this point, and, jointly with troops of the 47th Army, dislodge the Germans from Novorossiisk and seize the key Wolf Gate pass. To mislead the Germans about the landing area and zero hour Soviet sea patrols would simulate a landing off the town of Anapa.

Operation Mountains was to be directed by General Petrov and Operation Sea by Admiral Oktyabrsky.

Before delivering the main blow Petrov decided to test the enemy strength by two distracting strikes. The first such strike was delivered by the 46th Army in the direction of Neftegorsk and Maikop. The Germans were driven out of their trenches and were slowly retreating, holding on to every position of advantage on their way. To avoid being trapped, they started withdrawing from some key mountain passes.

The 47th Army dealt a blow at the Germans entrenched at Krymskaya. The weather and the terrain, however, favoured the Germans. The roads were slushy from continuous rain alternating with snowfall and Soviet artillery could not keep step with the troops. The Army finally bogged down.

The 56th Army had sliced the German lines and was forging ahead for all the efforts of the Germans to stop it. Thus, within a fortnight of fighting the Black Sea group, having overrun the German positions south of Krasnodar, captured twenty kilometres of territory.

The troops of the Southern Front were scoring important successes, too. On January 23, 1943 the command of Army Group A sent a message to Hitler's headquarters:

—Rostov had been sealed off by the Russians. They are bound to get significant reinforcements once their forces at Stalingrad are released and concentrated for a powerful thrust. . . . The Russians may also break through Voroshilovograd to the Sea of Azov. Then it will hardly be possible to fight them off and escape entrapment.—

Now that the avenues of retreat from the North Caucasus through Rostov were blocked, the German High Command turned the 17th Army towards the Taman Peninsula. The German forces in that area were moving towards a head-on collision with Petrov's troops.

That was a drastic change in the situation. On January 23, 1943 the General Headquarters ordered Petrov to move his forces into the Krasnodar area, saddle the river Kuban and strike out along both its banks. His main forces were to capture Novorossiisk and the Taman Peninsula and forbid its invasion by the Germans. In the meantime the troops of the Southern Front would block the route of German retreat at Bataisk and Azov.

The next task of the Black Sea group was to seize the Kerch Peninsula. The directive of the General Headquarters said that the troops of the Southern and Transcaucasian Fronts were to encircle and wipe out 24 enemy divisions in the North Caucasus to emulate the troops of the Don Front who had surrounded 22 enemy divisions at Stalingrad and were now destroying them.

Petrov's Black Sea group went into action as ordered. German resistance ceased gradually as it advanced across rugged and roadless country and captured one town after another—Khadyzhensk, Neftegorsk, Neftyanaya—on its way to the oil town of Maikop. It was finally taken by the guerrillas as German resistance crumbled all along the front.

In the early days of February the North Caucasian forces came up to the Sea of Azov in the area of Novorossiisk. It was time Operation Sea got under way.

The landing-force had been in training in the area of Tuapse and the Bay of Gelendzhik with over 60 warships and auxiliary craft readied for the assault. It was to be carried out by two landing parties at two different points of the shore.

On the night of February 4 Soviet seaborne troops were poised for action. Vice Admiral Oktyabrsky with his staff directed the operation from his command post at the naval base of Gelendzhik. The operation had been planned by the staff of the Black Sea Fleet under his guidance.

My story of the progress of that operation may be less injurious to the pride of its masterminds if I quote reminiscences of its participants whose prestige is taken for granted. Marshal Grechko recalls:

—The first flotilla of ships carrying the main landing force sailed off from Gelendzhik after a delay of 1 hour and 20 minutes caused by poorly organized troop embarkation and a gale-force wind. These were ships of different classes and speeds, so the fastest ones had to slow down to let their sluggish sisters overtake them.

—When there was only 48 minutes to go before artillery would open fire to soften the shore defences, Rear Admiral Basisty who was directing the landing force radioed about the delay to Vice Admiral Vladimirsky on the cruiser Krasny Kavkaz and to Vice Admiral Oktyabrsky, requesting a postponement of fire. Vladimirsky immediately transmitted the request to all the ships. They were thus compelled to manoeuvre in front of the landing area in full view of the Germans.—

Thus the deadlines fixed for every stage of the operation and the rule of secrecy were breached. Marshal Grechko writes further:

—Vice Admiral Oktyabrsky realized that a delay would leave too little time for a landing before sunrise and ordered the operation to start as scheduled. His radio message, however, reached the flotilla 45 minutes after the zero hour. Thus, miscalculation and incoordination eventually resulted in defeat of the main landing force.—

Further developments were discordant with plans. The Soviet Air Force uninformed of the delays attacked the shore defences at the appointed time. This was followed by a landing of paratroops. In the meantime the Soviet ships fired more than 2,000 large-calibre shells at the German defences. All these strikes were in the wrong sequence.

Marshal Grechko continues:

—The grazing fire of naval guns caused no damage to the German firing posts and troops hiding in shelters on the far side of the coastal hills. After half an hour the cruisers ceased fire and headed for their bases.—

The landing force to be protected by this fire was too slow to take advantage of it.

Lieutenant General Shiyan testifies:

—The landing force in the area of Yuzhnaya Ozereika came under lethal German machine-gun, mortar and artillery fire. Six ships were hit and crippled. Gunboats and other ships came close to the shore but were driven back by German artillery.

—Rear Admiral Basisty ordered his flotilla to retreat to Gelendzhik and Tuapse to avoid further losses. The assault troops who had seized a foothold on the shore had a strength of about 1,500 men and 16 tanks. They captured the German shore defences and carried the fight further, towards the next German strongpoint at Glebovka.—

Here they met with stiff German resistance. For three days they kept on fighting against overwhelming odds, suffering heavy casualties. They had run out of ammunition. Communication with the naval command had been disrupted, so they did not know if they could hope for aid or rescue. A small group fought their way to the area of Stanichka where the auxiliary force had landed, and 25 men joined the paratroopers and were later rescued by the Navy.

The auxiliary landing force in the area of Stanichka carried out its operations without a hitch. Coastal artillery, rocket launchers and gunboats knocked out German firing posts by accurate hits, and torpedo boats set up a smokescreen along the shore. Within an hour Major Kunikov who was in command of the landing force reported success and requested the second wave to go into action. The third wave followed shortly, and the landed troops soon drove the Germans out of their fortified positions. The operation, however, had to be called off in view of the disastrous failure of the main landing force at Yuzhanya Ozereika.

On the whole Operation Sea—designed to expel the Germans from Novorossiisk—ended in a debâcle. Hundreds of Soviet troops died, many ships and a lot of military equipment were lost. Vice Admiral Oktyabrsky was dismissed from command of the Black Sea Fleet and appointed Commander of the Amur Naval Flotilla in the Far East.

On February 1, 1943, Hitler promoted Kleist to the rank of Field Marshal, as he said in his message, ". . . in recognition of your distinguished record and the services of your troops during the decisive battles in the East. . . ." In his message to the Führer Kleist expressed his thanks in the pseudochivalrous language of a vassal addressing his suzerain: ". . . My lofty title is an award to my intrepid soldiers serving under your supreme command."

In another message transmitted to Hitler the very same day Kleist requested a licence to carry out numerous death verdicts passed on his "intrepid soldiers" by the divisional tribunals. His request was promptly granted.

Thus, Petrov's third top-ranking opponent was also a Field Marshal. The first was Antonescu, who captured Odessa vacated by Petrov's Maritime Army. The second was Manstein who was unable to take Sevastopol during a 250-day siege with vastly superior forces resisted by Petrov's bleeding army cut off from the rest of the country.

It is true, Kleist's 1st Panzer Army had been advancing swiftly from Rostov to the Terek. At this line, however, its power was completely exhausted and it rolled back to Rostov for a full 500 kilometres. Army Group A under Kleist's command suffered a devastating defeat. Was it a good reason for making him a Field Marshal? Hitler's motive must have been different. He had deposed many high-ranking generals and now was evidently trying to form a trustworthy following in the Wehrmacht. Kleist was a time-tested loyal minion.

Petrov was still a Lieutenant General at the time of these events.

Marshal Zhukov

Early in 1943 the German High Command and the Führer himself found themselves in a quandary. Manstein's Army Group South which had recently been trying hard to rescue Paulus' 6th Army trapped at Stalingrad was now in danger of total destruction. Kleist's Army Group A faced a similar prospect. Catastrophe was imminent, and urgent measures were needed to find a way out of the critical situation. On February 19, accompanied by a retinue of generals and aides-de-camp, his private physician and valet, Hitler boarded his personal plane he had named "Kondor", and flew off to Zaporozhe in the Ukraine for a conference with Manstein and Kleist.

Manstein admitted to the Führer that his front at Rostov would crumble unless reinforcements arrived from the Kuban theatre. Kleist objected: his own troops in the Kuban valley were hardly able to hold off the Russians threatening them with a second Stalingrad. The conference broke off unexpectedly. Hitler's aide-de-camp Below burst into the room, gasping for air after a quick run: "My Führer! Russian tanks are attacking the airfield!"

Hitler's valet Lange started packing hastily, his master nervously helping him. When Hitler climbed into his car, Below reported again: "My Führer! That was a different airfield south of the city. The tanks have turned back." Hitler heaved a sigh of relief.

The German High Command was taking feverish steps to check the Soviet offensive in the North Caucasus by feeding into battle divisions released from the front shortened as a result of the German retreat to the Taman Peninsula. Aircraft were transferred to this sector from airfields in the Crimea and the Donets basin. Bombers were flown in from Tunisia and the Netherlands. Building up strength in this sector, the Germans expected to check the advance of Soviet troops on the Gothenkopf (Goth's Head) Line they had started to build here.

Hitler and other Nazi leaders reposed great hopes in this line, which, as they were confident, would allow them to remain in control of the Kuban bridgehead for another offensive on the Caucasus.

On March 28, Chief of the General Staff Zeitler transmitted Hitler's directive to the Commander of Army Group A:
—The Führer has determined that the 17th Army should hold the Gothenkopf Line which includes Novorossiisk.—

That inclusion caused no end of trouble to the Germans. Though Novorossiisk was still in their hands, Soviet troops had seized a bridgehead in close proximity to it, the Little Land, as it was called, which threatened the German key positions on the Gothenkopf Line.

The German Command planned Operation Neptune to deal with this danger but all their efforts to dislodge the Soviet troops from the Little Land proved futile.

After taking Krasnodar the Soviet forces continued their offensive for some time, but stiff German resistance soon brought it to a halt almost all along the North Caucasian front.

The Soviet offensive had been successful on the whole. The towns of Nalchik, Pyatigorsk, Cherkessk, Mineralniye Vody, Stavropol, and Armavir, were free again. The Black Sea group had expelled the Germans from Maikop and Krasnodar. The Southern Front troops had taken Rostov on February 14 and cut off the German group in the Caucasus from the German forces in the Ukraine. The German 17th Army now had the Sea of Azov and the Black Sea behind its back.

For all that the Soviet High Command was dissatisfied with the results of the offensive, mostly because the German group on the Taman Peninsula had not been trapped as planned.

On Stalin's instructions a group of top-ranking Soviet generals led by Marshal Zhukov flew to Krasnodar to confer with General Maslennikov, Commander of the North Caucasian Front, and study the situation on the spot.

Zhukov was a man of action and strategic foresight, so when staying in the Caucasus he thought of securing the southern flank of the gigantic operation that would come to be known as the Battle of the Kursk Bulge. In conversation with Stalin shortly before his visit to the North Caucasus he had spoken of the German 17th Army entrenched in the Taman Peninsula as a pain in the neck to his staff planning to defeat the Germans in the summer campaign of 1943. Like a good chess player he planned his moves well in advance of the decisive battle.

Zhukov carried out the operation against the 17th Army in a thorough-going manner. The Soviet forces were regrouped. The 56th Army, which was to deliver the main strike, was reinforced with artillery from the Supreme Command Reserve and sizeable air forces withdrawn from other fronts. Trains of fuel, ammunition and military equipment were coming in to the area of troop concentration in rapid succession. On April 21, the Soviet Air Force started massive strikes at German defences, supply bases and airfields. The German troops besieging the Little Land were attacked by groups of up to 200 aircraft.

General Shtemenko, who was an eyewitness of those events, writes:

—Finally, the D Day of April 29 came. Soviet artillery opened up at 7:40 and kept on pounding the German defences for 100 minutes. Soviet air strikes followed one another at short intervals. The fire was then lifted, and infantry went into attack against the main German strongpoint at Krymskaya. The Germans were fighting back ferociously.

—The 56th Army was advancing at the rate of two kilometres a day, the Germans counterattacking it doggedly, particularly at the right flank. Six to eight such attacks were beaten off every day.

—On May 4 the Germans were taken in pincers and driven out of their fortified defences at Krymskaya. That was a formidable strongpoint with a dense network of trenches, dug-outs and other shelters cemented for added protection against artillery and air strikes. The approaches to the station were defended by tanks buried in the ground up to their turrets.

—In the next few days the offensive was just as slow, and eventually bogged down on the line of the Kurka and Kuban rivers. Reconnoitering parties reported that the Germans had fallen back onto a strongly fortified line of defence works, which was the so-called Gothenkopf Line. Attempts to pierce it with a rush proved to no avail, and further attacks would be meaningless. On May 15 the operation was called off. Another operation was required for breaking through this line, another concentration of forces and armaments.

—Thus, the Taman Peninsula remained in German hands. We knew that Stalin would be angered by our failure and were prepared for a dressing down. To our surprise, however, he displayed lenience and only dismissed the Front Commander Maslennikov, whose post was taken over by General Petrov. Under his direction the Soviet forces cleared the Taman Peninsula of German troops within five months.

A Front Commander

As Commander of the North Caucasian Front, Petrov now had eight field armies and two air armies in his group, as well as The Black Sea Fleet and the Azoz Naval Flotilla subordinated to him operationally. Their total strength ran to hundreds of thousands of officers and men. That was a Marshal's post though he was still a Lieutenant General. The next man up the chain of command was the Supreme Commander Stalin himself.

The general situation in the southern theatre of war at that time was as follows:

After the German retreat in the North Caucasus and the surrender of Paulus' 6th Army at Stalingrad Hitler nevertheless did not give up his plans of conquest of the oil fields of the Caspian. That seemed to be his fixed idea. It is definitely known today that the Nazis had no strength sufficient to carry out anything like Operation Edelweiss but Hitler believed that by mobilizing whatever forces were still available to him he could reverse the tide of hostilities and capture the coveted oil sources.

Generals Wagner, Philippi and Heim write in their reminiscences that in the period of retreat from Stalingrad the Führer was thinking not so much of holding Rostov as of retaining the positions on the Kuban and in the Taman Peninsula as a springboard for another offensive on the Caucasus.

A telpherway was built across the Strait of Kerch between the Crimea and the Taman Peninsula to supply German troops with whatever they needed for fighting the war. In addition, Hitler ordered construction of a permanent five-kilometre double-decker bridge across the strait for rail and motor transport.

The telpherway commissioned on June 14 carried 1,000 tons of freight a day, which was enough to meet the needs of the 17th Army.

However, before striking out in the direction of Baku from the Kuban bridgehead again, Hitler had to settle some political and strategic problems. Nazi Germany's severe setbacks had undermined its prestige among its allies. Therefore, in a discussion on April 8, 1943 the German Minister of Foreign Affairs von Ribbentrop assured his Italian counterpart Bastiniani that during the winter campaign of 1942 the Russians had exhausted themselves, so much so that the Red Army could now be vanquished by a series of repeated blows that would bring the war to a victorious end.

That diplomatic gamble had to be followed up by practical steps to regain the strategic initiative. In those days Hitler held a series of conferences with Army Group Commanders which culminated in a plan to give the Russians a decisive battle in the area of the Kursk Bulge. Here the Soviet forces formed a large arch-shaped protrusion in the deployment of the German forces and were thus exposed to the danger of convergent strikes from two directions under the base of this arch. By encircling them the Germans hoped to avenge themselves for Stalingrad and seize the strategic initiative.

That crucial operation required manpower and equipment for its success, while the German Army had been heavily depleted. The Nazis announced total mobilization of the nation's potential. All males under fifty were to be drafted into military service, and women and children were enlisted for work on the home front. German war industry had started mass production of up-to-date military equipment and weapons. Hitler pinned great hopes on the new T-6 "Tiger" and T-6 "Panther" tanks and the "Ferdinand" self-propelled gun, all of which had very thick armour.

By that time a new fighter plane, Focke-Wulf 190 A, had been designed and put into production. It was perhaps the best German aircraft in those years.

Within a record time about two million men were enlisted under a total mobilization plan and the strength of the German Army was brought up to 11,280,000.

In the summer of 1943 the Germans had 43 divisions more on the Eastern front than at the time of invasion of the Soviet borders.

In mid-April the operational plan was completed and codenamed Citadel, which was an allusion to what the Nazis thought was the last stronghold of Russian resistance.

On June 1, 1943 Hitler assembled at his headquarters in East Prussia all the commanders of the Army Groups, Armies and corps which would take part in Operation Citadel. In a long speech he praised the merits of modern German arms, tanks and aircraft in the first place, that would certainly give the German Army a great advantage over the Russians. He was confident of victory.

Army Group A opposed to General Petrov's forces was not to be directly involved in Operation Citadel but it was to assist it in accordance with Order

No. 5, which said in particular:
—The Command of Army Group A should be clearly aware of the central task of releasing forces for fighting on other fronts. . . . Army Group A is hereby ordered to hold the Kuban bridgehead and the Crimea at all costs. . . . The defences on the Crimean coast should be made as impregnable to enemy assaults as those in the West.—

The Battle of the Kursk Bulge ended in a German defeat, and laid the groundwork for the sweeping Soviet offensives of the next two years. This famous battle is not the subject of my story, but, though General Petrov did not take a direct part in the fighting at Kursk, he was doing his best on his own front. The most effective aid to the Soviet forces engaged in the Battle of the Kursk Bulge was keeping the German troops pinned down on the Taman Peninsula.

The Gothenkopf Line

In May 1943 Petrov had a pleasant surprise. His Chief of Staff recently appointed by Moscow was an old comrade. General Laskin had been commander of the 172nd Division in the Battle of Sevastopol and had since been in several key staff posts and taken part in the Battle of Stalingrad.

Immediately upon arrival Laskin hastened to the Front Commander's headquarters in a forest not far from the cossack village of Krymskaya. Petrov was waiting for him.

"Long time, no see, General", he smiled broadly as Laskin entered his dug-out. "It's good to have you back again. Congratulations! Stalingrad was good work, to be sure. We know from grapevine telegraph that it was you who captured Paulus, right?"

He shook his hand warmly. Laskin smiled back: "It's only partly true. It was my troops and I, but I took the Field Marshal to headquarters in my jeep."

As Chief of the General Staff Zeitler testified, at a conference held on February 1, 1943 at the Führer's "Wolf's Lair", his headquarters near Rastenburg, East Prussia, Hitler lapsed into a veritable hysteria on learning of Paulus' surrender. He was indignant: Paulus ought to have committed suicide.

Incidentally, Paulus had been promoted twice within two months. He had led the 6th Army towards Stalingrad as a Lieutenant General. On December 1, 1942, he received the rank of Colonel General, and on January 30, 1943 the rank of Field Marshal. Hitler presumed that this high title would oblige Paulus to shoot himself to escape captivity. It was a shock to the Führer to learn of his newest Field Marshal's surrender on the next day after his promotion.

* * *

After a long pause General Petrov concluded that Novorossiisk was the key to the Gothenkopf Line. Once it was taken the German defences would be unhinged. But how was it best to do it? By encircling, outflanking, or storming? One setback was enough. Those war graves and sunken ships were not to be forgotten. Worse still, the previous assault had alerted the Germans and made them reinforce their positions.

The chief adviser and opponent of a Front Commander is usually his Chief of Staff. Petrov invited Laskin for a conference.

"See here," he said and pointed at the map on his desk. "This is the Gothenkopf Line which cuts the Taman Peninsula from sea to sea. Its flanks rest on the Black Sea and the Sea of Azov. Most of the line is based on natural obstacles: swamps and lakes. The Germans have many troops on the peninsula, and here we'll have to fight Ruoff's 17th Army. We failed to break its back last time and had to pull back. Marshal Zhukov stayed with us for some time, analyzed the operation, berated us and left for Moscow. We hoped for aid, but in a couple of days a few artillery, antiaircraft and tank units were withdrawn from our front into the General Headquarters' reserve. Now we are under orders to defeat Ruoff and clear the Taman Peninsula with smaller forces. You have a competent staff, so get down to work."

After some time the operational plan based on Petrov's instructions was ready. The 18th Army and the Black Sea Fleet would converge on the Germans at Novorossiisk and free it. Seaborne troops would surprise the Germans in the harbour district. Their formidable fortifications, pill-boxes, coastal artillery and barbed wire entanglements would be rendered useless. This would be a race against time, but the factor of surprise and swift action were the clues to victory. The 18th Army would attack from the Little Land. The 9th and 46th Armies would attack simultaneously and block the movements of German reserves.

As was the general rule before a large-scale offensive, a representative of General Headquarters—Marshal Timoshenko—arrived in the North Caucasus. He stayed in a small house in the forest near the Front headquarters. General Petrov accompanied by Laskin came to see him and discuss the operational plan. Petrov spread a map on the desk, then described briefly the situation and the assault plan. The Marshal remarked:

"So you are going to take Novorossiisk in pincers and ram its waterfront? That will take a lot of firepower. The ferroconcrete shields of the Germans there need a real good punch to be broken. If you fail to crack them, your men won't be able to get to the heart of the city. The loss of life will be heavy."

Petrov explained: "That has been worrying us all along. But we have big ships to deliver that fire punch with their huge guns. Our 18th Army also has much cannon and their crews can work wonders, firing over their sights. As for the waterfront defenceworks, our navymen have come up with a plan. What can stand up to a massive attack by a swarm of torpedo boats? They will bore a hole in the shore defences big enough for a battleship to enter. Of course, we shall have many pillboxes razed by methodical gun fire before going into attack. This assault plan will work, as sure as sure."

"Now I see", the Marshal said. "I have no objections to your brainchild. The next step is to be taken by General Headquarters. I will support your plan."

Before long another representative of General Headquarters, Admiral Kuznetsov, who was People's Commissar of the Navy, came to the North Caucasus for a conference with the Front Military Council.

Petrov requested ships of the Black Sea Fleet to help with his plan to take Novorossiisk and give his troops a position of vantage to pierce the Gothenkopf Line. Kuznetsov, however, offered arguments against that request, as had already been decided at General Headquarters:

"We have weighed all pros and cons and have to disappoint you, General. Big ships will stay away from your battle area. They are built for combat, it is true, but the offshore waters here are heavily mined, the Germans have a large fleet of torpedo boats and many bombers. We cannot afford to put the big ships at risk. When Sevastopol had to be held at all costs, we sent our biggest ships to help its defenders. Now the situation is different: you have a mass of artillery, Katusha rocket launchers and aircraft concentrated on the approaches to Novorossiisk. Their combined fire power will be enough to bury the Germans in their pillboxes. We have yet to win this war, and its end is not yet in sight. We'll need those ships for a final settlement of accounts with the Nazis. But we know of your inventiveness, and we are sure you will break your opponent's neck anyway."

A Meeting with Stalin

At the end of August the General Headquarters finally transmitted its directive for a full-scale offensive in the Taman Peninsula. The North Caucasian front forces were to wipe out the German group here before it escaped to the Crimea. Petrov read the terse lines of Stalin's order which gave him a lot of leeway in handling the operation. That meant he was trusted more than he had expected.

He ordered his staff to prepare maps, reports and other documents for his visit to the General Staff and the Supreme Commander.

In Moscow his plan was approved by the General Staff and the Chief Naval Staff and he was invited to Stalin's office for its final endorsement. That was his first meeting with Stalin, and he was given some useful hints by his high-ranking well-wishers as to what it would be best to say to the overworked and tired old man in the few minutes Petrov would have to get his okay.

Petrov reminisced later:

—Stalin met me with a close, steady gaze, as though reading my mind. I was surprised to see pockmarks on his face, which was pale and pinched. He was slightly shorter than I was, which was unexpected, as I had always imagined him a bigger man. He shook my hand and motioned me towards a large desk where I could spread my maps, then said curtly:

"Okay, I'm all ears."

—I set out my plan in rough outline, knowing that every minute counted. Stalin was silent, his face inscrutable. General Antonov of the General Staff ventured a comment:

"We have examined it. Looks good."

Stalin spoke up, as if thinking aloud:

"You have the German 17th Army, a fortified line and difficult terrain to overcome in Taman. This Army, however, has its back against the wall, which is the Strait of Kerch. You have the Black Sea Fleet and the Azov Naval Flotilla to help you. Your two-year record of joint action with the Navy is commendable. Your task now is to drown the German army in the coastal lakes and the sea. We regard you as an expert on defensive combat. The defensive stage of the war is over and now you will have to win a name in offensive warfare."

—"That's all," and he shook my hand again. "I wish you nothing less than victory, General."—

Petrov returned to his troops on the same day. In the morning a radio call from Moscow informed him of his promotion to Colonel General. Stalin had evidently concluded that two stars were too few for such a battle-toughened veteran.

Now Petrov had a free hand to carry out what is known today as a classical battle, which is studied at military academies and discussed in research papers on the art of warfare.

The Battle of Novorossiisk

On the night of September 8 General Petrov moved to his command post near the shore. It was a windy and damp place. Dark clouds raced across the night sky driven by a rising gale. A few motor launches sent off to test the roughness of the sea had their decks swept by violent waves and turned back. A storm like that could play havoc with any seaborn assault yet he could not afford to call it off, knowing that any deferment of deadlines would make his troops nervous. Petrov waited for another day, and, when the storm had slightly abated, he ordered his forces to get under way. The largest force of 2,500 men was the 255th Marine Brigade under Colonel Potapov.

Another force of 1,100 men was the 393rd Marine Battalion under Lieutenant Commander Botylev and a third of over 1,000 men was the 1,339th Infantry Regiment under Lieutenant Colonel Kadanchik.

Every unit was led by a group of motor launches. Their crews were to clear surface and underwater obstacles and seize a foothold on the shore.

Petrov was watching the German defences. They were quiet. An occasional searchlight beam flashed here and there. Flares soared into the dark sky far beyond, in the Myskhako area. Were the Germans simply waiting for a signal to open fire?

In the meantime the wind was rising and heavy billows hid the shore from sight as the small vessels of the landing forces were heaved up and down by the rough seas. The tugs hauling barges with troops lagged behind faster ships and the zero hour had to be put off again, to 3 hours this time.

A group of Soviet bombers flew low over their heads and across the Bay of Tsemes, and flashes of bomb explosions were followed by booming reverberations as they dropped their loads on the German rear and artillery positions north and south-west of Novorossiisk.

The long-awaited moment of attack came at last. At 2:44 800 artillery guns and hundreds of mortars opened up and the thunder of thousands of exploding shells and mines rent the air. The shore and mountains at Novorossiisk were lit by a deathly glow.

The blazing arrows of Katusha missiles cut the darkness, hurtling towards their targets like comets. That was the first salvo of 227 rocket launchers. Flames and fountains of earth and debris shot up from the German positions.

Then bombers of the 4th Air Army flew wave after wave at different altitudes, raining bombs on the targets beneath: artillery positions, command posts and troop concentrations.

Vice Admiral Kholostyakov, who witnessed the landing on the shore of the Bay of Tsemes, tells this story:

—The ferroconcrete pillboxes built on the piers all along the waterfront were the first to come under attack. Torpedo boats racing at top speed burst into the harbour and fired a swarm of torpedoes at the shore defences. Thirty pill-boxes closest to the sea edge were blown up in a few seconds.

—The torpedo boats were followed by motor launches carrying Marines who invaded the shore and attacked the Germans in their trenches. The first lines were captured in fierce hand-to-hand fighting. The surviving defenders ran for their lives and were pursued by the attackers into the city. Within half an hour 800 Marines were fighting the Germans on the streets and advancing towards the railway station.

—As they fought their way through the German defences, enemy resistance steadily stiffened. During house-to-house fighting at night effective troop control was impossible. Groups of Marines had to rely on their own judgement as how to carry on the attack, but they were tough people who never lost their presence of mind. And, as we know, "when the going gets tough, the tough get going".

—Not all men of the landing force were lucky to set foot on solid ground. A few craft had run aground in shallow waters off the coast and men with their rifles, machine pistols, machine-guns, mortars and ammunition boxes jumped overboard and waded towards the shore under deadly German fire.

—The Germans finally realized where the danger was greatest and converged the fire of their artillery and six-barrel mortars on the landing area.

Shells exploded in the midst of Soviet troops and many were killed. Seven barges and launches were sunk in a matter of minutes. Survivors swam to shore but not all could make it.

—Nevertheless, most of the men of the three landing units were now fighting on the ground.—

Simultaneously, units of the 18th Army went over to the offensive northeast and south of Novorossiisk. The city was under attack from three directions. The Germans were exposed to powerful strikes along a 100-kilometre front. Their defences, however, were so formidable and their fire so well-aimed that regiments of the 18th Army were unable to capture even the first defence line. Soviet artillery had evidently left too many fortifications and firing posts undamaged. Petrov realized that now that the Germans had held their positions here they could move reinforcements to the landing area to drive the Soviet Marines into the sea. He requested General Vershinin of the Air Force to send his attack planes and bombers to help the Marines and scatter whatever German reserves would be on their way to the city.

At dawn, however, the Luftwaffe also joined battle in large numbers. Soviet fighters were scrambled on short notice and numerous dog fights were seen in the clear sky, Soviet and German planes chasing one another and leaving long trails of black smoke as they were hit and crashed into the ground or the sea.

And yet, as was increasingly obvious, the first day of fighting gave no advantage to the Soviet attackers. The foothold seized at Novorossiisk was there, it is true, but it was very insecure, and the Marine brigade defending it was under constant attacks by German artillery and aircraft. The Marines were tenaciously holding their ground and beating off German panzer attacks.

The groups that had captured key points in the city were having a bad time fighting off German tanks which had come within range. Botylev's 393rd Marine Battalion which had taken the German stronghold at the Seamen's Club had only 40 men left on its strength and 90 men heavily wounded. All the others had died in the fighting.

The 1,399th Infantry Regiment had captured all the port installations, but towards the day's end the Germans had pressed its men to the edge of the sea by several violent counterattacks.

The group which had taken the railway station had repulsed many German panzer and infantry attacks and their position was precarious.

Was it another setback? It seemed all had been planned, timed and targeted to a T. Yet the results were small compared to the big effort. Laskin recalled later:

—The German defences on the southern battle front and in the Novorossiisk area were stronger than any other sector of the Gothenkopf Line. The enemy took advantage of the system of ferroconcrete gun emplacements and great fire density: 60 machine-guns, 20 mortars and up to 25 artillery pieces per kilometre of frontline. Not all of them had been identified and knocked out in advance.

—In the Battle of Stalingrad and the Battle of Kursk the Soviet side had 160–180 pieces of artillery per kilometre of frontline, whereas in our operation the relevant figure was only 25 and, counting mortars, no more than 45. That was only one seventh of what was needed for complete success.—

Petrov was determined to press on with the offensive. He ordered a build-up of forces in the landing areas and another thrust by the 18th Army's two flanking groups to take the city in pincers. The 9th Army was to pursue its offensive with greater tenacity to prevent German troop withdrawals from its sector.

On the second night of the offensive Soviet artillery and night bombers resumed their strikes. Sea-borne troops began landing in all sectors of the shore.

In the morning Soviet artillery kept pounding the German defences and lifted fire to hit targets behind the enemy lines. Groups of aircraft made frequent sorties from nearby airfields. Then a deafening thunder of Katusha missiles shook the ground, which was a signal for the regiments of the 18th Army to encircle the city from east and west. Soviet infantry went over the top and attacked the Germans in close combat. During the day the eastern group of the 18th Army wedged itself into the German defences for one kilometre and the western group advancing from the Myskhako bridgehead overran the first German lines.

In the city and the coastal area of the Bay of Tsemes the Germans were making desperate efforts to drive the Soviet Marines back into the sea. The groups holding the railway station and the Seamen's Club were fighting off vastly superior German forces. Each of them had repelled about 20 attacks in the last two days.

Finally, more gladdening reports started coming in: Bulbulyan's 1,337th regiment had linked up with Kadanchik's regiment and, by a joint attack, had captured two factories. The 142nd and 327th battalions had been joined by scattered units of their brigade and formed a continuous battle front.

On the morning of September 13 Petrov ordered General Leselidze to commit to action his reserve—General Bushev's 176th Division—from the Myskhako bridgehead and add punch to the blow east of Novorossiisk with Colonel Safarian's 89th Infantry Division.

Now it was time his own reserve was thrown into battle. That was the 55th Infantry Division of the Guards under the command of General Arshintsev. The division attacked in force and broke the German lines. The divisions on the Little Land also went into attack. Fierce battles continued for a full day, hand-to-hand fighting was carried on until both sides were utterly exhausted, but the tide of hostilities had not yet been turned.

General Trusov reported to Petrov: "The Germans have committed two fresh divisions: the 125th and the 101st. Ruoff seems to have guessed our intention to defeat him at this critical point."

Petrov knew that success now hinged not only on the commitment of reserves but also on the speed and accuracy of his steadily hardening strikes. To increase their impact he assigned Colonel Shurenkov's armoured brigade of his own reserve to General Leselidze's army and reinforced it with an antitank artillery regiment, one infantry and one engineering battalion. That was a strong fist he would use to knock out his opponent at the right time.

In the meantime large German infantry forces with a lot of artillery of various calibres were moving towards the city from the north. Petrov phoned to Vershinin: "I have a job for your airmen, General. There are four German columns on the move. We expect you to deal with them as best as you can, okay?"

Soviet air strikes at the German reinforcements followed shortly. These reserves were dispersed and herded into shelters in which they stayed while they were needed desperately to prop up the German defences.

Arshintsev's division and Shurenkov's armoured brigade were forging ahead in the face of stiff German resistance. Yet Petrov's fresh reserves were tipping the balance of the battle. Therefore, he took the next resolute step: handing over to Leselidze from his reserve the 414th Infantry Division of Colonel Kurashvili.

Now the Germans had used up all their reserves, and it was time to finish them off. Though they were still fighting desperately, the Soviet forces had gained three to four kilometres of ground all along the front at Novorossiisk.

On the morning of September 14, Petrov resolved to complete the rupture of the Gothenkopf Line and carry the fight into the depth of the Taman Peninsula. The 56th and 9th Armies were ordered to mount a decisive offensive the harassed enemy would be unable to hold off.

No, he wouldn't let Ruoff recover his wind and have a respite, he would dislodge him from his stronghold here.

The last few hours were the hardest time for the Marines fighting for their lives in complete encirclement. Few of them had survived. Wounded men stayed at their firing posts. The famous sniper Rubakho, his legs crippled by bullets, was carried by his comrades from place to place, taking accurate shots, and killing 70 Nazis. But rescue was near.

The western and eastern groups of Leselidze's army were stubbornly advancing towards the city's centre. The Germans realized that they would soon be trapped and started a hasty retreat from the city.

At dawn Vershinin reported excitedly: "They are fleeing! My airmen see them fleeing!"

On the morning of September 14 Novorossiisk was free. The operation had lasted for five days; the Gothenkopf Line was now broken at its strongest point.

*   *   *

Petrov was looking at the city, its ruins still smoking, and saw in his mind's eye the troops of his three armies carrying on the fight on the plains. The Germans would not give up the Taman Peninsula without a fight, that was clear as daylight. Only the first belt of the Gothenkopf Line had been sliced open. A few others were yet to be overcome.

The Taman Peninsula was like a sponge soaked with water: lakes, rivers and swamps, roads and fields turned to slush by autumn rain. Troops loaded with heavy weapons were wading through knee-deep mud, pushing and hauling artillery and vehicles and shouting at horses slipping at every step.

The Germans, of course, had the same hardships to endure but for a defender an impassable terrain and nasty weather are not a disadvantage as soon as he is entrenched and prepared to meet an attacker. For Petrov, therefore, riding on his opponent's back in close pursuit and breaking into his new positions would be the best plan to follow. Yet that would simply give him almost equal chances with the enemy, but he thought of gaining a greater advantage to make his success doubly sure.

He determined to move ahead of the Germans and capture their rear positions before they reached them. His troops would thereby cut the avenues of retreat of the German main forces to the sea ports in the western part of the peninsula.

The width of the battle front from the Sea of Azov to the Black Sea was slightly over 100 kilometres and the distance to the Strait of Kerch, that is the depth of the German defences, was roughly eighty kilometres. That was, in fact, a fully fortified area where the Germans had moved into the second line of defence and regrouped for effective resistance. That would take another breakthrough and a heavy loss of life. Petrov found a way to obviate a frontal attack.

On his orders the Black Sea Fleet landed a force of Marines and infantry in the area of Chaikino and the Cossack village of Golubitskaya in the German rear to saddle the roads leading to the Strait of Kerch.

On the morning of September 21 Soviet warships burst into the harbour of Anapa, shelled the coastal defences and landed another force of Marines, while Shurenkov's armoured brigade and regiments of the 318th and 56th Divisions of the Guards drove the Germans out of the village of Rayevskaya and approached Anapa from the other side. These accurately timed simultaneous strikes from the sea and on land took the Germans by surprise, so much so that they failed to escape on the sixteen ships riding at anchor in the harbour of Anapa in expectation of troop embarkation. In Anapa alone Soviet tankmen and Marines wiped out hundreds of German troops, who were fleeing in panic, captured 49 pieces of artillery, 180 machine-guns, 77 mortars, 4,000 rifles and machine-pistols, and 40 warehouses stocked with military stores and provisions.

The 18th Army was fighting its way forward along the narrow isthmus between the sea and the Kiziltash coastal lake.

On the night of September 25 more sea-borne troops landed in various areas, cutting off the routes of German retreat to the town of Taman from where a sea lift would take the German 17th Army to the Crimea as had been planned by its command. That plan codenamed Krimgilda was the Germans' last hope.

The Soviet 9th Army was advancing on the town of Temryuk at the Kuban estuary, the 56th Army in the central sector was storming a German fortified line guarding the sea ports, and attack planes of two Soviet air force regiments made hundreds of sorties to batter German manpower and artillery and assist the Marines holding their bridgeheads on the sea coast.

On the night of September 27 Colonel Terekhin's and Major General Sevastianov's troops outflanked the Germans at Temryuk from two sides and at dawn launched an all-out attack on the eastern district. The Germans attempted a retreat to the south-west but ran into the Marine units landed at Chaikino. Now they were under fire from three sides. Fearing entrapment, they started an exodus to the sea ports in the west.

Chief of Reconnaissance Trusov reported to Petrov:

"German infantry and artillery are retreating to the ports of Kuchugury, Taman, and Ilyich." This was the finale at last. Petrov felt a surge of joy. He radioed to the 4th Air Army Commander Vershinin:

"Alert all your crews to attack troops and equipment on the roads and embarkation sites in sea ports. Sink all escaping transports in the Strait of Kerch."

The Black Sea Fleet Commander Vladimirsky gave the same order to the naval air forces. Soviet airmen made five to six sorties a day, bombing and strafing troop concentrations and ships, and completed the German defeat. Hundreds of barges, launches, boats and various small craft were sunk, and many German planes attempting to aid the evacuation were brought down by Soviet fighters.

On October 1, Petrov's armies stormed the last fortified defence line on the approaches to the Strait of Kerch.

The town of Taman was freed on October 3. On the night of October 8 the Black Sea Fleet landed a force of Marines on Cape Tuzla and cleared it from the Germans towards morning.

On October 8, fierce battles were still being fought for the ports of Kuchugury and Veselovsky. The Germans, driven to the edge of the sea were wiped out or taken prisoner.

At 0900 hours on October 9 Petrov radioed to Stalin about the rout of the German group on the Tamain Peninsula and its complete liberation. His message was worded in expressive language:

"... No Germans except POWs have survived on the Kuban and the

Taman Peninsula."

The Battle of the Caucasus was over. Operation Edelweiss was buried in Nazi archives. The bridgehead which had nurtured Hitler's hopes for another march on Baku was now liquidated.

Petrov was promoted to the rank of General of the Army and decorated with the Order of Suvorov First Class, which, in accordance with its statute, was to be awarded to generals who had defeated superior enemy forces in offensive combat. This was a recognition of General Petrov's skill in offensive warfare which had disproved the view that he was good only as a master of defence.

Some Implications

The Battle of Moscow had buried the Nazi idea of blitzkrieg, a lightning war. The Battle of Stalingrad had turned the tide of hostilities in the Soviet theatre of war, as well as the Second World War as a whole. At Stalingrad the Red Army had seized the strategic initiative from the Wehrmacht and held it until the end of the war. Stalingrad had been the farthest point of the Nazi invasion of the USSR, and the starting point of the Nazi retreat. The Battle of Kursk had brought the Nazis to the brink of catastrophe, and secured the Soviet strategic initiative for good.

That is a matter of common knowledge. But why is the Battle of the Caucasus not listed among the crucial battles of the war? The Nazis were, indeed, a stone's throw from Baku. If they had taken the oil fields, fuel shortages would have made further struggle impossible and the war might have been lost.

I predict vehement objections to such a conjecture. True, to think of defeat when the country is at war would be tantamount to high treason. But now, many years after victory, we are obliged to analyze our failures and setbacks. This will not detract from the significance of our victory but will emphasize the price we paid for it.

It will be recalled that only 7 per cent of the Soviet fighting forces were deployed in the Caucasus. That, of course, was not enough for averting an almost inevitable disaster which threatened the Caucasus. Nevertheless, the Soviet forces won that battle.

The German débâcles at Stalingrad and in the Caucasus undermined the Nazis' prestige among their allies. Turkey, which was prepared to attack the Soviet borders, gave up its plans. So did Japan.

The morale of the German soldiers declined, and the Nazi chieftains saw the writing on the wall.

When fighting was in progress on the Terek River in August 1942 Nazi Germany was still at the zenith of its power. The Third Reich held sway over Europe from France to the Caucasus and from Crete to Cape Nordkyn in Norway.

The Wehrmacht's top brass and the leaders of Germany's war economy were now determined to inject the oil of the Caucasus into their war machine for the conquest of the Middle East and India. The Führer's frantic personal ambitions maintained the momentum of this plan. Eventually, the Wehrmacht lost about two million men in southern Russia and was driven back to where it had started one of its biggest operations on the Eastern front.

The Soviet victory in the Caucasus, like Nazi Germany's defeat in Russia in general, had yet another aspect. It stopped the impending invasion of the Eastern countries by the 20th century barbarians—the German Nazis obsessed with the idea of world supremacy. For a few centuries Russia has shielded the West against conquest by the Mongols and thus saved European civilization. After the invasion of Russia the Mongols did not venture to advance into Europe with the unsubdued Russians in their rear. In a century and a half a Russian army led by Prince Dmitry Donskoi would defeat Khan Mamai's hordes in the Battle of Kulikovo and deliver Europe forever from the danger of a barbarian invasion from the East.

And now, in the 20th century, Russia protected the East against an invasion by the Nazi barbarians. Indeed, India, Iraq and Turkey, as well as other countries, had already been assigned their places on the German strategic maps, while their lands and national wealth figured in the tentative estimates of Nazi war trophies. The Nazis had been on the threshold of the East. So the Battle of the Caucasus was of historic significance for the destinies of the Eastern nations.

A Strike Across the Straits

In July and August 1943 the Red Army inflicted a devastating defeat on the Wehrmacht in the Battle of Kursk, which was a ferocious contest between armoured and air forces on a scale never witnessed in the history of war. The German Army Group Centre under Field Marshal von Kluge and Army Group South under Field Marshal Manstein had concentrated 70 per cent of the panzer forces and over 65 per cent of the air forces operating on the Soviet–German front—a total of 2,700 tanks and self-propelled assault guns and about 2,050 combat aircraft, about 10,000 pieces of artillery and mortars and over 900,000 troops for the summer offensive in the area of the Kursk Bulge. Many of the German tanks and aircraft were of the latest models, on which the German High Command had reposed great hopes.

The Red Army, which had recovered from its setbacks of the early period of the war, confronted them with a powerful force of 3,444 tanks and self-propelled guns, 2,172 combat aircraft, over 19,000 pieces of artillery and mortars and 1,336,000 troops.

The ferocity of the fighting was exemplified by the tank battle at Prokhorovka, in which up to 1,200 tanks and self-propelled guns were involved on both sides. In the biggest tank battle of the Second World War the

Germans lost 400 tanks and over 10,000 troops killed in one day, which was July 12. The German panzer force was routed.

In the Battle of Kursk the Wehrmacht lost about 500,000 troops, 1,500 tanks, over 3,700 combat aircraft and 3,000 pieces of artillery. Following that battle Nazi Germany and its allies had to shift to the defensive in all theatres of the Second World War.

At the end of September the Red Army forced a breach in the German defences on the Dnieper and seized a large bridgehead on its far bank.

Now it was time the German 17th Army was finally wiped out in the Crimea. While his forces were still mopping up straggling German groups on the Taman Peninsula, General Petrov was thinking of a way to effect a crossing over the Strait of Kerch to surprise the German forces in the Crimea. In general outline his plan provided for an attack on a broad front to make the Germans disperse their forces to fight Soviet sea-borne troops without a chance to concentrate for a strong counterattack.

That would require many landing craft and many supporting ships with powerful artillery, but these were not readily available after so many sea battles while many crippled ships were under repair. There was some time left before the operation, so Petrov resolved to take advantage of this respite to increase the fitness of his troops for the impending sea-borne attack. He ordered all commanding officers to train troops in every detail of embarkation, disembarkation and fighting for a foothold on a beach. Training went on round the clock, and nobody complained despite the fatigue of the battles that had just ended. All realized that efficiency would have to offset the disadvantages of an attack against an entrenched enemy relying on a formidable system of fortifications and immense firepower.

Who was Petrov's opponent this time? After his setbacks on the Taman Peninsula, Colonel General Ruoff had been dismissed. The new commander of the 17th Army was Erwin Eneke, its former Chief of Staff, who was quite familiar with the fighting conditions in this area.

In a directive of September 4, 1943, Hitler said:

—The defences of the Crimea should be organized to bar any Soviet ships from entry into the Straits of Kerch. These should be mined and blocked and exposed to the fire of German artillery.

—The German and Rumanian forces in the Crimea should hold their ground and form a wedge in the Red Army's rear for a further German offensive in the Ukraine.—

The German High Command took urgent steps to reinforce the 17th Army heavily depleted by the fighting on the Taman Peninsula. Troop reinforcements were coming in by sea and by air from France and the Netherlands. The Luftwaffe was also building up its forces in the Crimea. The 17th Army consisted of 12 divisions, of which five were German and seven Rumanian, with a total strength of 200,000.

The German shore defences were based on a system of strongholds with numerous gun emplacements, surrounded with mine fields and a dense network of wire entanglements on the beaches and within a few dozen metres of the shoreline. All coastal waters were mined to prevent the entry of hostile ships. The Germans had a fleet of naval vessels based in the ports of Kerch, Kamysh-Burun and Feodosia—a total of 37 torpedo boats and 25 gunboats, 6 mine-sweepers and over 60 high-speed self-propelled barges. There were three defence lines in the depth of the Crimean Peninsula.

Petrov carefully considered the balance of forces in the impending battle, looking for a flaw on the German side that would let his troops burrow into their defences that seemed impregnable. He kept counsel with his Chief of Reconnaissance Trusov.

"Now I know enough about German strength," he said. "What about their weaknesses? Have you any ideas?"

Trusov said: "The 17th Army can be supplied only by sea or air. It is, in fact, cut off from the main German forces and their deep rear now that the 4th Ukrainian Front forces have come up to the Perekop Isthmus and the mouth of the Dnieper."

Petrov commented: "So they are in a trap. We'll pounce upon them in a few places at the same time. Each of our attacks should be strong enough to make them think it is our main strike. In the meantime we will rip their belly where they expect it least of all."

The asssault was scheduled for the night of November 1. To make the Germans disperse their forces, Petrov ordered two secondary strikes to be delivered on the flanks of the main landing force, which was to attack a few sectors of the shore defences.

The embarkation had lasted until dark, and at 21:00 a command rang out along the piers of the harbour of Temryuk: "Full steam ahead!" All the 150 ships of the Azov Naval Flotilla assigned for the assault with a total of 30,000 men on board set sail for the Crimean coast. The sea was rough, a gale force wind driving huge billows that were pounding the small vessels, spraying the crowded decks. It was a distance of 30 kilometres to the landing area near Kerch, the main German stronghold.

Another force was on its way to the Eltigen district. The weather unexpectedly worsened, the storm threatening to scatter the ships before they reached their destination, which would help the Germans more than their firepower. Petrov called off the attack but the flotilla had already entered the Strait of Kerch.

General Gladkov, who was in command of the 318th division, recalls:

—The violent wind whipped our faces and cold sprays showered us from head to foot. The hulls of the overloaded vessels boomed under the blows of huge waves and the storm was driving the ships off course but they were stubbornly making headway. A searchlight far away occasionally cut through the darkness of night with its blazing beam and lit the foamy crests of the waves for an instant. Then the beam would shoot upwards and fade in the heavy black clouds. A voice called out: "Beware! We are passing a mine field!"

—We were quite close to the shore when German searchlights discovered us. A blinding light dazzled me. Covering my eyes with my hand, I looked around and saw near the flagship dozens of launches, motor boats, barges and rafts floating on empty iron barrels. All of them were diving into the foaming waters, surging upwards and downwards and running like an avalanche towards the shore. The German searchlights had taken hold of us and would not let us go. A thought flashed through my mind: "Now we are in for a thrashing."

—Red flares soared into the sky from the motor boats in the vanguard: a request for covering fire. Immediately, the friendly shore of Taman behind us lit up like lightning. Hundreds of shells of heavy artillery whizzed overhead, piercing the thick, damp air. A steady continuous thunder reached us from the Taman Peninsula. Simultaneously, the drone of numerous engines announced the raid of Soviet bombers against German coastal artillery.

—We were eagerly looking ahead at the shore lit with the flashes of shell explosions. Pillars of smoke rose from the ground and collapsed. Tongues of flame were seen here and there.

—All of a sudden the deck swayed under my feet. There was a blinding flash and an explosion in the ship's bows. Somebody screamed. A few sailors ran past me and came back carrying a stretcher with a man covered with a black trench coat.

—"Who is that?"

—"Captain Third Rank Sipyagin. Killed. . . ."

—Towards 5:00 in the morning the assault groups on flat-bottomed craft reached the shore. We could hear that from the rattle of German machine-guns.

—I asked the officer who had taken over from Sipyagin: "When will you start disembarking and land my staff?"

—"I'm sorry, Comrade Colonel. The boats haven't come back."

—That was the gravest mistake in the assault plan. Many flat-bottomed vessels that were to take the assault groups from ship to shore had been sunk by enemy fire or had run into mines. Others were swept by the surf to the shore and crushed on the rocks.

—The Captain addressed me: "I've got a wireless order to take all deep-draught ships to Taman."

—The ships were turning back and sailing away from Crimean shores. Far away at the edge of the sea a man's figure was raising his arms towards us. What were the men of the assault groups thinking of our retreat?—

During the night about 3,000 men were landed on the Crimean coast. They had only 18 artillery guns with much ammunition. The flotilla had taken on board the wounded and returned to its Taman bases at dawn. More than half of the motor boats and launches were lost. Many of the surviving vessels needed repairs.

But what happened to the landed troops? Another eye-witness, Lieutenant General Koveshnikov (Ret.), gives this story:

—We were discovered some three kilometres offshore. Then hell on earth broke out. German machine-guns and mortars opened fire. Searchlights and flares helped German artillery to score accurate hits. We were fully exposed to view and had nowhere to hide. Long trails of tracer shells and bullets were flying to our boat where we stood on deck pressed to each other like in a tram car. Our boat was speeding towards the shore, defying German fire; the shore would give us a chance of survival.

—. . . Within some 200 metres of the shore our vessels ran aground. I called out to my men: "Abandon ship!" and they started jumping overboard, holding their weapons above their heads. The water was neck-deep and cold, and we waded to the shore, struggling with the waves threatening to drown us.

—We seized a foothold on the shore and prepared to repel counterattacks. We knew that the Germans would soon recover from their surprise and drive us back into the sea from the flat ground we were holding. We badly needed their trenches on the heights beyond Eltigen that would give us relative safety.

—Captain Miroshnik's company was the first to fight its way to these heights. Tulinov's company captured the hills to the left. When the Germans had their panzer ready to attack, we were already entrenched and prepared to fight them. The Germans, of course, soon found out that our numbers were few and that other Soviet forces had not yet landed. We were bombed and strafed, and attacked by tanks and infantry. General Petrov encouraged us and supported us with long-range artillery fire and air attacks on the Germans. We would have been wiped out if it had not been for that aid.

—One must have guts to fight a tank single-handed. On our small bridgehead such fights were a matter of course. We had no artillery to repel attacks and had to rely on our antitank rifles and hand grenades. The Germans attacked us in waves: one line of tanks and infantry was followed by another and another at intervals of a few hundred metres. Towards the end of the day they had pushed us to the steep edge of the sea. We were fighting on a small patch of land with our wounded in the middle. Our strength was waning and we knew that we would not hold on much longer unless we took some strong action. I called a conference of surviving officers: the political instructor Movshovich, Captain Zhukov, Captain Belyakov, Major Borzenko, a war correspondent, the mortar company commander Tsikaridze, the Komsomol organizer Alekseyev, and my staff.

—"Now we have two alternatives," I told them. "Either we stay here and die, or counterattack in force and—come what may!"

—We knew that our best chance was to engage the Germans in hand-to-hand fighting. They had not expected such a ferocious attack from battle-weary, bleeding men, and we fought our way into their trenches and used pistols and rifles, knives and bayonets to drive them out.—

Petrov realized that the men on the bridgehead were in a critical situation. It was not humanly possible to hold it without artillery and tanks, so the landing of a large force near Kerch could be the only way to rescue them. But the storm of wind force 8 still raging in the Strait of Kerch and the Sea of Azov would not allow him to mount a full-scale attack.

He sent one infantry and one artillery regiment, food and ammunition to the bridgehead, however. Fierce fighting at sea and on land flared up. Thirty Soviet vessels were destroyed but reinforcements were landed. German panzer and infantry were keeping up their pressure on the bridgehead. In the morning German artillery unleashed its full fire power on the Soviet troops and up to thirty German bombers escorted by Messerschmidt fighters attacked them.

Immediately Soviet fighters were scrambled on the Taman coast, Ilyushin attack planes sped across the strait and Soviet long-range artillery opened fire from its positions on the Taman Peninsula. It was a battle of all arms and services for a small piece of contested ground on which the fate of the operation hinged.

In the meantime the storm was subsiding and Petrov ordered embarkation of Turchinsky's 2nd Division of the Guards. A convoy of ships, some with loaded rafts in tow, sailed off towards Crimean shores.

Five naval units carried on board two regiments of the 2nd Division of the Guards and the 369th Marine Battalion. Boats with assault groups came up to the shore one after another, troops jumped overboard, and engaged the Germans in close combat. Ships returned to the Taman coast and came back in rotation, bringing in more troops throughout the night. Before long two regiments of the 55th Infantry Division of the Guards joined the fight. After some time two full Soviet divisions were attacking the Germans on the bridgehead near Kerch. On the next day the landed troops repelled nineteen counterattacks. The Germans were hurled back. The casualties on both sides were staggering. More than 1,000 Soviet troops were wounded in one day.

The Soviet forces mounted a full-scale offensive from the Kerch bridgehead on November 11, but scored only tactical success. The strongly fortified German defences could not be breached with one strike. Petrov, with a group of staff officers, set up his headquarters on the bridgehead which was only 4 to 6 kilometres deep and was exposed to the fire of German field artillery. His staff officers were accommodated in a former German pillbox not far from his command post in a small house near the village of Mayak. A few trenches were dug nearby to provide shelter against artillery and air attacks. It was certainly against regulations, because a Front Commander was obliged to stay a few dozen kilometres away from the front line. Petrov, however, wanted to see the battlefield with his own eyes and personally direct the course of combat at the most critical points. As more Soviet troops arrived, the pressure against the Germans steadily grew but the rate of advance was slow. Towards the middle of November the Soviet forces had approached the north-western outskirts of Kerch. The units of the 16th Corps had encircled and wiped out a German group there. More than 1,500 German troops were killed, but Kerch was not yet taken. The 11th Corps of the Guards had also got bogged down. The German forces were being reinforced continually, and now seven enemy divisions were resisting the Soviet advance. The bridgehead had been widened to 25 kilometres long and 12 kilometres across, but the Soviet forces came up against the second German line of defence.

In the meantime the Germans continued their attacks on the small bridgehead at Eltigen in an effort to cleave it in two and wipe out its defenders. Petrov ordered the Commander of the Black Sea Fleet to evacuate them. However, the Germans had sealed off the coast by torpedo boats and high-speed self-propelled barges with artillery on board. The bridgehead defenders had been fighting for thirty-six days. The landing of Soviet forces at Kerch relieved the German pressure upon them but the situation on the bridgehead was disastrous. A link-up with Soviet troops besieging Kerch would mean the loss of the bridgehead held at the cost of so many lives, but the survivors were too few to fight on against German tanks, aircraft and artillery which had turned the narrow strip of land defended by the landing force into a smoking moonscape where any life seemed unthinkable. Yet the brave men never thought of surrender. They were worried about their wounded, sheltered in half-ruined trenches and dugouts and waiting uncomplainingly for medical aid.

Kerch was 25 kilometres away, too long a distance for them to be carried by their comrades fighting on their way, and the shore was sealed off by German sea patrols. Yet Soviet motor launches occasionally managed to evade their pursuers and brought food and ammunition, taking away as many wounded men as they could carry on their way back.

Finally, only those who were fit to fight remained on the bridgehead, and a force of 2,000 desperate men led by Colonel Gladkov suddenly attacked the Germans at night, cut through their lines and raided their rear, wiping out whatever happened to be in their way—headquarters, artillery positions, and logistic services. They left a trail of fire and destroyed German equipment in their wake, and they burst into Kerch, a crowd of shouting men, firing wildly, who could have died so many times that death meant nothing to them now.

They captured the strongly fortified Mt. Mitridat dominating the city and entrenched themselves. The Germans alerted to this new danger came down upon them from all sides. Gladkov radioed to Petrov:—We are running out of ammunition. We have too few men to hold Mt. Mitridat which is the key to German defeat in Kerch. But we will not give up. We expect aid by air.—

Petrov ordered the 16th Corps to mount a massive attack and break through the German defences towards the mountain, but these proved too strong. He knew that Gladkov's men would be doomed unless rescued immediately and ordered their evacuation.

On the night of December 10 launches came up to the nearest shore under cover of artillery fire and picked up the survivors. They were taken to Taman for a rest. That was the end of their ordeal that went down into the history of the war as the heroic Eltigen landing operation.

Now Petrov's whole army was in the Crimea. In the meantime the General Headquarters were planning the further conduct of the Crimean operation. As General Shtemenko of the General Staff writes: —Stalin ordered a coordinated strike of Tolbukhin's and Petrov's forces from two directions with the aid of the Black Sea Fleet and the Azov Naval Flotilla and sent the old veteran Voroshilov as his representative to report on the progress of the operation.—

D-Day was set for January 10. The thunder of Soviet artillery announced an all-out attack of the 11th and 16th Corps. German resistance was so stiff that they could not capture more than two miles of ground in a full day. A landing force under Glavatsky attacked the Germans north of the main battlefield and came under fierce air, artillery and panzer strikes. Nevertheless, its men captured a few heights and linked up with the main forces.

Fierce fighting was going on on the outskirst of Kerch but the Germans were firmly holding their ground. General Shtemenko writes further:—The General Headquarters were worried: street fighting usually entails heavy losses and limits the use of artillery, tanks and aircraft. In a message to Petrov and Voroshilov, Stalin said that the Soviet forces outnumbered the Germans in men, artillery, tanks and aircraft but this advantage was cancelled by the disadvantage of fighting for every street and every house against an entrenched enemy. He ordered the battle to be carried to an open field, limiting the attacks in Kerch to supporting action.—

The Soviet forces withdrew and regrouped for a large-scale offensive across the Crimean plains. And then, the unexpected happened. Shtemenko writes:—A special train suddenly arrived, bringing the new commander, General Yeremenko, to replace Petrov. He was dismissed and summoned to Moscow.

—We at the General Staff concluded that the limited success of the operation at Kerch had caused Stalin's doubts about Petrov's competence, though his army was fully prepared to liberate the Crimea as its further success would make perfectly clear.—

An entry in Petrov's personal file reads:—Relieved of his duties and assigned to the General Headquarters reserve. Demoted to Colonel General for mismanagement of a combat operation.—Such are the fortunes of a career military officer.

The immediate cause of that development had been the heavy losses sustained in the landing of Glavatsky's 166th Guards Regiment on Cape Tarkhan. It had been put off repeatedly because of the rough seas and incoordination with the forces landed at Kerch. Voroshilov was impatient, and the landing was finally launched on the night of January 10.

It was only 15 miles to the landing site but the overloaded barges and motor boats pounded by the huge waves were making slow progess. Though effected after a delay the landing was successful on the whole, but on their way back the ships were caught in a heavy storm. A few ships were in distress and their crews had to abandon them, some others were missing.

Petrov would later tell me of his interview with Stalin about the Kerch affair.

—I arrived in Moscow and was waiting for a summons to Stalin. Like all my comrades in the Crimea I had expected another high appointment. I was a Front Commander after all, and my Front was about to be abolished. I was invited to Stalin at last and, as I entered his office, I saw him standing in the middle of it and eyeing me sullenly.

—"Report!" he uttered stiffly without greeting me.

—"Report what, Comrade Stalin?"

—"Just how many men and ships you have lost in the Straits!"

—I was at a loss for words. He blurted out angrily: "You shipped all your army to the Crimea. Why the hell did you need new landings? You should have attacked from the bridgehead. You sacrificed men and ships for nothing."

—That was unfair. I was silent for a while and then I felt I could not hold my temper and protested:

—"That's not my fault, Comrade Stalin."

—He watched my face closely: "Whose then?"

—"Let the General Staff examine it and report", I said.

—Stalin went on quietly but menacingly: "No dodging here, Comrade Petrov. I have no time for long deliberations. Who is the one responsible?"

—That was when I did the wrong thing and I still regret it. A thought crossed my mind: why should I answer for what I had never done while those who are to blame have chickened out? That was an ugly thought, and it pains me to this day.

—I told Stalin that the landing had been initiated by his own representative. Stalin looked at me for a long while and then said very quietly, waving his finger from side to side in front of his face:

—"We will not allow you to hide behind the broad back of Comrade Voroshilov. You were in command and you will be held responsible. Over!"

—That was followed by my demotion by one rank. I deserved it. Not for the casualties which were indeed not my fault but for my stupid answer which made Stalin think I was trying to exonerate myself.

General Petrov would be repeatedly appointed a Front Commander again and he would do his duty with the same dedication and would be relieved of his post again, each time unfairly. In short, that was the life of a general who often fell into disfavour but, when required in an emergency, was again requested to do his stint in the service of his country.

The Last Battles

Expectation

February 1944 was a snowy time in Moscow. The earth and the sky were monotonously grey and bleak, the clouds hanging low and the snow dirty with soot. The days were dull and short, and the grim mornings were followed by grim evenings after a short spell of daylight. The nights were long and dark, with the shaded lights of patrol vehicles darting here and there like fireflies.

Petrov stayed at the Moskva Hotel, expecting a verdict that would seal his fate. He was haunted by misgivings, and his heart was heavy.

Quite recently he had dreamt of a full night's sleep at least for once, but he could not afford more than a short nap in his jeep shuttling between the different sectors of the front. Now that he had plenty of time for his dream to come true, he was suffering from insomnia. A good sleep requires peace of mind, but that was something long forgotten.

It was not the first crisis in his life, of course. In the past, however, he had somehow managed to escape the worst and carried on with redoubled energy. This time his chances were slim: he would certainly be dismissed and demoted in rank.

Thoughts about developments at the front were obtruding on his mind. He was thinking of his officers and men of the Maritime Army he had left in the Crimea. Listening to the war communiqués broadcast by radio and reading the terse lines of newspaper reports, he tried to imagine what was going on far away in the south. It was the end of March but there was no news yet of any large-scale operations in the Crimea. Was it likely that General Yeremenko appointed in his place had decided to revise all earlier plans? The front line in the Ukraine was steadily drawing closer to the Rumanian border, and the German troops in the Crimea had been cut off from their main forces. But why were the Soviet forces marking time before taking Kerch? Indeed, at the time when Petrov was dismissed from command of the Maritime Army, it was poised for that thrust.

Petrov was thinking also of his own destiny. From time to time he came up to the window and looked at the Kremlin. He saw the red-brick fortress walls and the towers and green roofs of the palaces beyond. Stalin was probably busy with some urgent and important affairs in his office. Petrov realized that the Supreme Commander had more important things on his mind than Petrov's case. Yet he knew that Stalin would finally utter a few words that would seal his fate. But what could Stalin possibly say? Petrov recalled his apprehensive thoughts in the waiting-room of Stalin's office when he was looking at its heavy door behind which the careers of Marshals and Ministers at times took unexpected turns.

Petrov smoked much and stayed awake almost until sunrise.

One day his long waiting came to an end. The phone in his room gave off what seemed to him a shrill and demanding ring. He hurriedly took up the receiver.

A voice in the earpiece said in a peremptory tone:

"General Petrov, you have been appointed to command of the 33rd Army. Come over for a briefing and orders."

He felt blood surging to his head and a great relief as if a tremendous burden had been taken off his shoulders. He was needed after all! But where was that Army? In the north or in the south? Who would brief him? Questions raced through his mind. His painful expectation was over at last. The receiver had long been emitting short busy signals but his hand was still gripping it.

To give the reader a general idea of the situation at the Soviet–German Front and the position of the 33rd Army on it, I will briefly describe what they were at the time of Petrov's new appointment.

The Battles of Karsk and the Dnieper completed the turning of the tide in the Soviet Union's national war and the Second World War as a whole. The Red Army had finally seized the strategic initiative and was firmly holding it.

The earlier battles had proved that the Red Army's fighting capability had grown tremendously while the morale of its officers and men was higher than ever before despite all the casualties and retreats of the initial period of the war. The heroic efforts on the home front had enabled the Soviet war industry to boost the manufacture of whatever was needed by the fighting forces. Therefore, the Soviet High Command was determined to pursue the autumn offensive without a respite all along the length of the Soviet–German front.

In the winter of 1944 the Soviet Army Groups operating in the south advanced by more than 200 kilometres, encircled and wiped out a large German troop concentration at Korsun-Shevchenko, expelled the invaders from the cities of Zhitomir, Kirovograd, Rovno, Lutsk, Nikopol, and Krivoi Rog, thereby laying the groundwork for a further offensive campaign.

In the north the Germans had been driven back from Leningrad. The ancient city of Novgorod was freed, and Soviet troops carried the brunt of their offensive into the territory of Estonia.

In the centre of the enormous Soviet–German theatre of war, however,

Soviet successes were modest. Troops of the 2nd Baltic, Western and Byelorussian fronts were fighting offensive battles but had so far failed to effect a decisive breakthrough.

The 33rd Army Petrov now commanded was part of the Western Front (Army Group). I was at the time a reconnaissance officer in the 39th Army of the 1st Baltic Front commanded by General Bagramian.

In January 1944 troops of our Army Group were fighting heavy offensive battles to close the ring of encirclement around Vitebsk which the Nazis had turned into a major stronghold on the northern flank of Army Group Centre under Field Marshal Ernst Busch.

Collecting material on General Petrov's record as commander of the 33rd Army, I met Lieutenant General Toloknyuk, now retired, who had been close to Petrov in those days and very well informed. This is his story:

—We were fighting hard as we advanced on Vitebsk. Our Army, decimated by earlier fighting, had got bogged down and could not gain much ground in the face of ferocious German resistance. The Army Commander, Colonel General Vitaly Gordov, had been in command of the Stalingrad Front before his latest assignment. On learning of the arrival of Petrov, also a Front ex-commander, some of our officers joked: "Our Army is a penalty box for demoted generals."

—Gordov, however, was not to blame for the 33rd Army's setbacks. During the last few months he had undertaken a few offensive operations but all of them had failed because of time trouble, inadequate artillery support and bottlenecks in ammunition supply.

—The Front Command realized the futility of these attempts of course, but they were to secure the performance of a larger task. Other Army Groups were on the offensive to the south and north of our Western Front while our operations were intended to hold the enemy forces pinned down to prevent reinforcements being moved from the German Army Group Centre to more critical areas.

—In the first half of April a commission of inquiry appointed by the State Defence Committee arrived at the Western Front. Among its members were Malenkov, Shtemenko and Shcherbakov. That was, indeed, a representative body, which indicated serious faults brought to its scrutiny.

—They examined the fighting record of the Western Front. Though it looked like a stalemate, the commission resolved that the Front Command was not guilty, because it had insufficient strength to pursue a full-scale offensive.

—Nevertheless, soon upon their return to Moscow the Supreme Commander issued a directive to abolish the Western Front and establish two new Fronts in its place: the 2nd and 3rd Byelorussian Fronts commanded by General Chernyakhovsky and General Petrov respectively.

—We were sorry to part with our new commander; in the short time of his service with us all of us had come to respect his demanding attitude backed up by long experience and excellent competence.

Petrov's new appointment evidenced that despite his alleged earlier failures he commanded high prestige within Party and military circles. His candidature had been proposed by a joint commission of top-ranking party and military leaders. Their opinion, of course, could have been vetoed by Stalin, so the fact that the Supreme Commander had endorsed it proved again that he valued Petrov's competence. He had probably foreseen the inevitable difficulties a new Front Commander would have to deal with in realigning his forces for an eventual full-scale offensive. Perhaps the unfairness of Petrov's dismissal had now become apparent.

It was now more than two months since Petrov's recall from his command post on the outskirts of Kerch, when his troops were within a few hundred metres of its centre, and it had taken all that time to negotiate that distance before the Soviet forces could finally take the city and advance into the Crimean hinterland.

His high appointment showed that justice had triumphed after all. That, however, was not a complete reinstatement. His rank of General of the Army had not been restored to him.

Commander of the 2nd Byelorussian Front

In April when Petrov received his new appointment the general situation on the Soviet–German front looked as follows:

In the south the Red Army had reached the Rumanian border and was already aiming its thrusts at Bucharest. More northerly, the Germans had been driven back from the Dnieper and retreated into the Carpathians. In the north Soviet forces had forced the Nazis to lift the siege of Leningrad and approached Lake Chudskoye, Pskov and Novorzhev. Thus, between these flanks which extended far westwards, there remained an enormous projection in the direction of Moscow. It was known as the "Byelorussian Bulge". The frontal part of this bulge passed along the line of Vitebsk, Rogachev and Zhlobin not far from Moscow.

The German forces deployed in this area (Army Group Centre of over sixty divisions) were barring the way to the west for Soviet troops. Moreover, the German High Command took advantage of the dense network of railways and highways to manoeuvre its forces quickly and strike at the flanks of the Soviet forces advancing south and north of this bulge. From here the Luftwaffe made bombing raids against Soviet troop concentrations in the north and south. The danger of air raids over Moscow was still there.

At the same time the German troops deployed in the bulge were exposed to Soviet flanking strikes from the south and north and hence encirclement. To effect an encirclement on such a vast scope, however, enormous forces were necessary. For that, the Soviet force had to defeat Army Group North in the Baltic and Army Group Northern Ukraine in the Ukraine, and only after that would it be possible to take Army Group Centre in pincers.

The German High Command had foreseen this course of hostilities. Field Marshal Model, commander of Army Group Northern Ukraine, for instance, stated categorically that the Russians would begin their offensive across his left flank by a strike under the base of the "Byelorussian Bulge". Model was not much mistaken. That direction was, indeed, very advantageous to the Soviet side. By liquidating the "Byelorussian Bulge" the Soviet forces would wipe out one of the biggest concentrations of Army Group Centre, and liberate the long-suffering Byelorussia, which had been under occupation for three years. They would further liberate Poland and advance by the shortest route to the border of Nazi Germany, carrying the war into its territory.

Therefore, the Soviet High Command resolved to carry out this complex operation and started preparations for it. One of the measures in the context of this plan was the division of the Western Front into the 2nd and 3rd Byelorussian Fronts, the appointment of new Front commanders and other high-ranking officers, a regrouping of troops and logistic services.

At Stalin's suggestion the part of the summer campaign to liberate Byelorussia was codenamed Operation Bagration. In accordance with its plan the troops of four Soviet fronts were to deliver penetrating thrusts at the main forces of Army Group Centre, liberate Byelorussia and establish springboards for a further offensive in the western areas of the Ukraine, in the Baltic, in Poland and East Prussia. The German defences were to be pierced in six sectors simultaneously and German troop concentrations dismembered and wiped out one by one. At the same time powerful groups of the 3rd and 1st Byelorussian Fronts swiftly advancing on the flanks were to link up in the Minsk area, encircle and defeat the German forces driven back by Soviet frontal attacks.

That was Operation Bagration in general outline.

Before the Strike

The tense work of the General Headquarters, the General Staff and the command personnel of the Army Groups to be involved in carrying out that operation, one of the biggest in the course of the war, lasted for over two months. The General Headquarters called a conference of top-ranking generals to hammer out a competent master plan, finalize all the details and delimit the areas of personal responsibility.

General Shtemenko reminisced:

—The General Headquarters discussed the plan on May 22 and 23. Among the conferees were Zhukov and Vasilevsky, Commander of the 1st Baltic Front, Bagramian, Commander of the 1st Byelorussian Front, Rokossovsky, members of the Military Councils of these Fronts, as well as General Staff officers headed by Antonov. Chernyakhovsky was absent for health reasons. General Petrov did not attend because his troops were operating in an area of secondary importance.—

Shtemenko explains the last phrase:

—The 2nd Byelorussian front was assigned the task of holding down as much German strength as possible to forbid the German High Command from feeding reinforcements into the areas to be outflanked by the troops of the 3rd and 1st Byelorussian Fronts. Petrov was a dependable general with a long experience of such operations and we had implicit faith in him.

For all that, Petrov was the only one of the Front Commanders to have not been invited to that conference of critical importance. The reason for that was not, of course, negligence on the part of General Headquarters personnel: nobody would have ventured to ignore a Front Commander. The reason was certainly the Supreme Commander's own decision.

Despite his high opinion of Petrov as a general, Stalin probably did not want to see him so soon after their unpleasant conversation. At any rate Petrov's absence at the conference evidenced that his position might very likely be precarious.

General Petrov was not discouraged. He was wholly engrossed in the enormous work being carried out at his headquarters and all the sectors of the 2nd Byelorussian Front. He realized that successful operations of his troops would dispel or mitigate whatever doubts Stalin might have about his aptitudes.

Troops were being re-grouped in conditions of top secrecy and attacking positions were being thoroughly prepared. Hundreds of trainloads of ammunition and supplies were being secretly brought to the front line. Faithful to his principles, Petrov was training his troops and commanding officers in the conduct of offensive combat.

It is common knowledge that the success of a large-scale military operation is largely dependent on its efficient preparation and organization, a competent re-grouping of troops before attack, the standards of combat training and operational planning, trouble-free logistic supply and effective co-ordination of the actions of all arms and services.

During April and May Petrov and his staff, the commanders of units, formations and armies had brought all that enormous work to perfection, which secured the devastating effect the Soviet thrust had on the opposing German armies. General Shtemenko commented on the successful completion of Operation Bagration:

—The German generals taken prisoner in the Minsk area were dumbfounded by the ease with which the Soviet forces had defeated the crack divisions of the Wehrmacht opposing them. For us, however, that was not unexpected at all. That outcome of the operation had been anticipated well in advance when it was still in the preparatory stage.—

Petrov's contribution to that success was indisputably of crucial significance.

It would be fair to mention another important event that took place in the period of preparations for Operation Bagration and facilitated its success, too.

On June 6, 1944 an Anglo-American expeditionary force landed in Normandy, France. That had happened 17 days before Operation Bagration got under way.

I have sought to present an objective description of the operations of the German forces, and it would be fair to apply this principle to all belligerent sides, our Western Allies included. The fact that the Anglo-American leadership had delayed the opening of a Second Front at the most critical time of the war when we had to fight the powerful German Army single-handed remains on their conscience, so to speak. D-Day finally came, however, and thousands died for the common cause of the Allies. Of the 122,000 officers and men who were killed in the invasion of Normandy, 73,000 were Americans and 49,000 were Britons and Canadians.

Not just the war dead but also the survivors of that most terrible of all wars deserve a truthful account of themselves and our respectful thanks: indeed, they were prepared to die for our common cause and bravely defied death to bring about the defeat of our common enemy.

Following my plan to track down the eyewitnesses of the events of my story and to visit as many former battlegrounds as I could, I came to England to meet the veterans of Operation Overlord. That visit was fairly hard to arrange, and after long and tedious arrangements this part of my plan came to fruition. My efforts were richly rewarded.

I had been to England before, so I knew where to go first. I tried to meet as many war veterans as I could possibly find, and had discussions with Admirals, Generals, officers and privates. In London I visited Winston Churchill's HQ. It is housed in a cellar converted to a bomb shelter under an enormous building in central London.

The equipment of all services and the Prime Minister's office have been carefully preserved exactly as they were in war time. There is a large desk in this office with a green shaded lamp, old-fashioned telephones, and a wide bed encased in glass in a corner. Other glass cases contain maps and documents. In one case—the English never lose their sense of humour—is an old battered heavy pistol that Sir Winston had brought from the First World War and kept under his pillow. It is displayed side by side with a white ceramic chamber-pot that the Prime Minister used to obviate the need for long walks to the toilet through the countless rooms and corridors.

All clocks at the HQ show the hour of signing the Act of Germany's surrender.

In the coastal city of Portsmouth I visited the HQ of General Eisenhower, Supreme Commander of the Allied Expeditionary Force in Western Europe. A large map with coloured chips indicating warships and their bearings occupies the full length and breadth of a wall in his office.

I also inspected the field HQ of Field Marshal Montgomery consisting of several specially equipped vehicles which were his office, a conference room and sleeping quarters with a toilet. . . .

On the occasion of the 40th anniversary of Operation Overlord a D-Day museum was opened in Portsmouth. In addition to ordinary exhibits the museum walls are decked with a giant applied tapestry depicting scenes from major battles at sea and on land. A documentary about Operation Overlord is shown in the cinema hall of the museum.

I also went to the Imperial War Museum to continue my researches in its library and rich repository of war-time archives. With much interest I read the running commentary of War Correspondent Colin Wills who watched the fighting on the beaches of Normandy from one of the assault ships of the invading force.

I also visited the British Military Academy, its war relics rooms and central library. The memorial book of the Academy's church lists the names of 20,000 officers killed in the Second World War.

The Marines Museum is a majestic building containing a rich collection of exhibits and documents on the history of the Marines since its early days when their boarding parties attacked and seized enemy ships.

However, the most interesting and valuable information that I gleaned in Britain came from living eye-witnesses of Operation Overlord: Admiral Goeritz who after our official meeting invited me to his home in the small cosy town of Salisbury, General Multon and General Tupp, Brigadiers Alexander Breeden and James Hill.

My sincerest thanks go to Mr. John Roberts, Director of the Great Britain–USSR Association, who organized my trips and meetings in Britain and to Mr. Baridge, President of the Veterans of Normandy Association. At his home in Portsmouth he introduced me to his friends, veterans of the Second World War, and we had a frank and friendly conversation as between soldiers about our wartime experiences.

All this deserves a separate story, but, as it distracts me from the main subject, and I have said enough to show the reader that I have worked hard on collecting authentic information for this chapter, I shall only give an outline of the operation that opened the Second Front as is required for my narrative.

Our war-time allies explain their delay in opening the Second Front by the need for long and thorough preparations. In the days when this subject was first raised that the Allies pledged to land an invasion force in France but there were neither troops nor ships in adequate numbers in British ports. The assembly, training and equipping of forces took quite some time. The H-hour was repeatedly put off until a later date.

Finally, on the morning of June 5, Supreme Allied Commander Dwight Eisenhower issued his orders to launch the invasion. An enormous armada of ships sailed off towards the French coast across the English Channel, which varies in width from 32 to 180 km.

The Allies had planned to land sea-borne troops and paratroops on the coast of North-Western France, seize a bridgehead and, towards the 20th day of the operation, widen it up to 100 kilometres along the coast and up to 100–110 kilometres in depth.

The invading force consisted of 39 divisions, 12 separate brigades, 10 units of Commandos and Rangers. According to British sources, Operation Overlord involved a total of 3.5 million officers and men, 1.5 million of them Americans, as well as 4,126 landing craft under cover of 1,213 warships, 1,600 auxiliary ships, 3,500 motor launches and hydroplanes. Air support was provided by 111,500 planes. The Second American and the First British Airborne Divisions were landed behind enemy lines.

This armada was to land 150,000 troops on the first day, which was carried out within 16 to 17 hours. The casualties on the day of the landing operation were not heavy: not more than 11,000.

German resistance stiffened as the Allied forces advanced further inland. Fierce fighting flared up here and there, and soldiers, as veterans told me, had sometimes to pay with their blood for every inch of the ground they gained.

It was disappointing to learn, however, that these brave men did not know that in those days of bitter fighting Soviet troops were also on the offensive against the main Nazi forces.

"We didn't know that", Mr. Baridge said. "I don't think, however, that we were deliberately kept uninformed. The landing was followed by a terrible confusion, so we received no letters or newspapers for a fortnight."

All veterans of Operation Overlord praised the friendliness and assistance of the French people during the Allied invasion of Normandy.

Towards July 25, that is on the 20th day, strictly according to schedule, the Allied forces had gained a strategic foothold on the Continent. The biggest landing operation of the Second World War had been successfully completed.

That success was mainly due to skilful camouflage and misinformation of the enemy, which deluded the Germans with regard to the areas and time of the landing. The movements of large forces of the Army, Navy and Air Force were efficient and well-coordinated. The courage and morale of the officers and men was high. They had great faith in their just and common cause of struggle against the Nazi tyranny which had caused untold suffering to the nations of Europe.

The German High Command had been aware of the Allies' preparations for crossing the English Channel and even knew that in June 1944 the Allies would launch their invasion. Two German Army Groups "B" and "G" subordinated to the "West" Command headed by Field Marshal Rundstedt were stationed in France, Belgium and the Netherlands. Early in June 1944 there were only 58 German divisions there, while a total of 239 divisions, of which 181 were German, were operating on the Soviet–German front.

The main forces of the Wehrmacht were fighting the war in the East, of course, but now all of them and the German High Command felt that the Allies had finally changed over from verbal declarations to practical actions in the West.

Operation Bagration was carried out between June 23 and August 29 and largely contributed to the Allies' success, because the Soviet forces securely held the German High Command in check, forbidding it from moving reinforcements to Normandy to thwart Operation Overlord. These two operations are a model of action the Western Allies would have done well to follow.

A concerted all-out attack in East and West would have shortened the war and saved innumerable lives. It is a sad realization that not all on the Allied side had precisely that aim in mind for the prosecution of the war.

Operation Bagration was a brilliant masterpiece of the art of warfare, which threw into salient relief the high competence of the Supreme Commander Joseph Stalin, the talent of Georgy Zhukov, Alexander Vasilevsky, Konstantin Rokossovsky, Ivan Chernyakhovsky, Ivan Bagramian, Georgy Zakharov, and Stanislaw Poplawski, Commander of the Polish First Army.

In that operation Soviet troops liberated the heroic Byelorussia, which the Nazis had been unable to bring to its knees during the long three years of occupation. The Red Army advanced by 500–600 kilometres across Polish territory as far as the border with East Prussia. A few German troop concentrations were encircled and none of them managed to break out of the iron grip. Seventeen enemy divisions and three brigades were wiped out completely and 50 divisions lost more than half of their strength.

More About Myself

After the second part of my book was published in a magazine I received many letters from readers requesting me to give more details of my own life. That, however, would make another book. Yet there was one event that would fit the context of my story about General Petrov.

In 1942 I was doing my bit on the Kalinin Front a hundred miles from Moscow and got into scrapes on quite a few occasions. My fighting record caught the eye of my commanding officers and was commended.

I was not decorated, of course, because no war medals were awarded to members of penal battalions. The highest award they could attain was reinstatement as an ordinary honest citizen. A penal battalion man was expected to expiate his guilt by shedding his blood in fighting, that is by getting killed or wounded. Exemplary courage in battle was another motive for a release from penal service in exceptional cases. In fact, however, only the dead or wounded were pardoned, as a rule.

Along with a few other men who had miraculously survived unscathed fierce attacks and hand-to-hand fighting I was not eligible for pardon. We were enlisted in another penal company which had just arrived. And again I went through a few hand-to-hand fights without a scratch. This time, however, I received my first award, a small square sheet of paper I still keep together with my war medals. This is a priceless document and a war relic for me. It reads:

Certificate of Pardon

Issued to serviceman Vladimir V. Karpov to certify that in accordance with the Decree of the Presidium of the Supreme Soviet of the USSR of December 14, 1941, and the resolution of the Military Council of the Kalinin Front of February 20, 1943 (No. 016) and in recognition of his distinguished record of service in the war against the German Army of invasion the verdict of the Court Martial of the Central Asian Military District of April 28, 1941 to sentence him to five years' imprisonment under Article 66-10, part I, of the Penal Code of Uzbekistan (Article 58-10, part I, of the Penal Code of the Russian Federation—V.K.) has been declared null and void.

February 20, 1943
Secretary of the Military Council of the Kalinin Front (Signed).
Seal of the Court Martial of the Kalinin Front.

Now that I became an equal member of the Armed Forces, I was enlisted in the 629th regiment of the 134th division to which my former penal company was attached.

My regimental commander, Lieutenant Colonel Alexei Kortunov, learned of my prewar achievements as a boxer. He commented: "Well, a pugilist must be a good match for a scout team." That settled my choice. I became a foot scout in my regiment. That was the lowest position in the complex, dangerous and indispensable combat intelligence work. I was, speaking figuratively, at the other end of the line from the romantic figure of Isayev alias Stirlitz familiar to Soviet TV audiences from a serial about Soviet intelligence work against Nazi Germany.

Any form of intelligence work is risky but necessary in wartime. As for the romantic aura with which novelists and script writers surround this work—it is a source of some amusement to the professional intelligence officer. In fact, an intelligence agent or a frontline scout is simply more exposed to the risk of death than other people. Death is omnipresent in war: it may cut you down with a bullet or a shell, splinter or crush you with a bomb.

These chances to die are equal for all in war, speaking in general, but death can still be avoided by hiding in a trench or a dug-out or some other shelter. A scout, however, fights death single-handed, as it were.

Going behind enemy lines to carry out his hazardous task, a scout defies death. He survives if he can outsmart the enemy, relying on his intelligence and presence of mind, shrewdness and physical fitness. Lieutenant Colonel Kortunov was right: a good boxer can indeed make a good scout. A boxer fights well if he is quick on the uptake. In training and at contests I had learned to take prompt decisions, to keep my temper under a hail of blows, to plan in a split second how to parry the opponent's next thrust and then counterattack. That gave me an advantage over the enemy in critical situations, helping me to do my duty and survive.

There was yet another reason why I strained myself to the utmost, trying to excel my mates. I knew that, should I survive the war by some miracle and return home, life with the label of a former "enemy of the people" would not be easy for me. Would I be admitted to a University or allowed to take a good job? What would I do for a living? I did not know any civilian trade after all. Musing over all these things, I took this decision: I have guts and must be on my mettle. That would earn me a war medal which would make life easier for me. Before the war I had seen that a bemedalled person had all doors open to him.

Before long I was awarded a medal "For Valour" followed by a Red Star, and now I dreamt of a third award. I was young and impatient; in 1942 I had just turned twenty.

My enthusiasm caught the eye of my commanding officers and I was promoted to squad commander and a sergeant's rank. After some time I was commissioned as a junior lieutenant and then lieutenant in command of a reconnaissance platoon. Regimental commander Kortunov encouraged me, and our regiment was never short of identification prisoners. Our good fame spread all along the Kalinin Front.

Scouts, just like airmen, were usually nominated for the top award—the title of Hero of the Soviet Union—not only for an exceptional valorous deed but also for a spectacular combat record. According to an unwritten law, an airman was nominated for 20 to 25 kills and a scout for 15 to 20 captures.

There came a day when my personal score reached 45 captures. Kortunov later explained to me that the blemish on my reputation in the past had been the reason for abstaining from putting me up for the top award when I had 20 captures to my credit. He had been biding his time before my score became as high as to rule out any risk of rejection of my nomination for the title of Hero of the Soviet Union. With a record of 45 captures my nomination seemed double sure and was forwarded up the chain of command.

Time went on and I continued to do my routine scout duty, but there was no response from the top. Once I was ordered to report to the regimental commander. A summons to headquarters was a matter of routine to me, because I was given the next task almost every day. I reported to Kortunov and stood to attention. He was seated at his desk and his face was gloomy. I felt uneasy, wondering what was wrong. He uttered curtly: "Now read this!", and he pushed the papers on his desk towards me.

I read a letterhead: "Recommendation for Award". Then followed my name, biography and a description of my fighting record for which I was nominated for the title of Hero of the Soviet Union. Large red letters ran across the sheet, as though nullifying its contents. "Think twice before you recommend!" The signature was illegible and just as angry, as if consisting of exclamation marks.

Kortunov comforted me: "Don't be upset. Justice will triumph in the end."

His kindness eased the shock of realizing that my dream of that high distinction had not come true. In fact, I had already done at least as much to deserve it as other scouts already decorated with a Gold Star. My record was praised in newspapers and my colleagues called me a No. 1 scout.

In a couple of weeks I was again summoned to headquarters. It was early morning when scouts were usually asleep after their nightly combat work and were not to be disturbed. Sullen and angered, I entered Kortunov's dug-out and saluted him. He glanced to one side, and I saw a stranger holding out his hand to greet me. He was in a General's uniform, thick-set and strong, with a Gold Star shining on his chest.

Kortunov said softly: "This is Major General Boiko, Military Council member of the 39th Army."

The General shook my hand and looked at me with frank interest. "I know a lot about you, Sergeant Karpov, but mostly from papers and phone calls. Sorry we have awakened you, but I'm pressed for time. I want to have a word with you. Let's get out of this stuffy hole and walk, o'kay?"

We strolled together towards a hollow that would shelter us from stray bullets and shell splinters.

"I've read your file and now want to hear your story right from the horse's mouth," Boiko said.

I told him of my school days and boxing matches and my victory at the tournament of Central Asia. I spoke of my admiration for my former school commandant Petrov.

Boiko remarked: "He deserves it. His defence of Odessa and Sevastopol made history. I know him well."

When I came to the most unpleasant part of my story, I stopped hesitantly. "Go ahead, get it off your chest", he encouraged me. I wished to be frank but I had second thoughts about telling him what I felt about my bad luck. It was human malice or misunderstanding that was to blame for my conviction. Was it the right time to stir painful memories?

Boiko read my mind and changed the subject. He asked my opinion of the Communists and Komsomols of my reconnaissance platoon, and I gave him a full story of my dare-devil mates, a close-knit team of skilful fighters who would rather die than back down before danger. Konstantin Kamilevich had hurled himself at a German machine-gun nest and wiped it out with a hand-grenade to rescue an ambushed group of scouts by sacrificing his own life.

Boiko asked suddenly: "Isn't it time you joined the Party?"

The question stunned me. "Are you sure I'm the right man for it? You know I served time in a penal battalion."

"Let bygones be bygones," Boiko said. "Time is the best judge of men. You're a first-class scout and have proved your allegiance and dedication to duty many times over. We have complete trust in you."

"I would be happy to join, but I doubt if I would be admitted. Who would recommend me?"

"Your doubts are unfounded. Your comrades know all about you. A man's true worth is clearly seen in the firing lines. . . ."

I joined the Party in the same year 1943, as I understand, not without the solicitation of General Boiko and Lieutenant Colonel Kortunov.

The events in the foregoing story were an introduction, as it were, to the developments where I was close to General Petrov in the days of preparations for Operation Bagration. General Voloshin, Chief of Reconnaissance of the 39th Army, who was the top commanding officer in my line of service, describes the situation on the 3rd Byelorussian Front in his book "Scouts Lead the Way":

—The combat duties of the scout teams became more complex, but their skill had grown tremendously. Now they carried out raids far behind the enemy lines and even infiltrated Vitebsk occupied by the Germans. Vladimir Karpov, I have repeatedly mentioned above, disguised in German uniform, made his way into the city to collect copies of important documents from the Resistance and safely came back.

—At the time Karpov carried out special assignments from the Front Chief of Reconnaissance. The latter had phoned me once, asking to pick an experienced scout officer to handle a task of paramount importance. I named Karpov without a moment's hesitation.—

What happened following that call is described by Akram Sharipov in his war novel "General Chernyakhovsky".

—. . . General Chernyakhovsky was thinking of vulnerable spots in the German Army Group confronting his forces. There must be some, but where? He finally ordered his Chief of Reconnaissance Major General Aleshin to plan a scouting raid behind the German lines in front of Lyudnikov's Army. The plan was ready soon, and the right man for the mission was on hand. He was Senior Lieutenant Vladimir Karpov.

—"The Front Commander needs battle intelligence badly," the General said to him. "And he wants to brief you personally."

—Karpov became nervous. Aleshin reassured him:

—"Nothing to worry about. He's a remarkable man."

—Chernyakhovsky received them at his command post. He shook Karpov's hand respectfully and asked him to sit down.

—"I have been informed that you are one of the bravest and brightest men in your line of duty. We have a task that fits you all right. It will be very hard to accomplish but we know we can rely on you. Very much depends on whether you will make it."

—"Comrade Front Commander, I am expecting your orders. I know my duty."

—"I trust you, young man, and I wish you all the luck in the world. We have agents in Vitebsk, and you will have to find them. They have photographed German fortifications but cannot smuggle the film to us. The city commandant, General Helmuth, was recently ambushed by partisans and narrowly escaped death, so the Germans are now spying on every civilian. It's eighteen or so kilometres from here to the city. This is a tactical zone filled with troops. A safe landing by parachute is unthinkable. A group of scouts will be easily discovered, too. So it seems best to go alone. And you must be prepared for any mishap."

—"I can see that," Karpov moved to stand up.

—"Wait a minute. You will start out today. There's no time to be lost. Have you everything ready, General? A pass, ciphers?"

—"We have done everything to a T, Comrade Front Commander."

—Chernyakhovsky embraced the scout. "It's a hell of a task, young man. Take care of yourself. And remember: a reconnaissance man must have a lion's heart and a snake's caution."

—Disguised in civilian clothes, Karpov stole his way through the German lines and reached the city without any unpleasant encounters. He found the right people in Vitebsk and collected intelligence. On his way back he was stopped by a German patrol, but after a short scuffle managed to escape.

—On the next night he came close to the back of the German lines. In the very first trench he ran into a sentry and knocked him out with a blow on the head with his heavy pistol before the man could raise the alarm.

—He had not yet moved far enough from the trench to reach no man's land when the sentry, who had evidently come to life, started calling for help. Flares shot up into the night sky, and he was discovered at once. German machine-guns opened fire from a few nests simultaneously but by some miracle he was not hit. He hugged the ground and crawled.

—Soviet artillery responded instantly, bringing down a hail of shells on the German lines. Karpov wormed his way to a wire entanglement, and here a German bullet got him at last. Almost fainting, he gathered his last strength, cut the wires and kept on crawling until he passed out.

—When he regained consciousness, he saw the faces of his comrades looking at him with concern. He was in a dugout and out of danger.

—As he learned later, he had been rescued by scout patrols in the corps defence sector, while the entire Soviet artillery was pounding the German lines on Chernyakhovsky's special orders to protect him.

—Karpov's daring mission proved invaluable to the Front Command. The intelligence he had retrieved confirmed that the German defences on the flanks were poorly fortified and shallow in depth. At the central front and within the city itself, however, they were truly impenetrable.

—Concentration of Soviet fire and attacks on the right flank allowed Soviet troops to effect a breakthrough and rip the belly of the German defences by a strike from behind them. Vitebsk was free again.—

To the best of my knowledge, intelligence about the "Bear Line" was transmitted to the neighbouring 1st Baltic and 2nd Byelorussian Fronts. Marshal Bagramian writes:

—As Commander of the 1st Baltic Front I regularly read battle intelligence reports and often came upon the name of Senior Lieutenant Karpov.

—It is a pleasure to know that this brave scout is now a well-known writer who has published a fascinating novel, "To Capture Alive", about the difficult and dangerous work of gathering battle intelligence. A faithful portrayal of combat and the routine of trench life in meticulous detail is to my mind one of the finest merits of this work written by an author who knows all about his subject. In fact, he was a participant in the events of his story. Karpov was fighting the war on the front of my Army Group and in the sector of the neighbouring 3rd Byelorussian Front and, to the best of my knowledge, was highly regarded by its Commander Ivan Chernyakhovsky.—

Bagramian's testimony warrants my conjecture that General Petrov also read my battle intelligence reports, and it gladdens me to know that I was useful to him, however slightly, when he was in command of the 2nd Byelorussian Front.

An enormous number of German troops were taken prisoner in the course of the Byelorussian operation. The victors displayed magnanimity and humaneness to the captive invaders. They were taught an object lesson in common sense without a shade of vindictiveness or derision let alone rough treatment. On their way to POW camps the captives were escorted through Moscow, so they had a chance to see the Soviet capital, which had been reduced to ruins by the Luftwaffe according to the frantic outbursts of Goebbels' propaganda.

The march of POW columns through the city was a very unusual spectacle and was filmed for posterity. I happened to be in Moscow at the time, recuperating from a wound, and watched that display of defeated vanity. It was a sad and edifying scene.

The generals were walking unhurriedly in the front ranks. They were different types: lanky, swollen with fat, moon-faced, hook-nosed. Golden insignia glistened in their collar tabs. Shoulder straps of twisted strands resembled fancy cakes. Chests were hung with medals and coloured ribbons. They stared ahead impassively, exchanging casual remarks.

They were followed by a column of officers marching in broken lines and obviously trying to look defiant and unsubdued by captivity. One of them, a clean-shaven strapping man, met my eye and quickly showed me his hefty fist. My answer was instant: I described a noose around my neck with my finger and pointed it upwards. The Nazi looked back at me several times, baring his yellow teeth, evidently swearing. "Bastard", I thought, "too bad you weren't done in at the front."

The next column was a countless multitude of non-coms and privates marching in lines of twenty and flooding almost the whole length and breadth of Gorky Street.

Soviet cavalrymen with their sabres drawn and infantrymen holding their rifles atilt were escorting the columns.

Crowds of Muscovites on both sides of the street were grimly and silently watching the procession. Only the shuffling of thousands of feet disturbed the unusual silence on the street filled with people as far as the eye could see.

On July 17, 1944 a total of 57,600 German prisoners of war were marched through Moscow. They were a part of the enormous number of German troops who had recently surrendered to the Red Army at the 1st, 2nd and 3rd Byelorussian Fronts.

Some time before that an unforgettable event had taken place in my life. How does one learn of his decoration in wartime? When he is with his military unit, he receives a message of congratulation. I, however, was in hospital and away from my regiment.

On June 6, 1944, strolling along Gorky Street in Moscow, I caught sight of an old woman pasting a fresh newspaper onto a house wall. I came up to it and glanced at the front page news. My head swam. Printed in bold type in the latest decree was my full name. The woman asked sympathetically:

"Are you unwell, young man?"

"Quite the contrary, Ma'am. I'm in better shape than ever before. May I kiss you?"

"Why?"

"Because I am happy. See here. I am a Hero!"

The woman hugged me and kissed me on both cheeks.

"May God bless you, good boy! I wish you all the happiness in the world."

After a few days I received an invitation to the decoration ceremony in the Kremlin. On the appointed day a group of awardees, me included, assembled in the Sverdlov Hall. An Air Force Captain with a row of war medals on his chest was seated next to me.

"What am I supposed to do when my name is called out, Captain? Do you know the rules?" I asked him.

He shrugged his shoulders: "No idea. I received all my medals at the front."

The ceremony began with the awarding of Heroes. There were three of us, and my name was called out first. I came up to the presidium table and stood still in confusion. President Mikhail Kalinin with his invariable goatee and iron-rimmed spectacles greeted me with a broad smile. My Gold Star and the Order of Lenin were shining on the red velvety cloth and I looked at them as if mesmerized. Kalinin handed me my diploma and awards and cordially shook my hand.

"Comrade Karpov, I congratulate you on your high title of Hero of the Soviet Union!"

I answered mechanically according to army regulations: "I serve the Soviet Union!"

Kalinin looked at me with fatherly compassion. I did not look like a hero at all. I was thin and pale after my discharge from hospital, and my army tunic loosely hung from my shoulders.

"How old are you?" Kalinin asked.

"Twenty-two."

"Good age. We admire you, young hero!"

Commander of the 4th Ukrainian Front

The Byelorussian operation was developing successfully. When Operation Bagration was at its height, the forces of the 1st Ukrainian Front, taking advantage of the favourable situation created by the swift advance of the Byelorussian Fronts, passed to the offensive, too. The Germans were doing their level best to check the advance of the 1st and 3rd Byelorussian Fronts, which threatened to trap a large enemy troop concentration by linking up in the Minsk area. The German High Command had moved in large reinforcements here.

The 1st Ukrainian Front forces under Marshal Konev dealt their strikes in the direction of Rava-Russkaya and Lvov, which was liberated on July 27. Carrying on their offensive, Soviet troops reached the Vistula and seized a bridgehead on its far side and enlarged it in time to 75 kilometres long and to 50 kilometres across. Fighting to capture that bridgehead the Soviet forces had taken the town of Sandomir, which gave its name to the famous Sandomir springboard from where the Soviet armies were aiming their thrusts at Berlin, while the armies of the left wing of this Front engaged the Germans in the foothills of the Carpathians.

In the south the forces of the 2nd Ukrainian Front under Marshal Malinovsky were poised for a thrust into Rumania. These two powerful Soviet Army Groups were separated by the enormous arch of the Main Carpathian Range up to 400 kilometres long and more than 100 kilometres wide. The convex part of this arch consisted of a few parallel mountain ranges, which were a formidable natural obstacle not to speak of the enemy fortifications there.

All the roads, mountain passes, and gorges were blocked by German nests of resistance, while the Main Carpathian Range had been turned into a defensive line, called Arpada, with ferroconcrete fortifications all along its length. The left flank of the 1st Ukrainian Front and the right flank of the 2nd Ukrainian Front faced this mountain range. It was naturally hard for the Front Commanders to organize and direct combat on such rugged or flat terrain, each of which would require a specific method for the conduct of warfare.

The Soviet High Command, therefore, resolved to establish the 4th Ukrainian Front. The forces of the new Front were to fight in the mountains. But who had sufficient experience of mountain combat to lead them? General Petrov was the best suited. His record in this field extended as far back as the Civil War when he had fought in the Pamirs. In the early months of the war he had led the Maritime Army across the Crimean Mountains to Sevastopol in the face of stiff German resistance. The great battles in the Caucasus had also been fought mostly under his direction.

The General Staff was aware of Stalin's ambivalent attitude to Petrov but, nevertheless, proposed his candidature. The Supreme Commander consented, evidently in recognition of Petrov's merits and competence.

By a directive of General Headquarters of August 3, 1944, Colonel General Petrov was placed in command of the 4th Ukrainian Front. His Army Group included the 1st Guards Army, the 18th Army, the 8th Air Force Army, the 17th Corps of Infantry Guards and special units.

Two infantry armies were not enough for an effective offensive, and it slowed down as they advanced into the foothills of the Carpathians. Petrov, therefore, was under orders from the High Command to organize a deeply echeloned defence to protect the flanks of Konev's forces on the Sandomir springboard and Malinovsky's forces fighting in Rumania lest the Germans take advantage of Carpathian roads and attack the flanks and rear of the 1st and 2nd Ukrainian Fronts.

On September 3, 1944, however, General Headquarters issued another directive ordering Petrov to take the offensive. New developments required an urgent revision of earlier plans.

In Czechoslovakia beyond the Carpathian ridges confronted by Petrov's forces a popular uprising had long been brewing, and developments had come to a head.

As the war went on the resistance movement in Czechoslovakia was steadily growing.

As far back as December 12, 1943, the Soviet Union and Czechoslovakia had concluded a Treaty of Friendship, Mutual Assistance and Postwar Co-operation. Under this Treaty the Soviet Government gave Czechoslovak resistance fighters great assistance, supplying them with weapons and ammunition and whatever was necessary for a struggle against the Nazis.

The resistance movement needed a competent leadership. The staunchest fighters against fascism, Czechoslovak communists, were either killed in the invasion of Czechoslovakia by Hitler's army in 1939 or were imprisoned in concentration camps or went into hiding or exile. Between 1941 and 1943 four attempts were undertaken to bring back to Czechoslovakia some leading functionaries of the Communist Party of Czechoslovakia who had escaped to the USSR. All of them were tracked down and detained by the Nazis.

The fifth attempt made in the summer of 1943 was successful. A group of Communists formed the Central Committee of the Communist Party of Slovakia headed by K. Schmidke, G. Gusak and L. Novomeski. The Slovak National Council was established to direct the national liberation movement in Slovakia.

The Council was headed by a presidium, which consisted of representatives of different parties, including Communists. K. Schmidke was one of the co-chairmen of the Council.

The Czechoslovak government-in-exile, which had its seat in London, also laid claim to leadership of the popular resistance movement.

The government-in-exile pursued its own political aims, intending to use the Slovak Army to achieve them. That Army existed legally as an ally of Nazi

Germany. In 1939 Slovakia had been declared an independent state under the "protection" of Nazi Germany. Therefore, it had its own government headed by Josef Tiso and its own army. The government-in-exile was planning to use that army for a quick seizure of all key positions and establishing bourgeois administration before the Red Army moved into Czechoslovak territory.

The Command of the Slovak Army was allied to the government-in-exile. It had been instructed to delay the national uprising, to carry out a coup before the entry of Soviet troops to Slovakia and restore the rule of the government-in-exile.

Developments, however, thwarted these plans. In August 1944 the partisans stepped up their operations in Central and Northern Slovakia. The people resorted to arms in various other areas. Growing numbers of units of the Slovak Army mutinied against the puppet government. Troops moved into mountain areas for punitive operations against the partisans fraternized with them. Many defected to their side, bringing their weapons and ammunition.

The high tide of the liberation movement threatened to topple Tiso's puppet regime. The government, therefore, took a treacherous step: it appealed to Hitler for an immediate invasion of Slovakia.

On August 29 the Defence Minister of the Tiso government in a broadcast message announced the entry of German troops into Slovakia for the "restoration of law and order". On the same day the Slovak National Council broadcast an appeal to the nation for a general uprising and armed struggle. The people responded enthusiastically. That was the beginning of the Slovak national uprising. Towards evening it spread throughout Central Slovakia and part of Eastern Slovakia. The centre of the insurrection was the city of Banska Bistrica freed by the Slovak partisans on the night of August 30.

On September 1, the Slovak National Council announced the takeover of legislative and executive powers. Its leaders appealed for aid from the Red Army.

The Soviet High Command resolved to open an immediate offensive with the forces of the 1st and 4th Ukrainian Fronts and by a strike across the Carpathians to come to the assistance of the insurgents as quickly as possible.

The arch of the Carpathian Mountains, which seems to have been made for defence by nature, lies across the flat part of Central Europe. It is a row of ridges 1,000–1,300 metres high rising in altitude successively. The Main Carpathian Range could be crossed over a few passes. The road network was sparse, and paved roads were absent. The steep mountains are overgrown with forests and shrubs. In rainy weather the roads became muddy and almost impassable. It was September, which is a season of rain and slush. The Soviet forces had to traverse hundreds of kilometres of this formidable terrain, fighting enemy troops entrenched in prepared positions on every ridge and shooting at the attackers from these points of vantage.

Numerous rivers, rivulets and streams cut the Carpathian Mountains in various directions. In summer they are shallow and quiet but in autumn with its torrential rains all of them turn violent. The thick fog reduced visibility almost to nil. The mountain summits, however, were already covered with snow and blizzards were raging there.

In the days of Soviet preparations for attack across the Carpathians the German High Command took vigorous steps to protect the Moravian industrial area which was crucial to the war effort. A few divisions were withdrawn from the front and moved into Slovakia. The Nazis acted quickly and cruelly. The command of the East Slovakian Corps, which was to capture the mountain passes and help Soviet troops to come to the aid of the insurgents, offered no resistance to the invaders. The corps had not been alerted for combat and was taken by surprise. The Germans disarmed its officers and men during the early days of September. Many were detained and shipped to concentration camps, part of the corps escaped and joined the partisans.

Across the Eastern Carpathians

The forces of the 1st and 4th Ukrainian Fronts were to deliver their blows at the junction of their flanks. The 38th Army of Colonel General Moskalenko went into attack in the main direction on September 8. It was to defeat the Germans in the Carpathian foothills and by a swift advance of its cavalry and armoured corps to seize the Duklin pass with the aid of the Slovak troops who had pledged to attack the Germans in the rear. The Army was to drive the Germans backwards by 90–95 kilometres within 5 days.

On the next day, September 9, the 1st Guards Army of Colonel General Grechko also passed to the offensive. The 38th Army had bombarded the enemy positions for 125 minutes and advanced by 12 kilometres before it was bogged down after repeated attacks on September 9. As Marshal Moskalenko recalls, "In two days of fighting the units of the 38th Army proved unable to break through the tactical zone of defence and rapidly advance towards the Carpathian passes."

At the 4th Ukrainian Front developments took a different turn. One corps of the 1st Guards Army attacked on September 9 and during the first day of fighting burst open the German defences in a 12-kilometre sector and advanced by 6 kilometres. The German Command started bringing up reinforcements from other sectors of the front to check the Soviet advance. Petrov immediately ordered the 17th Guards Infantry Corps of Major General Gastilovich to join battle. In three days the corps advanced up to 15 kilometres in the centre and 30 to 60 kilometres at its flank and came close to the main mountain passes in its area.

In an effort to stop Soviet forces now in this sector the Germans moved in reserves from neighbouring areas. Petrov promptly moved the units of the 18th Army into action, leaving only two divisions along the remaining length of the front. That was a risky decision, but Petrov realized that the Germans had panicked and were trying to stop up the breaches in their defences and would not venture to attack elsewhere.

Within five days troops of the 18th Army overran the German defence positions in a sector over 30 kilometres in length, and carried the offensive into the areas beyond to a depth of about 40 kilometres. General Petrov's foresight and competent analysis of the situation made the whole operation of the 4th Ukrainian Front a spectacular success.

That was, indeed, a model of mountain warfare. One episode exemplifies its complexity. On September 20, 1944, Vedenin's 3rd Mountain Corps entered the territory of Czechoslovakia. The left-flank forces of the 38th Army, however, were stalled by dogged German resistance, and the right flank of the 3rd Mountain Corps remained exposed to German attack. The Germans immediately took advantage of that, and an SS panzer division struck at the junction between the 3rd Mountain Corps and the 38th Army. The latter's units beat a retreat.

At a critical moment when the SS panzers were close to winning the battle Petrov committed to action three antitank regiments which broke the back of the German counter-attack. German tanks knocked out by accurate hits flared up like torches all over the battlefield. The 318th Division under the command of Gladkov, the hero of the Eltingen landing, counter-attacked in force and drove the Germans backwards.

The forces of the 4th Ukrainian Front, which had just enough strength for defensive action, went over to the offensive jointly with troops of the 1st Ukrainian Front in a 300-kilometre wide sector, and fought their way to the mountain passes of the Main Carpathian Range.

The East Slovakian Corps, which was to assist the capture of the mountain passes by attacking the Germans from the rear, failed to live up to its pledge, but the forces of the 4th Ukrainian Front burst through the German defences ahead of the 38th Army of the 1st Ukrainian Front, which was to deliver the main strike.

The Command of the 1st Ukrainian Front and the 38th Army Commander Moskalenko never left out of focus the central task of assisting the Slovak National Uprising outlined in the directive of the General Headquarters. For the same motive Marshal Konev moved the 4th Tank Corps into the sector of the 38th Army to turn the tide of hostilities.

The 1st Czechoslovak Corps incorporated into the Soviet forces was in the second line of attack, the brunt of the battle being borne by the 38th Army as its Commander Colonel General Moskalenko had planned. The Czechoslovak Corps Commander General Kratohvyl, a protégé of the Czechoslovak government-in-exile seated in London, had proved an unreliable ally, going out of his way to hold back his units in the second echelon which were to join battle.

General Shtemenko writes: "General Kratohvyl was appointd commander of the 1st Czechoslovak Corps on the insistence of the Beneš government. Rather than do his duty, he was sitting out the battle at his headquarters far in the rear, drinking British whisky in quantities larger than were good for him, while the officers and men of his corps were storming the formidable German defences in the Carpathians, suffering heavy casualties.

"Therefore, Konev suspended Kratohvyl from command of the corps and replaced him with General Ludvik Svoboda. Stalin approved of his action. . . ."

On October 6, 1944, the Czechoslovak troops led by their new, energetic and skilful commander set foot on their native soil. Jointly with their Soviet ally they had taken the Duklin pass in a swift offensive lasting a few days.

Thus, despite its smaller forces and auxiliary role in that operation, the 4th Ukrainian Front secured a faster pace of advance than its neighbours on the 1st Ukrainian Front. Stalin commended Petrov's actions and the courage of his troops in a special order of the day, which announced their breakthrough along a front of 275 kilometres from 20 to 50 kilometres in depth. Moscow saluted the valiant forces of the 4th Ukrainian Front with twenty salvoes from 224 artillery guns.

That was on October 18. Within a week Petrov's troops captured Mukaczevo, the industrial centre of Transcarpathian Ukraine, in Czechoslovak territory and a major German stronghold at the southern spurs of the Carpathians. On the next day his forces captured another stronghold, Uzhgorod, the capital of Transcarpathian Ukraine. That was followed by Stalin's new order of the day, this time addressed to General of the Army Petrov. He was finally promoted in rank.

The 4th Ukrainian Front under Petrov's command overran the German defence line in the Eastern Carpathians. The final liberation of Czechoslovakia was now a matter of months.

Uzhgorod had, in fact, been taken without much bloodshed. The Germans, of course, were determined to hold on to the city as long as possible and decimate the Soviet attackers, taking advantage of the mountainous terrain, rain and slush, and the numerous defence works they had built long in advance of the Soviet offensive, but Petrov, an old hand in mountain warfare, outsmarted them. His troops were fit to fight under any conditions, and their crash training under his guidance and battle experience were now to become the crucial factor of success.

He ordered mobile units to be formed of tanks, antitank and antiaircraft artillery for swift thrusts at vulnerable spots in the German defences, to defeat the Germans by superior firepower added to the surprise factor. One of such units overpowered the German defenders in one sector and unexpectedly attacked the main German forces from the rear. Uzhgorod was now within easy reach.

Petrov was impatient to watch the battlefield with his own eyes and, ignoring danger while the battle was still in the balance, drove to the fighting area. The city was veiled in smoke and the thunder of guns echoed by the mountains made his eardrums ache. A column of Soviet tanks standing still not far from the city outskirts caught his eye. His jeep was there within minutes, and he stood up and called to the tankmen: "What happened? Who is in command here?"

An officer ran up to him and saluted: "Major Morus, commander of the 5th Tank Brigade."

"What's holding you back here? There's no time to be lost."

"All bridges have been blown up, sir. The River Uzh is deep in this area, and its far bank is steep and clad in concrete. My tanks can do nothing."

"Okay, young man, let's go and look for shallow waters elsewhere." Petrov motioned to the officer to get into the back seat and shouted to the driver: "Go!"

They drove by the riverside and after a few miles caught sight of a ford where the rapid current was foaming over large stones and pebbles visible on the bed. Morus jumped out happily and waded to the opposite bank through the knee-deep water, searching for the best passage for his tanks. Petrov crossed the river in his jeep to take a look at the terrain beyond.

Suddenly, a German army truck burst forth as if from nowhere and raced at full speed towards them. Petrov and his men had no time to retreat and prepared to fight for their lives, but there were only three of them against at least twenty Germans armed with machine-pistols. That was, indeed, an ambush.

Morus, however, proved to be a man of foresight. One of his tanks had been following them on his instructions, and its crew saw their plight in good time. The tank turret turned slowly and its huge gun fired at the oncoming vehicle. The distance was too long, and it missed its target but the truck stopped, and the Germans hastily climbed out and hugged the ground, firing wildly.

But now the tank's machine-gun was rattling away, while Petrov and his men kept on firing at their assailants from the machine-pistols his driver had providently stowed away in the jeep.

The tank gun fired again, and this time the truck was hit and went up in flames. The gunner was an accurate shot, to be sure, and the next shell exploded right in the midst of the Germans. Human bodies flew into the air in a fountain of earth, and the German survivors ran for their lives. The gun fired again and again, the shells hitting the ground and exploding in front of them, and the Germans stopped abruptly and ran back, hurling their weapons away and raising their hands pleadingly.

The tank crew held their fire, as did Petrov and his men. They stood up and watched the approaching Germans, their weapons at the ready. That was the first batch of prisoners in the battle for the city. In a few hours they would be joined by numerous others.

The tank brigade alerted by radio from their saviours was already on its way to the crossing point, and its vanguard could be seen in the distance. "Well, a good beginning is half the battle!" the General exclaimed cheerfully. "Thank you, commander!" and he waved goodbye to Morus. "And give my thanks to the gunner. That was marksmanship at its best."

That battle was an extraordinary event: the Commander of an Army Group fighting in close combat like a rank-and-file soldier and taking prisoners at peril to his life. It was definitely against regulations, but Petrov felt satisfied: his old mettle was still there.

The 5th Tank Brigade, now in full assembly, attacked the Germans by a flanking thrust, taking them by surprise, and overran their positions around Uzhgorod. Dozens of German trains loaded with equipment and ready for departure were captured at the railway station. German troops surrendered by the thousands, and the city and its inhabitants were spared the horrors of street fighting, artillery and air bombardment.

After the capture of Uzhgorod and Mukaczevo, the troops of the 4th Ukrainian Front invaded the plain along the River Tisza and completed the East Carpathian operation. It went down in the history of warfare as the first large-scale battle in which a formidable mountain range—the Carpathian Mountains—was overcome by a large mass of troops along a front of over 300 kilometres.

That successful operation was followed by an historic event of vital significance for the Ukrainian people. On November 26, 1944, the 1st Congress of People's Committees of Trans-Carpathia adopted a manifesto on the reunification of Trans-Carpathian Ukraine with its historical heartland—the Soviet Ukraine.

On June 29, 1945, the governments of the USSR and the Czechoslovak Republic would sign a treaty to satisfy the formal request of the people of Trans-Carpathia for a reunification with the Soviet Ukraine.

Another important aspect of that battle was assistance to the insurgent people of Slovakia. Though Petrov's forces were sufficient only for defensive fighting, their dedication to their internationalist duty fortified their spirit. Petrov's energy and skill matched their determination to win the battle.

The art of warfare is comparable to mathematics in terms of precision. In a confrontation between two belligerent sides all "pros" and "cons" are carefully balanced, all the possibilities down to every piece of artillery and the fitness of every officer and man are taken into consideration.

On a battlefield where no sufficient manpower and weaponry are available for a sweeping attack, let alone an offensive across such formidable heights as the Carpathians, the competence, courage and presence of mind of the General planning and leading the attack are as crucial to success as superior numbers and weapons.

The loss by the Germans of Uzhgorod and Mukaczevo left a gaping hole in their defences, so they stiffened their resistance and counter-attacked the advancing Soviet troops continuously. General Petrov, however, was planning another breakthrough. As he had done more than once before, he divided his work into routine duties which demanded his immediate attention and strategic planning, which demanded examination of his opponent's potential for long-term defence.

Assessing the current situation from the angle of the immediate and longer-term prospects, General Petrov worked out the plan of a new operation and reported it to the Supreme Commander on November 5. He intended to begin it on November 15–17, that is he had requested 10 to 12 days to prepare it.

This plan was examined at the General Headquarters for four days and approved on November 9. General Headquarters, however, asked Petrov to explain how he would carry out the first part of the operation, if half of all the divisions deployed on the front were pulled out into reserve and the Front by his own decision.

Petrov explained his plan, but evidently the General Headquarters were not satisfied. A new instruction was issued to him on November 14:

"In view of the fact that the 2nd Ukrainian Front is advancing with all available forces and their operations are closely co-ordinated with those of the 4th Ukrainian Front, the offensive of the troops of your Front should be kept going at the same rate.

"The General Headquarters believes, therefore, that the number of divisions taking part in your offensive is not sufficient for advancing to the line of Medzilaborce, Gumenne, and Michalowce. The General Headquarters interprets the withdrawal of almost half of the divisions into the reserve of the Front and the armies as motivated by your intention to account only for the interests of your own front, ignoring your neighbour's situation and the common cause.

"You are, therefore, ordered to proceed as follows:

"1.   Leave five or six divisions in reserve and commit all your other forces to action, taking full advantage of artillery and aircraft cover as soon as the weather improves to advance to the line of Medzilaborce, Gumenne and Michalowce. Commit the reserve divisions to action, if necessary. . . ."

Thus, General Petrov was required to attack with full strength and assist the forces of the 2nd Ukrainian Front fighting on his left flank.

On November 14, however, he received another directive from General Headquarters: to hand over the 30th Infantry Corps of three divisions and the 18th Infantry Corps of two divisions of the Guards to the 2nd Ukrainian Front.

The forces under his command consisted of only two armies; so anyone would understand that the 4th Ukrainian Front would now have a hard time, fighting to attain its targets. Petrov expected a change in his offensive plan to be handed down from the High Command, but no new instructions were issued, and his tasks remained the same.

He had to rely on his own resources of competence and inventiveness to deal with that new situation. His best resource was thorough preparation and training of his troops for combat where less manpower and firepower were now under his command. The Commanders of the 1st and 18th Armies assisted by his staff got down to work to hammer out a plan of fighting good enough to compensate for this depletion in strength.

There was not sufficient artillery cover, which was the chief obstacle to effective infantry manoeuvres.

General Petrov remembered that even having a small number of guns and scant ammunition the enemy could effectively be fought by accurate firing and skilful manoeuvring.

Soviet artillery went into action at 8:30 on November 23 and kept pounding the German lines for a full fifty minutes. German troop control was deranged, gun and mortar emplacements were levelled to the ground, and numerous German firing posts in the trenches were knocked out by accurate hits.

A German prisoner of war testified that the German companies and battalions had lost almost half of their strength in the fierce barrages of Russian artillery. The earlier order to fight to the last ditch until a new winter defence line was built in the Kosice area, where retreating troops could hold on for a long time, was now just a scrap of paper. The Soviet gunners had broken the backbone of the German defences.

The Soviet 107th and 11th Infantry Corps of the 1st Guards Army punched a 16-kilometre-wide hole in the German lines and advanced up to 11 kilometres into enemy territory. The Germans attempted a few counter-attacks but the momentum of the Soviet offensive was too strong to be reversed. The Soviet troops were steadily forging their way in the direction of Michalowce.

In that operation the 18th Army under Major General Gastilovich, General Petrov's personal choice for that post, struck out across a swampy terrain from where the Germans had expected danger least of all.

Explaining his plan to Petrov, Gastilovich had pointed out some vulnerable spots in the German defences confronting his forces. The Germans had no deep trenches in that area and hence were exposed to the fire of Soviet artillery and mortars. The main German strongholds were in the villages which stood on dry land, so massive attacks against them would secure concentration of fire power where it was needed most of all.

General Petrov commended his logic and endorsed his plan. Moreover, he instructed Commander of the 8th Air Army, Lieutenant General Zhdanov to detail 400 combat aircraft to support the operations of the 18th Army. Petrov advised him to refrain from air strikes along the routes of Soviet attacks and concentrate air power where German reserves, especially panzer units, could come to the aid of the retreating troops and bar the Soviet forces from breaking through in decisive sectors. Gastilovich's Army would thus be guarded against attack by German reinforcements and have enough strength to rout the Germans in their first line of defence.

At 9:00 on November 20 the thunder of Soviet artillery shook the vast swampy plain south-west of Uzhgorod. After being under fire for 45 minutes German resistance was ended. German strongpoints in the villages were heavily damaged. The enemy casualties in manpower and weapons were staggering. Indeed, as it later became known, the German Command had never expected a Soviet attack across this almost impassable terrain.

Soviet troops were slowly advancing, hauling artillery, carrying mortars and machine-guns on their backs, their feet sinking into the swampy ground, every mile of their advance being a record of endurance. They were bypassing German strongpoints, avoiding fights, to gain as much ground as possible on that incredibly treacherous terrain.

Towards the day's end the Soviet breakthrough had widened to 15 kilometres and the Germans now had a 16–17 kilometre long Soviet wedge in their defences.

Thus, the 1st Guards Army and the 18th Army were advancing at a fairly good rate, but the 95th Infantry Corps under Major General Melnikov had come up against stiff German resistance. Petrov immediately went to its sector.

In addition to natural obstacles and German fire, the Soviet attackers had to deal with another difficulty: the Rivers Laborec and Ondawa had flooded the lowlands following a few days of torrential rain. A violent torrent of water up to 10 kilometres wide protected the German lines against their assailants.

The bridges and whatever could be used as makeshift crossing facilities had been swept away or remained under water. Besides, German artillery on the far side of this new obstacle was shelling the Soviet troops on the bank of the Ondawa. Petrov realized that the enemy should on no account be given a respite and a chance to recover from their defeats, and prepare themselves for another defensive battle with more manpower and weapons at their disposal.

Major General Melnikov recalls his predicament in that almost hopeless situation and Petrov's ingenuity in dealing with it. He inspected the crossing points chosen for building bridges and the remaining pillars, driving in his jeep from site to site, ignoring German fire and encouraging the teams of engineer troops.

His plan was to distract German forces from the key sectors where no decisive action was contemplated by the Soviet side and then deliver a blow in the strategic direction, taking advantage of our superior strength at the breakthrough points. As a result, the 1st Guards Army overran the positions of the German units deployed on its front and took the towns of Gumenne and Michalowce towards the end of November 26.

Thus, the 4th Ukrainian Front forces accomplished their tasks set by the General Headquarters. Their courage and the skill of their commander compensated for the withdrawal of two corps from their complement. Both towns were important road junctions and strongholds in the German defence system. On November 26, 1944, the Supreme Commander commended General of the Army Petrov in a special order of the day, and Moscow saluted the valiant forces of the 4th Ukrainian Front.

A New Directive of the High Command

Marshal Konev's work as Commander of the 1st Ukrainian Front was complicated by the situation of the 38th Army. His next target was Berlin, he was preoccupied with his new battle tasks. The 38th Army was fighting in the Carpathians though it was not formally subordinated to the 4th Ukrainian Front under General Petrov who was directing the Soviet offensive across the Carpathians. That discrepancy was causing problems of incoordination, so General Headquarters issued a directive subordinating General Moskalenko's 38th Army and General Ludvik Svoboda's 1st Czechoslovak Corps to the Commander of the 4th Ukrainian Front, General Petrov.

New demarcation lines on the front and new tasks were set by the Supreme Commander. On November 30 he radioed the following order to the 4th Ukrainian Front:

—1.   Carry on the offensive with the left wing and centre of your Front to take the line of Zborow, Bardeew, Presow and Kosice by December 12–15, 1944. Your general direction: Novy Targ and Poprad.

—2.   Prepare the 38th Army for attack and interaction with the left wing of the 1st Ukrainian Front to take Krakow in early January 1945 at the latest.

—3.   Submit your detailed plan of action and deadlines towards December 3, 1944.—

General Petrov worked out the plan of a new offensive jointly with his Chief of Staff, Lieutenant General Korzhenevich. They were hard pressed for time, because the fighting on the front continued unabated, and they had only a few days at their disposal to finalize the details before submitting the plan to the Supreme Commander.

. . . On December 9, following an artillery preparation of 45 minutes, the divisions of the 1st Guards Army attacked the Germans and relentlessly forged their way ahead, forming a deep wedge in the German defences. The last few mountain ridges lay between the attacking troops and the vast Trans-Carpathian valleys. The German High Command realized only too well that once the Soviet forces burst out onto the plains, no force would be able to check their further advance. Therefore, the command of "Heinrici" operational group went out of their way to bring the Soviet advance to a stop here in the mountains. Having concentrated up to four divisions in a small area, the Germans struck at the base of the wedge driven into their defences by the units of the 1st Guards Army. The Soviet forces were brought to a standstill. A brief lull followed in the course of hostilities.

On December 16, however, following a 35-minute artillery attack, the 11th Infantry Corps forced a crossing over the River Ondawa and seized the town of Dargow. Taking advantage of this success the neighbouring 107th Corps made a rapid thrust and took the town of Davidow. During the whole day on December 18, the units of the 1st Guards Army were repelling fierce German counter-attacks; there were nine of them in the sector of the 107th Corps alone.

General Petrov stayed in the firing lines round the clock, looking for a flaw in the German defences and a chance to develop his success. On the night of December 20, the 1st Guards Army secretly moved to the left flank of the battle front and surprised the Germans by an all-out attack. That allowed the Soviet troops to make some progress in the face of ferocious enemy resistance.

Petrov was watching the battle through a periscope set up in a trench. In the mountains there was no frontline in the true sense of the word and some units were far ahead of others. Unlike forces fighting a battle on a plain they were at different heights in relation to each other, which made troop control difficult. He saw soldiers climbing precipitous rocks and labouring through deep snow held up by bushes and trees. Their trenchcoats and high boots were thoroughly wet from sweat, rain and thawing snow. At greater heights there were frosts down to 20°C. Ice-cold winds were biting the face, numbing the fingers and chilling the body, hot from physical strain. Soaked trenchcoats grew stiff with ice, making every movement a great effort and well-aimed firing impossible.

Soviet soldiers had been fighting under such incredibly hard conditions of mountain warfare for months at a stretch, and they were almost at the end of their tethers.

Indeed, they were exhausted and underfed; there were the difficulties of food supply over a roadless terrain, along narrow and steep mountain trails exposed to deadly enemy fire, where men, horses and donkeys slipped and fell on ice-crusted rocky ground. This added to the problem of ammunition shortages which constantly plagued the advancing Soviet forces.

Higher up, near the mountain tops to where the Soviet troops were climbing with such dogged determination, they were awaited by an enemy armed to the teeth and lavishly stocked with food and ammunition. The Germans enjoyed the relative safety of expertly planned networks of trenches and pill-boxes and whenever they were forced to retreat they pulled back into prepared positions with plentiful supplies of whatever was needed to carry on the fight.

Once they had climbed up close to the German trenches, Soviet soldiers who had survived the lethal fire mustered up their remaining strength and engaged the Germans in hand-to-hand fighting. And they invariably overpowered their well-fed, well-armed and well-rested adversaries.

That was a truly heroic exploit. Every Soviet soldier was a hero, but none of them regarded himself as one. They believed they were simply doing their routine wartime duty. As Petrov watched these simple people of inflexible will and dauntless spirit his heart went out to them. It was fatherly love mixed with reverential admiration. It occurred to him that at their young age when they have so much to lose—the priceless gift of life—they are as fearless as the gods.

He was eager to help these courageous people, and he did not spare himself to give them practical aid. He brought pressure to bear on his subordinate commanders, headquarters, artillery, air force, logistic, transport and medical services, giving a dressing-down to whoever was guilty of delays and accepting no excuses. Nobody felt hurt by his harsh demands, because all realized why the Front commander was so impatient with them; they all knew of his noble motives.

All these difficulties were an additional burden on his shoulders, if one were to compare the battles on his mountain front with the battles on other fronts, which, for all their ferocity, were fought with better odds for the Soviet side.

A theatre of war, however, cannot be improved or replaced, so a general has to accomplish his tasks in the theatre that falls to his lot. As for the combat and political situation, however, it may be more or less complicated and can be influenced, that is changed for the better for the friendly forces and for the worse for the hostile forces. This is not a simple thing to do and is not possible for every general.

In the battle for the Carpathians all the factors seemed to be working against Petrov: a mountain theatre, poor weather, insufficient manpower, a strong enemy, formidable defences, inadequate logistic supplies, a roadless terrain.

In addition, there was another problem which did not exist on the other fronts. This problem merits attention, because dealing with it required much additional effort on the part of the Soviet fighting forces. There were nationalist bands operating in the rear of the 4th Ukrainian Front.

Here is an excerpt from a document confirming that the Carpathians were assigned as a zone of operations to these Nazi underlings. It was circulated to several addressees: SS Sturmbahnfuhrer Pommering of the Central Imperial Security Department; Bierkampf, Chief of Security Police and SD in the Governor Generalship; SS Hauptsturmfuhrer Spilker, Chief of Sonderkommando IV-N-90/44; SS Brigadefuhrer Dimg, SS and Polizeifuhrer of the District of Galicia:

—Lemberg, 26 May, 1944.

Top secret.

Regarding the establishment of links between UPA (Ukrainian Insurgent Army) and the apparatus of the Wehrmacht, police, and civilian administration.

. . . The units of UPA, which can hardly oppose the Soviet troops in Galicia, should be redeployed to an area of hostilities where the relatively weak UPA units will have an opportunity to check the further advance of Soviet forces. Such a favourable area could be the Carpathians.

The German occupation authorities should realize that the concentration of UPA units in the Carpathians is directed exclusively against the Soviets and by no means against German interests.—

As can be seen from this document, not even all German headquarters and civilian authorities knew that Bandera's forces and OUN (Organization of Ukrainian Nationalists) were in collusion with the Nazis. They were posing as "freedom fighters" struggling for an independent Ukraine. Their true identity was thoroughly concealed and was unknown to many rank-and-file members of Bandera's and OUN organizations. They were tools in the hands of the leaders of these bands, who were regular agents of the German secret services.

Here is an excerpt from a Soviet document confirming this:

—In the autumn of 1940 State Security agencies intercepted an emissary of the central body of OUN. He was carrying instructions to nationalist organizations, which said in particular: In the German's future war against the Soviets the nationalists should regard the Germans as liberators and allies. Therefore, all organizations and their members are required to conduct active subversive operations even before the outbreak of hostilities to demonstrate to Germany the capability of her allies in the struggle against the Bolsheviks.—

The atrocities perpetrated by OUN forces against civilians in the Soviet Ukraine were part and parcel of their "programme" masterminded by the Nazis. Before Nazi Germany's attack against the USSR the Abwehr, the intelligence arm of the Wehrmacht, had smuggled in its groups of saboteurs to nationalists' secret bases. In a number of villages they murdered peasants to prevent their exposure.

After the invasion of the Soviet borders by the Wehrmacht, OUN gangs widened their subversive operations in the Red Army's rear; they spied on troop movements, raided logistic depots, planted time bombs and mines on roads and bridges, attacked trains and lorry convoys evacuating refugees and industrial equipment and other valuable property from the threatened areas. Bandits disguised in Red Army uniforms attacked small Soviet units, firing at them from rooftops and prepared positions. The notorious "Roland" and "Nachtigal" units of Stepan Bandera's forces crossed the Soviet border under Nazi banners as part of the German forces of invasion.

Thousands of Soviet civilians were shot, hanged or tortured to death in the areas of Lvov, Ternopol, Stanislaw in the early months of the war. They died at the hands of the nationalists.

On the orders of their Nazi masters Bandera and Stetsko, another nationalist chieftain, were assigned to Abwehrkommando-202 in Krakow at the end of 1944 to direct the operations of their gangs in the Carpathians.

The Abwehr appointed its agent Dmitry Klyachkovski as the first leader of the nationalist gangs. He was succeeded by Roman Shukhevich, the ex-commander of the Abwehr's "Nachtigal" battalion. Their minions forced Ukrainian peasant lads to join their gangs, taking advantage of their ignorance of the complicated political situations arising in the Nazi-occupied areas.

Bandits carried out sadistic massacres of civilians in the western areas of the Ukraine and Byelorussia, mercilessly killing anybody suspected of being a member of the Resistance or a Communist sympathizer. Even children and women were murdered in cold blood.

The Red Army's advance towards the western areas of the Ukraine forced the Nazis and the nationalists to camouflage their collaboration, which was steadily growing stronger as the prospect of final retribution moved into clearer view.

General Petrov was not, of course, involved in mopping-up operations against the nationalist gangs in the rear of his Front, but he was kept informed about them by the special forces. The safety of his troops from a treacherous attack from the rear was crucially important for their success on the main battle front.

Thus, Petrov and his staff planned and controlled the efforts of hundreds of thousands of troops on the 4th Ukrainian Front and hundreds of miles behind the Soviet lines. The fierce fighting that was going on in all parts of this area added complexity to his tasks. His forces, however, were forging ahead relentlessly and nothing could stop them now.

The Vistula–Oder Operation

The year 1945 came at last. All were confident it would be the last year of the war. The Supreme Commander publicly announced the tasks facing the Red Army in 1945:

—. . . To consummate together with the Allied armies the rout of the Nazi Wehrmacht, to finish off the Nazi beast in his own lair and hoist the Victory Banner over Berlin.—

It was with joyful excitement that General Petrov expected the victorious end of the war. He saw clearly that hostilities had entered the final stage. The troops of the 3rd Ukrainian Front jointly with the People's Liberation Army of Yugoslavia had marched into Belgrade. Bucharest had been taken, and Rumania had declared war on Nazi Germany; Rumanian troops were fighting the Germans side by side with the Soviet forces. At the end of December 1944 the forces of the 2nd and 3rd Ukrainian Fronts had completed the encirclement of the German Army Group in Budapest. The troops of the 1st Ukrainian Front and the 1st Byelorussian Front were poised for an onslaught on Berlin.

Confronted by a disastrous situation on the Eastern Front, Hitler resolved to try to change the fortune of war in his favour by mounting a great offensive in the West. Perhaps it was to a certain extent a demonstration of Germany's still existing military might or an outburst of anger against the Anglo-Saxons who had opened a Second Front at last.

Hitler evidently hoped to come to terms with the leaders of Great Britain and the United States and form an alliance with them on the basis of a joint confrontation with Communism. He also wanted to teach them a lesson.

Three German armies suddenly attacked the Allied forces in the Ardennes with a powerful panzer and air strike.

Between December 16 and 25 the Germans advanced by 90 kilometres. As the Allies stiffened their resistance at the cost of heavy casualties, German panzer units had ground to a halt at the end of December. On New Year's eve, however, Hitler gave them a "Christmas present": an armada of 1,000 aircraft made an unexpected raid over the Allied positions, and German divisions burst into Alsace.

The Germans were swiftly rolling forward. In a personal and secret message to Stalin on January 6, 1945, Winston Churchill asked for help: "... You know yourself from your own experience how very fragile the position is when a very broad front has to be defended after temporary loss of the initiative.... I shall be grateful if you can tell me whether we can count on a major Russian offensive on the Vistula front, or elsewhere, during January, with any other points you may care to mention...."

Stalin replied in a message to Churchill on the next day: "... It is extremely important to take advantage of our superiority over the Germans in guns and aircraft. What we need for the purpose is clear flying weather and the absence of low mists that prevent aimed artillery fire. We are mounting an offensive, but at the moment the weather is unfavourable. Still, in view of our Allies' position on the Western Front, GHQ of the Supreme Command have decided to complete preparations at a rapid rate and, regardless of weather, to launch large-scale offensive operations along the entire Central Front not later than the second half of January. Rest assured that we shall do all in our power to support the valiant forces of our Allies."

Faithful to their pledge of assistance to the Allies, the General Headquarters issued battle orders to the Soviet forces and those of the 4th Ukrainian Front in particular. In co-operation with the left wing of the 1st Ukrainian Front they were to deliver the main strike in the direction of Gorlice–Novy Soncz and advance further to Krakow.

The target date of the offensive was set for January 12, 1945.

To secure a dispersion of the German reserves, the General Headquarters determined that the troops of the 2nd Ukrainian Front would go over to the offensive on January 6. Their first attack was successful. During two days of fighting they wedged themselves up to 40 kilometres into the German defence area and besieged the city of Komarno. However, they failed to take it and cross the Danube.

The Germans' attention was focused precisely on that sector of the front. Taking advantage of that, the right wing of the 2nd Ukrainian Front, the neighbours of General Petrov's forces, struck out in force on January 12. Negotiating the steep slopes of Slovakia's Rudny Mountains, they were making steady progress.

On the same day the troops of the 1st Ukrainian Front and the 1st Byelorussian Front launched an all-out offensive. The Vistula–Oder operation had begun.

On January 12 General Petrov ordered his 18th Army to open an attack. At 10:00 two corps of the Army assaulted the German lines after a 40-minute artillery preparation. That was intended to distract the Germans' attention from the sector where his 38th Army was to deliver the main strike.

On January 13 the troops of the 2nd and 3rd Byelorussian Fronts went into action to carry out the East Prussian operation. Thus, the Red Army was on the offensive all along the Central Front. The Germans were now in a corner and had to fight for their lives. Their counter-offensive in the Ardennes had to be called off.

Until January 17 the units of the 18th Army had been fighting heavy battles in the mountains. Their active operations compelled the Germans to re-group their forces and bring in reinforcements to check the Soviet advance. The fighting was fiercest at the approaches to the city of Kosice which the Germans had turned into the main stronghold of their defence.

All the approaches to the city were covered by a network of fortifications on the western bank of the River Toris. The areas off the roads bristled with antitank obstacles, the roads and bridges across the Toris and the Hernad were mined, and all possible crossing sites were mined and exposed to aimed artillery fire.

The offensive of the tired and depleted Soviet forces was steadily slowing down and would soon come to a halt. On the morning of January 18 the 18th Army made another attempt to take Kosice, all to no avail. After a full day of fighting, its unit were thrown back to their initial positions.

There seemed to be no way out of that embarrassing situation. Petrov, however, would not accept defeat. He was thinking hard: if the Germans could stiffen their resistance here, they must have brought in some units from another sector. His reconnaissance had not detected any German reinforcements coming from the rear. But where was that sector? He ordered all his units to carry out thorough reconnaissance of the German forces confronting them.

Listening to reports, Petrov finally found what he was searching for. General Gastilovich, commander of the 18th Army, reported a reduction in German strength in front of the 159th fortified area held by his troops. Local residents testified that the Germans had moved part of their forces to the Kosice area the day before.

Petrov's decision was quite unusual. He ordered Gastilovich to attack the Germans with the forces of the 159th fortified area. That was a logical decision at first glance. It will be recalled, however, that a fortified area is intended exclusively for defence and is provided with weapons and field fortifications to ward off an enemy breakthrough. Its troops normally leave it when the battle in the other sectors is over. The force of a fortified area mounting an offensive was something without precedent on the other fronts.

Petrov was taking a great risk, of course. What would happen if the Germans suddenly attacked in this direction after the force had pulled out of its fortifications, the backbone of its strength?

But fortune favours the brave, as the saying goes. Major General Vingradov, who was at the time a colonel in command of the 159th fortified area, recalls:

—We threw into battle the reserves of the other battalions and, after an all night's fighting, ripped through the whole depth of the first German defence line and approached the second line. Though German strength was much less here, we could not take it at once. We were tired and undermanned, but an urgent breakthrough was necessary before the German command realized the danger and started bringing in reinforcements.

—We made a desperate thrust forward and, ignoring German fire and our own casualties, fought our way to the outskirts of Kosice.—

Exploiting that success, the neighbouring 318th and 237th Infantry Divisions engaged the Germans in their own sectors and hurled them backwards by tens of miles. That was a rich reward for inventiveness, indeed.

On January 19, 1945, the Supreme Commander issued an order of the day commending General Petrov, his Chief of Staff General Lieutenant Korzhenevich and the forces under their command. The order said in part: ". . . the forces of the 4th Ukrainian Front launched an offensive on January 15 from an area west of the town of Sanok, burst open a strongly fortified German defence line and during four days of fighting have advanced by up to 80 kilometres and widened the breakthrough up to 60 kilometres along the front."

The assault on Kosice started on the same day, January 19. The units of the 3rd Mountain Corps delivered a frontal strike, and the 17th Corps of Infantry Guards went into attack south-west of the city. The Germans put up a fierce resistance, because Kosice was a major road junction of Eastern Slovakia and its industry was important for the German war effort. The enemy was determined to hold the city at all costs.

General Petrov did everything necessary to speed up the advance. He left nothing to chance, and whenever his troops fell back or delayed, his skill and initiative immediately helped them out. General Gastilovich's 18th Army was soon fighting the Germans in the city. They were driven out of Kosice towards nightfall, suffering heavy casualties. Many were taken prisoner.

But who was the German general with whom Petrov had "crossed swords" with in those final battles?

Colonel General Ferdinand Schorner appointed on January 17 to command of Army Group Centre was Petrov's next and last opponent in the war who would be honoured by Hitler with the title of Field Marshal as a gesture of personal trust.

The Moravska Ostrava industrial area was practically the last source of supplies to the Wehrmacht in that final stage of the war. Hitler had chosen Schorner as a faithful follower to defend it as long as possible, still hoping for a separate peace with the Western Allies to save the Third Reich from its doom.

Schorner was indeed an experienced soldier. He had started his officer career as a Lieutenant in the First World War and was decorated for valour. In 1937 he held the rank of colonel in command of a mountain rifle regiment. He had taken part in the conquest of Austria, Czechoslovakia, Poland, Belgium, the Netherlands and France. At the time of Germany's attack on the USSR he held the rank of Major General in command of a mountain rifle division fighting in the Murmansk sector of the northern front. He was soon promoted to corps commander and served there until 1943.

Schorner had met Hitler as far back as 1920 and was, as he said himself, "one of the first German officers to join the National-Socialist movement at its inception". A fanatical anti-Communist, he proclaimed: "My enemies are the Bolsheviks!" He had fought the Communists wherever possible; in particular, in 1919 he had taken part in suppressing the Bavarian Soviet Republic and the revolutionary movement in the Rhine region.

His exploits in the invasion of European countries had earned him the Knight's Cross and, in 1944, the Oak Leaves were added to that high distinction. In the same year, Hitler, remembering Schorner's long devotion to the National-Socialist creed, appointed him Chief of Staff for the National-Socialist education of troops under the OKW (Oberkommand der Wehrmacht). However, Martin Bormann, chief of Nazi party affairs, interpreted that as a challenge to his own influence. They failed to come to terms, and Schorner was soon placed in command of Army Group A. Here, in the area of the Crimea and Rumania, Schorner demonstrated his main tactical and strategic principle: to hold his positions at all costs.

In July 1944, when the Red Army was on the offensive in the north along the Baltic coast, Schorner was made commander of Army Group North. On the eve of the New Year 1945 Hitler bestowed on him the ultimate award— diamonds to the Oak Leaves. Schorner was the 23rd man to have won that supreme distinction towards the war's end.

As evidenced by his colleagues, Schorner's chief character trait supporting his authority was cruelty. Small wonder, therefore, that his subordinates, from high-ranking officers to the rank-and-file, cringed in terror before him.

In the days of his appointment to command of Army Group Centre when he "crossed swords" with General Petrov, Schorner was embittered to the utmost and full of determination to "save Germany" as the Führer had ordered him during a private audience.

As we see, at the start of that contest Petrov had dealt Schorner two telling blows, which were praised in Stalin's orders of the day. The swift advance of the Soviet forces had thwarted the Nazi plans of razing the city of Kosice though many of its factories and historical buildings had been blown up. Kosice was Slovakia's second biggest administrative and industrial centre, and its liberation also had important political implications for the life of Czechoslovakia. It became the seat of its new government.

While directing the battle for Kosice, Petrov never left out of focus his main target—Moravska Ostrava. On January 15 he ordered the 38th Army to attack in that direction after massive artillery and air strikes at the German positions. On the next day his forces took the town of Jaslo.

In the meantime the troops of the 1st Ukrainian Front were swiftly advancing in the direction of Breslau (Wroclaw), Katowice and Krakow, which gave Petrov's right-flank forces a position of vantage. On January 18 he moved the 1st Guards Army and the 1st Czechoslovak Corps of Ludvik Svoboda into action in the key sector.

German forces were reeling on all fronts under Soviet blows following in rapid succession. Nevertheless, German reinforcements were being fed into the area of Moravska Ostrava as Schorner was making strenuous efforts to fulfil Hitler's order and hold this industrial region.

Despite the incredible difficulties of fighting in the mountains where every inch of ground had to be contested against an entrenched enemy under a skilful and tenacious commander, Petrov's troops kept dislodging Schorner's forces from their fortified defence lines.

At the end of January Stalin commended General Petrov, his Chief of Staff Lieutenant General Korzhenevich and their valiant troops in three orders of the day:

January 27.—The troops of the 4th Ukrainian Front continued their offensive in the difficult conditions of forested mountain terrain in the Carpathians and have taken by storm the towns of Vadovice, Spisska-Nova-Ves, Spisska-Stara-Ves and Levoca—important road junctions and enemy strongholds.—

January 28.—The troops of the 4th Ukrainian Front continued their offensive ... and have stormed and taken the town of Poprad, a major administrative centre of Czechoslovakia, an important road junction and enemy stronghold.—

January 29.—The troops of the 4th Ukrainian Front continued their offensive ... and have stormed and taken the town of Novy Targ, an important road junction and enemy stronghold.—

Moscow saluted the valiant forces of the 4th Ukrainian Front with a fireworks display. Having overcome the Western Carpathian Range they were now liberating towns and villages in three countries: Poland, Czechoslovakia and Hungary.

Early in February the 1st Guards Army and the 18th Army of the 4th Ukrainian Front engaged the Germans in the town of Belsko. Street fighting carried on for three days, with Soviet troops taking one building after another, and by noon on February 12 the town was liberated.

Belsko had been a key German stronghold, a veritable fortress blocking access to Moravska Ostrava. The troops and command of the 4th Ukrainian Front were congratulated in Stalin's order of the day again.

In fact, during the offensive of January and February these troops had negotiated the greater part of the Western Carpathians and advanced by 175 to 225 kilometres. It was a major contribution to the Red Army's great winter offensive to relieve the Allies in the Battle of the Bulge. The German front had been unhinged over a length of 1,200 kilometres. In East Prussia the Soviet forces had advanced by 270 kilometres, up to the lower reaches of the Vistula. From their bridgehead on the Vistula the Soviet divisions had fought their way to the lower reaches of the Oder, a distance of 570 kilometres, and from the Sandomir bridgehead they had advanced by 480 kilometres. During 40 days of fighting 300 towns were liberated, 35,000 German officers and men were taken prisoner, 3,000 aircraft, 4,500 tanks and 12,000 pieces of artillery were destroyed or captured.

In the successful operations of the closing period of the war many Soviet generals, Petrov's comrades-in-arms, and the commanders of the neighbouring 1st, 2nd, and 3rd Ukrainian Fronts Konev, Malinovsky and Tolbukhin respectively, had distinguished themselves by their skilful troop control. They were awarded the top ranks of Marshals and decorated with the Gold Stars of Heroes of the Soviet Union.

General Petrov certainly deserved equal recognition. Let us recall his tenacious defence of Odessa and Sevastopol, his role in the Germans' debâcle in their offensive on the Baku oil-fields, the prevention of catastrophe at Tuapse, the brilliant Novorossiisk operation, the rupture of the Blue Line and the liberation of Taman. On many occasions he had proved his courage and defiance in the face of death. Finally, there had been ten successive orders of the Supreme Commander congratulating him and his troops, and ten victory salutes in Moscow to honour them. Was that not sufficient for his promotion and decoration?

Unfortunately, there were reasons behind that unfair attitude to the veteran soldier. Dark clouds were again gathering over him, as will be seen in the following story.

The Battle of Moravska Ostrava

After the success of the forces of the 4th Ukrainian Front, its Military Council on February 13 submitted to the General Headquarters its plan of further operations. The plan was approved after three days.

General Petrov contemplated at first a partial thrust to improve his initial positions to be followed by a 450-kilometre penetration as far as the River Vltava and the liberation of Prague.

At the opening stage Petrov intended to capture the Moravska Ostrava industrial area. That large-scale offensive was thoroughly prepared in the period between late February and early March.

The overall strategic situation and the efforts of the Soviet forces on the neighbouring fronts favoured his own operations. The Red Army had freed the greater part of Poland and invaded Germany. After the Oder had been crossed, the distance remaining to Berlin was only 60 kilometres. The British and American forces were advancing on Berlin from the West.

Germany was heading for a catastrophe, both military and economic. Its formerly powerful industry lay in ruins and could not sustain the continued war effort. Moravska Ostrava was one of its few surviving arsenals with steel, chemical, engineering and cable plants, oil refineries and coal mines. Hitler went there in person early in March to address an assembly of high-ranking generals. He demanded that the area should be held at all costs and promised harsh punishment to be meted out to whoever would retreat under Soviet pressure.

It was explained to all officers and men that the area was the last hope of the Reich. A prisoner from the 473rd infantry regiment of the 254th Infantry Division testified:

—On March 4 the divisional commander Lieutenant General Bekker visited our regiment and addressed us with a speech. He said that Moravska Ostrava now accounted for 80 per cent of the war production. "If you surrender Moravska Ostrava", he told us, "you will give up Germany. . ."—

In addition to brainwashing and intimidation, the German Command pinned their hopes on the powerful fortifications around the city. East of it there was an old line of permanent defence works built in the twenties and thirties under the direction of French engineers, the very men who built the Maginot Line.

General Petrov was certainly not Fortune's favourite in wartime; he had to fight almost invariably against heavy odds—on sea shore, mountainous, or swampy terrain—with his own units undermanned and the enemy forces heavily outnumbering them.

In the closing battles of the war he was handicapped again. On other fronts Soviet forces had freedom of manoeuvre over vast battlefields, whereas Petrov's troops were facing formidable mountains and permanent lines of fortifications; in many areas the enemy had been defeated and paralyzed but his own forces had to pay with their blood for every inch of ground. Fierce fighting was going on in all sectors of his front. Nazi propaganda officers accompanied by Gestapo men were reading out to German troops a message reputedly written by Schorner himself:

—German soldiers! We are waging a life and death struggle. We have no reason to be scared of death. Death is predetermined for man at birth. Go to the firing lines and fight on. If you are taken prisoner, you will be shot by the Russians, if you desert to the rear, you will be shot by your own comrades, and if you defect to the Russians, your families will be liquidated at home. Now go forward and fight the enemy!. . .—

German reconnaissance patrols were operating in the rear of the 4th Ukrainian Front and were aided by Bandera's gangs supplying them with battle intelligence. The German command learned of the forthcoming offensive of the Soviet forces on Moravska Ostrava, which was later confirmed by captured enemy officers.

The target date for the offensive was March 10. On that day a gale-force wind had been blowing since dawn, the sky was overcast, visibility was zero due to heavy snowfalls. Aimed artillery fire, let alone air support, was impossible.

General Petrov arrived at the 38th Army's command post at 6:30. He grimly watched the area of the impending battle and the positions of his troops poised for attack. His mind was at work, weighing up the chances of success and the risk of failure, now that his superior firepower could not be brought into full play. In fact, it had been reduced by unfair weather to a fraction of what was needed to rip open the German defences.

His officers requested an extension of the zero hour for the same reason. Marshal Moskalenko, who was at the time in command of the 38th Army, writes:

—I reported to the General that my forces were in full readiness for attack but that artillery preparation would be ineffective. No targets were visible, and carpet firing would yield only limited results. I asked him to phone the Supreme Commander and request a postponement until the weather improved.

—Petrov objected: "The target date was fixed by General Headquarters and is final. My call won't help."

—He phoned to the Commander of the 1st Guards Army Colonel General Grechko and discussed the matter with him. The latter's opinion agreed with mine. After a long thought Petrov uttered: "It's war. We attack."—

Petrov might have been wiser to heed the opinion of his battle-wise Army Commanders rather than the direct orders from higher authority which had been made irrelevant by the circumstances, but he was a man of discipline and he also knew that a change in the offensive plan would be disapproved by General Headquarters. They would certainly have turned down his request for a postponement of his offensive at a time when the Red Army was poised for a strike at Berlin and the Wehrmacht was in fact on the brink of collapsing. He had ample reasons to presume that the morale and military might of Nazi Germany had been irreparably undermined. Twenty-six German divisions had been cut off in Courland in the north, 32 in East Prussia, and a large German group had been trapped and was being wiped out in Budapest. All these factors would favour his success in the offensive on Moravska Ostrava.

Thus, the offensive got under way at the zero hour set by the General Headquarters. The snow blizzard was going from bad to worse. The skyline was lost to view in a grey-white haze. Soviet artillery opened up precisely at

7:45. Its thunder was deafening, but only the flashes of the nearest batteries could be seen, and observation of targets hit was unthinkable. Gun crews fired at the German positions identified in advance and marked out on charts.

That was not enough for softening up the German defences, of course. The Germans, who had known of the zero hour from intelligence sources, had pulled out of the first line of defence, and Soviet artillery was pounding abandoned trenches, the main mass of the enemy forces sitting out the artillery attack in the second defence line. Both lines were shelled, it is true, but the German tactics worked and allowed them to preserve much of their strength for effective defensive combat.

The Soviet attackers met with stiff resistance as the Germans had come back to their first line, and the momentum of attack was lost. Next day the Soviet forces resumed their onslaught on the Germans and burst through their lines in a few sectors, but the pace of advance was slow. They could not gain more than three miles of ground for all their efforts during a full day's flight. The offensive was being bogged down and after a week it was clear that it would soon come to a halt.

Petrov took another decision: to take advantage of the success of his neighbours on the right flank—the troops of the 1st Ukrainian Front, which had engaged the Germans in the town of Ratibor, and to direct the main strike of Colonel General Moskalenko's 38th Army at Moravska Ostrava from the north. He re-grouped his forces and launched them into another offensive on March 24.

This time the weather favoured the attackers, and the clear sky gave the Soviet air force the long awaited chance to knock out gun emplacements and tanks and deliver punches at German troop concentrations in the vulnerable spots of the defence line. Simultaneously, Soviet artillery kept pounding the defenders for a full 45 minutes, the gunners working with clockwork precision now that their targets were in full view.

A solid wall of clods of earth and indescribable debris, flames and smoke rose from the German positions after every Soviet barrage. The ground shook under the impact of the explosions, as if during an earthquake. German guns and their crews which recieved direct hits flew into the air like rag toys, and heavy tanks were overturned by air blasts like empty tin cans. The gods of war seemed to have unleashed their wrath on the invaders.

Now Petrov's troops went over the top. The fight was short and fierce, and German resistance crumbled all along the line. Towards the day's end the Soviet forces had forced the Germans from more than twenty towns, including Zorau, which lay on the main route of the Soviet offensive stalled a few days ago.

During the night the German Command had massed large forces to check the Soviet advance, but it had already gathered momentum, and another Soviet artillery attack was followed by another breakthrough. Petrov fed the 1st Guards Army and the 18th Army into the battle to distract the German forces from the key sector of Soviet attack.

The offensive was going well, and the 38th Army took the town of Jory at the approaches to Moravska Ostrava. The city itself was only 15 to 20 kilometres away. In the meantime the 18th Army had gained about 70 kilometres of contested ground, while the 1st Czechoslovak Corps had besieged the town of Jilina. The troops of the 4th Ukrainian Front had advanced by 50 to 70 kilometres in the course of these battles.

German defeat was imminent, but Schorner, tough soldier that he was, did not despair and was determined to fight on and to stifle the Soviet offensive. He moved two panzer divisions to ward off the main thrust of the 38th Army and sent more troops to counter-attack the 1st Guards Army and the 18th Army, hoping to take the edge off the Soviet drive and bring it to a halt before the formidable fortifications of Moravska Ostrava.

The Soviet forces foiled his plan and were forging ahead at a steady rate, bypassing German pockets of resistance, which were to be mopped up by troops of the second echelon. The 38th Army widened its breakthrough to 20 kilometres along the front and captured 15 kilometres of enemy territory in frontal attacks during the second day of fighting alone.

Neither the old ingenious fortifications built by the engineers of the Maginot Line nor the modern defence works erected by German engineers could stave off the advance of the Soviet troops. The town of Loslau was taken on March 26, which meant a rupture of the main German line of permanent fortifications.

That was a spectacular success. General Petrov's skilful change of the direction of attack, when the battle seemed to be lost, had worked. His valiant troops had overcome all obstacles—tank traps, pillboxes, escarps and, most important of all, the bitter resistance of the German troops fighting to the last ditch.

This time, however, there were no congratulations from Stalin, no victory salutes in Moscow but, like a bolt from the blue, there was a strange order, just like one of those which had shaken his life before: he was dismissed from command of the 4th Ukrainian Front. The new Front Commander who had arrived to take over from him was General Yeremenko, the very same man who had replaced him in the Battle of Kerch.

What Happened?

Strange as it may seem, it is harder work describing events of real life than writing fiction. Inventing the plot of his story and its characters, a novelist is free to choose whatever and whoever his imagination suggests to him. When writing a work based on true-life situations and hard facts, he must be capable of reproducing a picture consistent with the historical truth from a wealth of material coloured with predilections and prejudice however true to fact. One must be capable of rising above the emotions, likes and dislikes of those who supplied this first-hand information. The next task is to rise above one's own subjectivity in making an assessment as close to what really happened and motivated his heroes as possible.

Once all the details have been sorted out and woven into a coherent picture, the succession of events can be played back and committed to writing. Let us now try to analyze the reasons for Petrov's demotion, relying on eyewitness accounts.

The renowned Soviet author Konstantin Simonov, who was staying with Petrov's headquarters as a war correspondent at the time, gave this account:

—I happened to witness in March 1945 the dismissal of General Petrov from command of his Front, which was as unexpected to him as to his staff. I can testify that nothing resembling a setback for his troops, even distantly, had occurred prior to that strange decision.—

General Shtemenko, Chief of Operations at the General Staff, who was familiar with all the events of those days, writes about Petrov's earlier dismissal from command of the 2nd Byelorussian Front as a result of his denunciation by Military Council member Mekhlis, remarking that the latter sent similar messages to Stalin from the 4th Ukrainian Front.

General Moskalenko recalls that General of the Army Antonov, recently appointed Chief of the General Staff, phoned him one night to find out about the progress of the offensive on Moravska Ostrava:

—The Supreme Commander wants to know the reasons for the setbacks on your Front. What's your opinion?

—But my information is limited, and then, can I speak for the Front Commander?

—Stalin has received a message from Colonel General Mekhlis and wants to know the details.—

Needless to say, sending messages up the chain of command is not reprehensible, if their author presents an honest and truthful interpretation of events, seeking to promote the common cause. Mekhlis, I am afraid, had different motives, appealing to what were by no means the better sides of Stalin's character.

The result was not long in coming. Everything was forgotten: congratulations on victories, salutes in Moscow, and even the fact that Petrov's divisions were undermanned and exhausted by the fierce battles for the Carpathians.

But let us be lenient on the late veterans. *Errare humanum est* (To err is human), the ancient Romans used to say. That might have been an expression of ingrained bias, probably well-intentioned, if not quite consistent with ethics. Mekhlis was a prominent statesman and party leader after all. He had good sides and bad sides, and I am writing about only one episode from his biography without adding to or detracting from it.

... General Petrov preserved his outward equanimity on learning of his dismissal without betraying anything like embarrassment or nervousness, but his inner tension can easily be imagined. He reflected bitterly on his chances of further service now that the war was coming to a victorious conclusion. A general who had done so much for victory was so unfairly denied his place among the victors.

Petrov knew that he had been denounced by Mekhlis, which is evidenced by his own story at a later time and the opinion of his colleagues familiar with all the details of his affairs.

To sum up the circumstances that had led to another sudden twist in his life, it may be recalled that the bad weather had played havoc with the opening of his offensive on Moravska Ostrava, that Petrov, ignoring the advice of his subordinate generals, had refrained from requesting the General Headquarters to postpone the zero hour, which can be blamed not on a lack of foresight but on his desire to avoid another complication in his relations with the Supreme Commander. As we can see, a memory of injustice may cause more harm. Even a battle-hardened general may falter at times under the heavy burden of sad recollections.

For all that, the offensive so difficult at the start, had steadily gained momentum and brought about successful, if not brilliant, results and, it would be relevant to recall, at the cost of fewer casualties than those suffered under identical battle conditions on the neighbouring 1st Ukrainian Front under the command of Marshal Konev.

Moreover, as Marshal Konev reminisced, "On March 24, following a short pause in hostilities, the 38th Army under its brave commander Moskalenko pushed forward again and by a series of resolute attacks dislodged the Germans from their positions facing the left flank of the 60th Army. In the area of Rybnik and Ratibor the Germans were now in danger of being trapped. Thus we had a good spring-board for storming these towns. The 60th Army captured Rybnik and crossed the Oder south of Ratibor."

On March 26 Petrov's forces ruptured the first line of German fortifications and took the towns of Zorau and Loslau and more than forty villages south of Moravska Ostrava. In the evening Moscow saluted the troops of the 1st Ukrainian Front, but the Supreme Commander's order of the day made no mention of the role of Petrov's forces in those battles.

The Battle of Berlin

General Petrov's apprehensions concerning his future proved unfounded. Early in April of 1945 he was appointed Chief of Staff of the 1st Ukrainian Front. Marshal Konev writes in his memoirs:

—... My Chief of Staff in the Battle of Berlin was General of the Army Petrov, who had taken over from General Sokolovsky assigned to serve as deputy to Marshal Zhukov on the 1st Byelorussian Front. Shortly before that I had had a phone call from Stalin who had asked me if I would agree to have General Petrov as my Chief of Staff.

—I was informed of Petrov's recent suspension, but his impressive war record spoke for itself, so I said yes. On the next day after his arrival, Petrov was requested to compile a daily battle report for the General Headquarters. We had usually completed it a couple of hours after midnight, and I mentioned that to him.

—"You needn't worry, Comrade Marshal. I will have it ready before midnight," he reassured me.

—I called him at 2:00 but the report was still pending, because full information about one of the Armies had yet to be gathered. I granted him an extension until 4:00, but he could not submit it until 6:00. As I was signing it after making a few amendments, Petrov said apologetically: "I'm sorry I couldn't make it on time. In fact, I'm new to this job, and I have yet to learn to handle such a vast scope of operations."

—"Never mind, General", I comforted him. "We live and learn."

—He is modest, I thought. That was a promise of good teamwork in our joint service. I was not disappointed, to be sure. Petrov was as good as his word. He had a sound knowledge of military doctrine, which commanded general respect, and his courage and presence of mind made him a popular figure in the Red Army.

—Petrov served as Chief of Staff on my Front until the last day of the war, in which, as I hope, we had done our part as best we could.—

Petrov's new duties were, indeed, a challenge to his competence and stamina. The troop strength on the 1st Ukrainian Front was much greater than he had ever had under his command, and the battle situation was accordingly more complex.

At the beginning of the Vistula-Oder operation the 1st Ukrainian Front under Marshal Konev's command consisted of eight Armies: Colonel General Zhadov's 5th Guards Army, Colonel General Gusev's 21st Army, Colonel General Koroteyev's 52nd Army, Colonel General Kurochkin's 60th Army, Colonel General Pukhov's 13th Army, Lieutenant General Korovnikov's 59th Army, Colonel General Gordov's 3rd Guards Army, Lieutenant General Gluzdovsky's 6th Army; two Tank Armies: Colonel General Rybalko's 3rd Guards Army and Colonel General Lelyushenko's 4th Army; Colonel General Krasovsky's 2nd Air Army. Finally, the Front contained separate armoured and mechanized corps, a cavalry corps, a few artillery attack corps and divisions, and many other units.

Planning battles and logistic supply for such enormous masses of men and machines and gathering intelligence to forestall effective enemy resistance and setbacks involved a responsibility where any error was unthinkable. His staff duties meant hard work almost round the clock.

Petrov arrived at the 1st Ukrainian Front at the time when work had just got under way to plan the final offensive on Berlin. That operation, without precedent in scope and force of attack in the history of the Second World War, was to be finalized in detail by the command of the Fronts involved, and Petrov as Marshal Konev's closest assistant took part in planning it along with other Chiefs of Staff, as General Shtemenko testified in his reminiscences.

It would be relevant to mention here a circumstance that compelled the General Headquarters and the staffs of the Front which were to fight in the Battle of Berlin to speed up its planning. The Soviet High Command had learned of a message that Winston Churchill had sent to President Roosevelt on April 1, which said in part that nothing would produce a greater psychological effect and cause greater despair among all German resistance forces than the fall of Berlin. It would be the most conclusive proof of defeat to the German nation.

... The Russian armies will certainly invade the whole of Austria and enter Vienna. If they also take Berlin, will they not form an exaggerated idea of their overwhelming contribution to our common victory and develop a mentality that will cause serious and very considerable difficulties in the future? I believe, therefore, that for political reasons we should advance in Germany as far eastwards as possible and that by all means we should take Berlin if it happens to be within our reach. This seems reasonable from the military standpoint as well. (*Re-translated from the Russian. Translator*).

Stalin immediately summoned Marshals Zhukov and Konev to Moscow for a conference. After General Shtemenko had read out Churchill's message to them, Stalin inquired:

"Who do you think will take Berlin: us or our Allies?" After a brief discussion with the Marshals and members of his staff, he concluded in a peremptory tone: "Berlin should be taken as soon as possible. There's no time to be lost. Your battle plan must be prepared at once. Is that clear?"

Marshals Zhukov and Konev came up with their tentative plan while they were in Moscow, and Stalin approved it. They flew back to their frontline headquarters and got down to work to draw up detailed battle plans. General Petrov's competence and ingenuity made his advice invaluable, and the plans for his Front were completed in record time, to Marshal Konev's tremendous satisfaction.

There was an interesting development in the planning of the Berlin operation. The Supreme Commander, who had recently placed his deputy, Marshal Zhukov, in command of the 1st Byelorussian Front, determined that Berlin would have to be taken precisely by the latter's forces. Stalin probably wanted to emphasize the special role of Marshal Zhukov, who had done so much for victory over Nazi Germany.

The Commander of the 1st Ukrainian Front, Marshal Konev, however, thought that decision unfair; he believed that he also had a right and a capability to take part in storming the capital of Nazi Germany. One only has to imagine what Berlin symbolized at the time to the Soviet soldiers who had been fighting for four long years and seen so many deaths and so much destruction in their native land to understand their impassioned desire to see that city with their own eyes and totally subdue it.

The General Staff had a direct order from Stalin to assign a different task to the 1st Ukrainian Front: to defeat the Germans south of Berlin, in the Kotbus area, to capture the Beelitz–Wittenberg line south-west of Berlin and advance to the Elbe. The main strike was to be delivered by three infantry armies and two tank armies. Marshal Konev reasonably believed that with such enormous strength in his hands and with other armies under his control he could not only cross the Elbe but also make a thrust at Berlin, especially as at the conference held at the General Headquarters on April 1 he had received instructions from Stalin to provide in his battle plan for a possible attack of his tank armies in the northerly direction, that is against Berlin.

As the participants in that conference recall, Stalin stood at the map for some time, thinking, then took a pencil and crossed out the part of the dividing line between the theatres of operations of the 1st Byelorussian and the 1st Ukrainian fronts, which separated the latter from Berlin, preserving only part of the line, up to Lübben, which is some 60 kilometres south-east of Berlin. Then he said curtly: "Let the one who will break into Berlin first take it."

Marshal Zhukov's 1st Byelorussian Front launched their attack in the dead of night on April 16. Hundreds of lorry-mounted searchlights were secretly moved into the assembly area shortly before zero hour and were turned on simultaneously to blind the German troops, while Soviet artillery opened fire at targets now visible as clearly as in broad daylight. This was a complete surprise to the Germans and caused panic in their ranks. Soviet tanks and infantry followed in the wake of the artillery barrages. They overran the German positions and were soon in close pursuit of the enemy fleeing to the second line of defence and seeking safety behind its powerful fortifications.

The 1st Ukrainian Front under Marshal Konev used a different way of surprising the Germans. Its forces were to cross the Neisse and attack the enemy positions on its western bank. The attack followed a very long artillery preparation; the German positions were pounded for 2 hours and 25 minutes to secure an effective suppression of German fire power.

Soviet chemical support troops, artillery and attack planes set up an enormous smokescreen all along the 310-kilometre front of attack. Marshal Konev recalls: "The wind speed was a mere half a metre per second, and the smoke was slowly crawling into the depth of the German defence area, screening the entire valley of the Neisse, which was exactly what we needed."

At 6:55 Marshal Konev's troops started crossing the Neisse under cover of smoke and artillery fire, and the first echelon reached the opposite bank after an hour, captured bridgeheads and pushed its way forward in the face of fierce German resistance. The 3rd, 5th and 13th Armies punched a 26-kilometre-wide hole in the German defences and advanced by some 10 kilometres in one day.

The fighting on that broad front varied in intensity in its different parts. Some divisions of Pukhov's 13th Army and Zhadov's 5th Guards Army had ruptured the second line of defence and were forging ahead towards the third line, and even reached the approaches to the Spree at some places, whereas on the battlefields of other Armies some corps had captured only the first defence line and some divisions were fighting in the second line. The flanks of Soviet units, therefore, often became exposed to desperate German counter-attacks and needed constant protection.

For that reason the average rate of the Soviet offensive in the early days of the Battle of Berlin proved slower than planned, because, as Marshal Konev said revealingly:

—We plan alone but we fulfil our plans together with the enemy, as it were, in accordance with his opposition.—

In an effort to stop and hurl back the attackers the German Command committed to action six panzer, one motorized and five infantry divisions during the first two days. Knowing that their days were numbered and that the final retribution was not far distant, the Nazis were desperately clinging to every inch of ground, throwing into battle whatever reserves they could still mobilize.

On the whole, however, the Soviet offensive was developing successfully. The clear sky favoured the Soviet Air Force. During the first three days Soviet aircraft made a total of 7,517 sorties, and fighters brought down 155 German planes in aerial combat over the battlefields.

Marshal Konev was in the vanguard of the advancing forces, directing the moves of his tank armies. One of Petrov's concerns was wiping out numerous German forces remaining in the rear of Soviet troops. Marshal of the Armoured Forces Rybalko writes in his reminiscences:

—We were rolling forward without a stop, and German divisions not yet destroyed remained behind us. We were not worried about our supply routes because we knew that the High Command had taken steps to protect our flanks and rear during the operation.—

The tank armies were fighting on the battle fronts, while the infantry armies on the flanks were fighting off German forces trying to close the breach made by Soviet armour.

. . . In the meantime, Marshal Zhukov's 1st Byelorussian Front was advancing on Berlin from the east, its troops mounting frontal attacks to break through the deeply echeloned German defences bristling with cannon, tank and infantry. Marshal Zhukov's troops were having a hard time fighting their way forward.

Knowing of the swift advance of the tank armies of the 1st Ukrainian Front, Stalin instructed Marshal Konev:

"The going is tough for Marshal Zhukov, so turn Rybalko's and Lelyushenko's armies towards Zelendorf, as we agreed at our last conference."

The two armies swung almost at right angles, one to the north, the other to the north-west. Rybalko's 3rd Tank Army was to force a crossing over the Spree on the night of April 18 and burst into the city's southern quarter at night on April 20. Lelyushenko's 4th Tank Army was to capture Potsdam and the south-western quarter of Berlin in the meantime.

. . . In 1984 the present writer visited the German Democratic Republic and went to the district where Rybalko's Army had swiftly turned and attacked Berlin from the south.

I travelled through that district, visiting its small towns and strolling in its fields and forests, trying to imagine what they had looked like on that distant day in April when thousands of tanks, their engines roaring and their caterpillars beating the wet soil into an ocean of mud, rushed forward to the German capital. These were the world's best tanks, built by Soviet workers, constantly underfed, underslept and exhausted by hard work during the four years of the war. The tankmen, their faces stained with oil and smoke, had not slept for three days but they did not feel tired. They were full of enthusiasm: victory was near, the hateful war would soon be over. They were spoiling for a fight which would be the last one.

I also took a walk in the vicinity of Zossen. On April 20, 1945, Rybalko's tanks had forced their way into it—a spectacular "birthday present" to the Führer and very symbolic at that: the town was the seat of the High Command of the Wehrmacht. It was here that the Barbarossa Plan of invasion of the USSR had been hatched. And then, a staggering denouement: Soviet tanks demolishing that devil's workshop which had unleashed war on humanity.

I considered the two- and three-storeyed mansions of pleasant design picturesquely located in a fragrant pine forest. The serene beauty of that place made me think of the cosy living of its former inhabitants, those who had caused so much suffering to the peoples of Europe and their own German people.

I imagined them paying visits to one another, raising their glasses in congratulation on the conquest of the cities of Poland, France, Belgium, Denmark, Greece and many other countries. They were bursting with arrogance and conceit, persuading themselves that they were definitely the choicest members of the "master race" when their troops had reached the Volga and the approaches to Baku. In these mansions they had plotted the routes and time-tables of their troop movements to Iran, Iraq, Afghanistan and India.

Although I fought the Nazis on my native soil, all that seems unreal today, as if it was a nightmare. Could I, a front line officer, imagine in 1942 that I would be walking some day among the buildings of Hitler's headquarters. Such an idea would not cross my mind even in a dream.

And now I was here nevertheless, forty years after the former masters of this place had fled, scared of being captured and brought to account for all the evil they had done. In my mind's eye I saw them scampering in confusion over the well-kept grass lawns, hastily burning their criminal plans, and then running away disguised in civilian clothes to avoid being caught and identified as Hitler's accomplices.

The Soviet author Boris Polevoi wrote in one of his wartime newspaper articles about the goings-on here in the final hours. Here is an excerpt from conversations between German military commanders in southern Germany and the Zossen communications centre manned by four drunken ratings trapped in their underground bunker.

—Edelweiss: Transmit this message to General Krebs immediately. We learn about developments from British broadcasts. Report the situation. We expect orders for further action. Signed A-15. Over.

—Zossen: We can transmit nothing. We are buried alive. Over.

—Edelweiss: Stop your silly jokes. Who is on the line? Call the duty officer at once. A-15. Over.

—Zossen: The officer has bolted. All have bolted. Over.

—Edelweiss: Who is the drunken beast on the line? Call the duty officer at once. Over.

—Zossen: Kiss your granny on the arse, you idiot. Over.

—Edelweiss: U-16 here. Urgent. Over.

—Zossen: Don't hurry your hangman. Over.

—Edelweiss: I don't understand, Repeat. Over.

—Zossen: You stinking moron. All have got away. The Russians are walking all over us. They will get you, too. Over.

—Edelweiss: I demand connection with Krebs. Report the situation in Berlin. Over.

—Zossen: It's drizzling in Berlin. Get lost. Over.

—Edelweiss: Who is on the line. Report your name and rank. Over.

—Zossen: You are a bore. All have left. Russian tanks are on top of us. You dirty pig. Shut up. Over.—

These days were very hard for General Petrov. While the tank armies were approaching the outskirts of Berlin, the situation on the flanks of the Soviet breakthrough had worsened. On April 20 the Germans mounted fierce counter-attacks and checked the advance of the 52nd Army, pushing the 2nd Polish Army a few miles to the north. The Kotbus grouping of enemy forces was threatening the base of the corridor formed by the thrust of the Soviet tank armies.

Fighting was going on in many parts both in front of and to the rear of the Soviet forces: on the right flank tense battles for Kotbus continued without a respite, in the centre of the front the Soviet troops met a stronghold of German resistance, on the left flank the situation in the Dresden sector was not shaping favourably for Soviet troops; another large group of German troops trapped in Breslau by General Gluzdovsky's 6th Army was desperately fighting back.

Thus, an area a few hundred miles long and across was like a boiling cauldron with fighting continuing relentlessly in all places.

The flanks of the 1st Byelorussian and the 1st Ukrainian Front were steadily closing around Berlin. By the end of April 22 Lelyushenko's tank army was within 40 kilometres of General Perkhorovich's 47th Army of the 1st Byelorussian Front, while Rybalko's tank army was 12 kilometres away from Chuikov's 8th Guards Army. Thus, two rings of encirclement around Berlin were being formed simultaneously. Stalin demanded that Marshals Zhukov and Konev complete this double encirclement by April 24, the first ring girdling Berlin and the second, the Frankfurt on Oder group of German forces.

But what was happening in the enemy camp at this time?

Evidently aiming to encourage his protégé, as he had repeatedly done before in relation to his other stooges, Hitler made Schorner a Field Marshal. On April 22, Schorner had his last meeting with the Führer in the Reichschancery. Hitler spoke to him in confidence, requesting the newly-promoted Field Marshal to give him a chance, at whatever cost, to negotiate a peace settlement with the Western Allies.

"It is necessary to fight on until a politically favourable withdrawal from the war has been prepared. Good prerequisites exist for concluding a separate peace with Great Britain and the United States, which detest the idea of Berlin falling to the Russians. Consolidation of the military might of Bolshevist Russia and an increase in her influence in Europe are not consistent with their interests."

Simultaneously, the Führer called off all resistance to the Allied forces in the West and ordered Wenck's 12th Army and Busse's 9th Army to come to the rescue of Berlin's besieged garrison and to break the Soviet pincers closing around it.

The thrust of Wenck's and Busse's armies were directed against the troops of the 1st Ukrainian Front as well. They had to cope with the formidable task of repelling these thrusts while carrying on their offensive on Berlin.

On April 24, the forces of the 1st Byelorussian and the 1st Ukrainian Fronts linked up in the rear of Busse's 9th Army and completely isolated it from Berlin. That night Rybalko's tankmen cut the inner ring of defence works protecting Berlin's central quarter from the south and burst into the city.

On the same day, the vanguard of Wenck's army engaged the Soviet forces besieging Berlin in an effort to relieve its garrison. Fierce fighting ensued.

The thrusts of Wenck's forces were opposed by Lelyushenko's tankmen and the airmen of Ryazanov's attack aircraft corps. The latter were known as past masters of antitank warfare capable of pinpointing their targets and hitting them at pointblank range by treetop flying. German panzers were soon turned into smoking scrap metal scattered over the battlefield as far as the eye could see.

Hitler, trapped in his bombproof bunker, was hysterical and euphoric at the same time, speaking with inspiration about his coming rescue by Wenck's troops, though it was increasingly obvious that his last hope had been dashed.

While repelling Wenck's strikes on his left flank, Lelyushenko was pursuing his offensive on his right flank. At noon on April 25 his tankmen linked up with the troops of Perkhorovich's Army. Thus, the two fronts had securely closed the ring of encirclement around the troops defending the German capital. Lelyushenko's tanks and Perkhorovich's infantry went ahead with their offensive on Potsdam, foiling Wenck's attempts to fight his way into Berlin. In the meantime, Busse's 9th Army was making desperate efforts to break out of its trap but was driven back, suffering heavy casualties.

On April 25 Stalin addressed his next order of the day to the two Army Groups besieging Berlin:

—To Marshal Zhukov and Colonel General Malinin.

—To Marshal Konev and General of the Army Petrov.

—The troops of the 1st Byelorussian front have severed all the routes from Berlin to the west and today have linked up north-west of Potsdam with the troops of the 1st Ukrainian Front, completing the encirclement of Berlin.—

On the same day, April 25, 1944, the troops of General Zhadov's 5th Guards Army of the 1st Ukrainian Front linked up with the Allied forces on the Elbe. Stalin's order of the day issued on that occasion read in part:

—The troops of the 1st Ukrainian Front and our Anglo-American allies have cut the German front by their strikes from the east and west and at 13:30 on April 25 have met in the area of Torgau in Central Germany. The German forces in Northern Germany have thereby been cut off from the German forces in Southern Germany.—

The Germans, however, were continuing the fight, and in the Dresden sector Schörner even ruptured the Soviet front at the junction between General Koroteyev's 52nd Army and General Swerciewski's 2nd Polish Army and burst out into the latter's rear. The 5th Guards Army had to deal with that new danger immediately in accordance with Konev's and Petrov's instructions. Petrov went to the battle area to handle the situation on the spot.

General Krainyukov, who was Military Council member of the 1st Ukrainian Front, recalls:

—The counterblow dealt by the German forces at the rear of the 2nd Polish Army definitely had a political as well as a military motive. German officers for National-Socialist training of troops were fomenting hatred of the Poles and calling for their extermination with the same ferocity as of the Russian Bolsheviks.—

The Polish Army Commander Swerciewski was an illustrious figure. He was a veteran of the October Revolution of 1917 in Russia who had joined the Bolshevik Party in 1918. He had fought the White Guards in the Civil War on the Western and other fronts. On graduating from the Frunze Military Academy in Moscow, he had served in various command and staff posts in the Red Army. He had fought in the Spanish Civil War for three years under the assumed name of General Walter as commander of the 14th International Brigade of Russian, Polish, American, British, Spanish, Italian and German volunteers. In the early period of the German invasion of the USSR he had been a divisional commander on the Western front and was later responsible for raising troops for the 2nd Polish Army.

The Soviet Guards and their Polish comrades hurled the Germans back and sealed the breach. The offensive on Dresden continued. Reporting the situation to Marshal Konev, Petrov remarked:

"The 1st Byelorussian Front was in difficulty at the early stage of the siege of Berlin, but now life is easier for our neighbours. Their rear is no longer threatened, while we are under attack from the west and east."

Indeed, the Soviet troops fighting in Berlin and holding off the German attackers trying to relieve its garrison needed regular supplies of ammunition, fuel and provisions. Not infrequently, Petrov had to organize full-scale battles to free the roads for Soviet logistic convoys. Busse's 9th Army trapped between the two rings of encirclement made an attempt to break them and link up with Wenck's army. The 9th Army was a large force with 14 divisions and numerous special units, a total of 200,000 officers and men.

Busse delivered his main strike in the direction of Kukkenwalde and at the peak of the fighting for Berlin his troops severed all communication lines between the headquarters of the armies besieging or encircling Berlin. The Soviet staffs had to rely on their radios, but troop control was fully preserved.

Busse's units trying to break through Soviet lines and escape to the west occasionally ran into key elements of the Soviet battle order. In one area the headquarters of the 4th Tank Guards Army came under attack. All staff officers with Army Commander Lelyushenko himself fought off the invaders with hand guns, machine pistols and hand grenades. They were helped out by the men of the 7th Motorcycle Battalion deployed nearby. No sooner had the fighting subsided than alarm signals came from the headquarters of the 9th

Fighter Aircraft Division. A stray German unit had attacked its airfield. The airmen and ground crews fought back with whatever arms they had at hand and repelled the first assault. The divisional commander Pokryshkin, the famous fighter ace with 59 kills to his record, took part in that battle. Soviet reinforcements were rushed in to rescue the airmen. In the fierce fighting that followed the Germans were dispersed and 3,000 of them were taken prisoner.

On April 28, General Hans Krebs, Chief of the General Staff, issued his last desperate order:

—All units fighting between the Elbe and the Oder are hereby enjoined to use all available manpower and weapons to bring their general offensive to a speedy and successful conclusion and rescue the capital of the Reich.—

It was a voice in the wilderness. Nobody responded. The Wehrmacht was in the agony of death and unable to save the Third Reich and its Führer from their doom.

At midnight on April 29 Alfred Jodl, Chief of the OKW Operational Staff and Hitler's chief adviser on military strategy, received the Führer's last message:

—Report immediately: 1. Where is Wenck's army? 2. When will it resume the offensive? 3. Where is the 9th Army? 4. What is its target area? 5. Where is Holste's corps?—

The answer was short and meaningful: 1. Wenck's vanguard is reportedly west of Lake Swilow. 2. The 12th Army is unable to advance towards Berlin. 3. The 9th Army is encircled. 4. Holste's corps is under attack.

By a series of concentric blows Marshal Zhukov's and Marshal Konev's troops finally routed the trapped German groups. Stalin commended them in his next order:

—The troops of the 1st Byelorussian and the 1st Ukrainian Front have defeated the German forces surrounded south-east of Berlin. Between April 24 and May 2 more than 120,000 laid down their arms.—

There was another gun salute in Moscow on May 2 and later in the day Stalin's next order and another gun salute announced the fall of Berlin.

The order said:

—The troops of the 1st Byelorussian Front under the command of Marshal of the Soviet Union Zhukov in co-operation with the troops of the 1st Ukrainian Front under the command of Marshal of the Soviet Union Konev, after a period of fierce street fighting, have completed the rout of the Berlin group of German forces and today, May 2, 1945, have established their full control over the capital of Germany, the centre of German imperialism and the seedbed of German aggression.

—The Berlin garrison which defended the city under the command of the Chief of Defence of Berlin, General of Artillery Weidling, and his staff has ceased fire at 1500 hours today, laid down their arms and surrendered.

—By 2100 hours on May 2 the Soviet forces in the city of Berlin had taken more than 70,000 German officers and men prisoner. . . —

Hitler's army, which had laid claim to world supremacy, now reached its final stage of degradation. One illustration of that is the scene of despair witnessed by Erich Kempka, Hitler's personal chauffeur and an SS man, after leaving the bunker where he had been sheltering along with the Führer's retinue:

—... A horrible picture caught my eye. Soldiers tired to death, wounded people left without care, and refugees lying against house walls, on the steps of staircases, on platforms. Most of these people had abandoned all hope of escaping to safety and looked indifferent to what was going on around them.—

Indeed, they had nowhere to escape. That was the ultimate end of all their illusions. Many of them who had once dreamt of a landed estate in the East, hoping for a share in the rich spoils of war, could now only hope for survival.

The Rescue of Prague

Before committing suicide, Hitler, who had wreaked so many disasters and untold suffering on his own German people, had attempted, nevertheless, to salvage the Third Reich and in his political last will bequeathed his powers to Grand Admiral Karl Dönitz, who became the head of the new German Government. By that act the Führer hoped to give a semblance of legality to the new governing body which would inherit his ideas and, because it was new, could hope for some lenience on the part of the victor powers.

The Dönitz government had fairly large forces at its disposal, and they were continuing the fight. These were Army Group Courland on the Baltic coast, the remnants of Wenck's 12th Army west of Berlin, and the largest group— Army Group Centre under Field Marshal Schörner's command in Czechoslovakia. The latter contained up to 50 divisions, many special units and new formations composed of the remnants of defeated regular forces. In Western Czechoslovakia the Allies were opposed by the German 5th Army of five divisions also subordinated to Schörner. In Austria the troops of Army Group Austria were keeping up their resistance, and in Yugoslavia Army Group "F" was fighting the Soviet troops and the units of the People's Liberation Army.

In his broadcast statement on May 1, Dönitz declared:

—The Führer has appointed me his successor. At this hour of trial for Germany I am assuming the duties of the head of government and am fully aware of the responsibility devolving upon me. My first duty is to save the Germans from extermination by the advancing Bolsheviks. It is only in the name of this goal that we continue to fight.—

The Dönitz government went out of its way to allow as many German troops as possible to retreat to the West and surrender to the Western Allies. Schörner was also instructed by Dönitz to promptly complete the withdrawal of his Armies beyond the Elbe into the zone of operations of the Anglo-American troops. Schörner, however, disagreed with Dönitz but not because he was unwilling to surrender to the Western Allies. As an experienced general he realized that as soon as his Armies pulled out of their fortified positions, they would be overtaken and routed by Soviet troops. He said that he could hold on to his lines for a long time and even suggested that Dönitz move his government to Prague and place it under the protection of his Army Group.

For the Soviet side the urgency of taking Prague was motivated not only by its desire to bring the war to an end as soon as possible but also by the recent developments in the city. Inspired by the successes of the Red Army, the people of Prague had risen in arms against the German invaders. Schörner ordered his troops: "The uprising in Prague must be suppressed by every means." Knowing of his ferocity, it is easy to imagine the ominous implications of this order.

German reinforcements were converging on the city from all sides. The insurgents of Prague were poorly armed and desperately needed prompt assistance. The leaders of the uprising appealed for help over the radio.

The Soviet General Headquarters ordered the Commanders of the 1st, 2nd and 3rd Ukrainian Fronts to plan and carry out what came to be known as Operation Prague and to support the insurgents.

Now Petrov's known skill in mountain warfare proved invaluable. Marshal Konev had avoided fighting in mountain areas. All his experience of earlier battles was based on operations carried out on flat open, forested or swampy terrain. Mountains, as he admitted, were good only for protecting his flanks.

General Krainyukov testifies:

—The Chief of Staff of the 1st Ukrainian Front Petrov played a crucial role in planning Operation Prague. As a former Commander of the 4th Ukrainian Front which had freed part of Czechoslovak territory he was familiar with geographical details of military significance, road networks and fortifications. He explained that the approaches to Prague were covered by the Rudny Mountain Range extending for almost 150 kilometres. To the north, in the Dresden area, there were gigantic sandstone cliffs and forested plateaux cleaved by the Elbe and its tributaries.

—"This locality of unusual scenic beauty has been dubbed a Saxon Switzerland", Petrov remarked, "but the mountains may cause us no end of trouble. If we get stuck up on the mountain passes or take a respite in this Saxon Switzerland, we may suffer unnecessary casualties and fail to cut off the avenues of retreat of Schörner's Army Group. . . ."

—The Front Military Council resolved to deal swift and powerful strikes at the German forces to straddle the roads across the Rudny Mountains and allow the Soviet mobile troops to break out onto the plains beyond.—

The Soviet Command expected the Germans to put up the stiffest resistance on the roads leading to Prague and hence decided to form special units which could bypass enemy strongholds by climbing steep rocks and stealing their way along narrow gorges behind German pockets of resistance, and then attack them in the rear. These units were made up of troops of various arms and supplied with engineering equipment for clearing obstacles and repairing roads and bridges to maintain a steady rate of advance.

A powerful group of three Infantry Armies commanded by Generals

Pukhov, Gordov and Zhadov respectively, Rybalko's and Lelyushenko's Tank Armies and Poluboyarov's and Fominykh's Tank Corps was formed for a thrust towards Prague. This group was supported by five artillery divisions.

In planning Operation Prague the speed of advance was given top priority lest Schörner's troops rolling backwards under Soviet blows had time to join up with the SS and other special forces. The latter were fighting to suppress the uprising and unleash their vengeance and blind hatred on the insurgents, massacre peaceful civilians and raze the city itself to the ground. Therefore, Rybalko's and Lelyushenko's Tank Armies advancing from different directions were to outstrip Schörner's forces, break into Prague and rout its German garrison. Their next move would be to attack Schörner's forces retreating towards Prague.

In the meantime, Pukhov's Army was to cut off the German avenues of retreat west of Prague and wipe out the enemy forces in co-operation with the troops of the 2nd and 3rd Ukrainian Fronts advancing on the city from the south and south-west.

General Krasovsky's 2nd Air Army was to support the operations of the Soviet main forces with 1,900 aircraft in the central sector and 355 in the auxiliary directions. The Soviet airmen were to prevent German troop redeployment and retreat to the West.

The Army Commanders were briefed at a conference called by Marshal Konev on May 4. "I want you to deliver a lightning strike", the Marshal said. "You should literally fly over the Rudny Mountains and the Sudetes. Don't engage in lengthy fighting for strongholds or towns, bypass them and push forward. The tanks will lead the way. The Germans left behind you will be mopped up by infantry. And I expect you to be humane to those willing to surrender. Avoid bloodshed when possible. Don't wipe out trapped German groups but send out truce envoys to persuade them to give up. They have in fact lost the war anyway."

Shortly before zero hour, on the night of May 6, the Czech National Council radioed an SOS:

—German panzer, artillery and infantry are advancing on Prague from all sides. We need help urgently. Send us planes, tanks and firearms. Help, help, help!—

The Soviet offensive was launched 24 hours earlier than planned, on the morning of May 6. The troops of Pukhov's and Gordov's armies went over the top and Rybalko's and Lelyushenko's Tank Armies attacked simultaneously. Zhadov's 5th Guards Army was not yet prepared to go into action and had to take precautions against Schörner's panzer and motorized divisions operating in the Dresden sector, which could turn their strikes to the base of the wedge driven into the German defences by the advancing Soviet main forces. Zhadov's army, therefore, went into the assault at night.

In the meantime, General Gluzdovsky's 6th Army was holding the German group under the command of General Nihoff trapped in the city of Breslau, which was in the rear of the Soviet offensive forces. As German prisoners testified, Schörner had planned a strong blow to be delivered in the direction of Breslau on May 7 to relieve the trapped group, but the Soviet offensive thwarted this plan.

General Nihoff realized that his situation was hopeless and surrendered. The Supreme Commander issued his next order of the day addressed to Marshal Konev and General Petrov:

—The troops of the 1st Ukrainian Front following a prolonged siege have today, on May 7, 1945, taken full control of the fortress city of Breslau.

—The German garrison under the command of the fortress commandant, General of Infantry von Nihoff, and his staff has ceased its resistance, laid down their arms and surrendered.

—By 19:00 on May 7, the Soviet forces had taken prisoner more than 40,000 German officers and men in the city of Breslau.—

Zhadov's 5th Guards Army pushed forward on the same day, taking Dresden in pincers from the north-west and north-east and came up to the city's outskirts towards nightfall. Fearing encirclement, Schörner ordered this flank of his Army Group to retreat. Taking advantage of that, Konev moved the left flank of his Front forward. The 2nd Polish Army, the 28th, 52nd, 31st and 59th Armies deployed on that flank went into attack. This was a gigantic offensive with an enormous mass of troops and military equipment moving over a broad front. Petrov kept all of them in his field of vision, responding promptly to any delay, assessing incoming information and reporting it to the Front Commander, who was staying with his vanguard in the sector of the main strike, and higher up to the General Staff and the General Headquarters. The strain was very great indeed for the Chief of Staff, but Petrov felt satisfied as his battle plan had proved flawless.

On May 7, reports started coming in from headquarters and commanding officers about foreign radio broadcasts announcing the end of the war. There were numerous inquiries, but Petrov could not comment on the news because no instructions had yet arrived from the General Staff, although he had also heard jubilant music, church services, and triumphant speeches on the air from Paris, London, Brussels, Amsterdam and other cities.

As became known later, the Supreme Allied Command had accepted a German surrender in Reims on that day. The German troops on the Western front, however, had long stopped all resistance to the Allies, so the acceptance of that separate surrender was a violation of the Allied commitments, and the Soviet Government protested against it. In the Prague area no surrender or armistice had yet been offered, and the forces under Field Marshal Schörner were fighting on desperately and perpetrating atrocities against the Czech freedom fighters.

General Petrov requested a briefing from the General Staff about the latest developments. He was informed that it had been agreed to consider the surrender accepted by the Western Allies, a preliminary act to be followed by the ceremony of Germany's unconditional surrender in Berlin on May 8, 1945.

The surrender would be submitted by the High Command of the Wehrmacht and accepted by Marshal Zhukov as Deputy Supreme Commander of the Red Army and representatives of the Supreme Allied Command. The signing of this act would mean the final termination of hostilities.

On May 7, however, Schörner issued the following order to his troops:

—Enemy propaganda is circulating false rumours about the capitulation of Germany to the Allies. I hereby warn the troops that the war against the Soviet Union shall continue.—

On the same day, General Headquarters ordered the troops of the 2nd Ukrainian Front under the command of Marshal Malinovsky and the 4th Ukrainian Front under the command of General of the Army Yeremenko to go on to the offensive. That left no hope for Schörner's Army Group, which was under attack on all sides.

On May 8 the main group of forces of the 1st Ukrainian Front was continuing its swift offensive on Prague. Fierce fighting flared up on mountain passes and in narrow gorges as Schörner's troops offered tenacious resistance to the advancing Soviet forces. Dresden was taken on the same day, and Moscow again saluted the victorious troops of the 1st Ukrainian Front.

Lelyushenko's tankmen reported destroying a large convoy of German staff vehicles and capturing a group of generals and high-ranking officers travelling under heavy escort, as well as a load of staff documents. The tankmen were in haste and could not afford the time to interrogate the prisoners or inspect the trophies. As it became clear later, they had run into the headquarters of Schörner's Army Group. The Field Marshal himself had had a narrow escape and was now hiding in the woods disguised in civilian clothes and looking for a chance to surrender to an Allied patrol. As he later himself recalled:

—On the night of May 7 my headquarters were on the move and in the morning of the next day they were rounded up by Russian tanks. Now I was no longer in control of my retreating forces. The breakthrough of Russian armour was a complete surprise to us. The night before the frontline had still existed.—

That most ferocious of Nazi generals was caught after all. Along with Kleist and other war criminals he was tried by a Soviet tribunal and sentenced to 25 years in prison. At the trial Schörner had resorted to the standard tactics of defence used by Nazi generals accused of war crimes: he had pleaded innocence as a subordinate who had to comply with orders from his superiors. In 1953 his sentence was commuted for humanitarian reasons. He was released and left for West Germany.

. . . On the evening of May 8 General Petrov was informed by the General Staff that in a few hours an act of unconditional surrender would be signed in Berlin by Field Marshal Keitel. He was requested to announce the news of

Germany's surrender by radio to all German troops in Czechoslovakia and suspend hostilities for three hours, until 2300 hours on May 8. Should Schörner's troops fail to listen to reason and continue their resistance, they were to be dealt a decisive blow and wiped out.

The Soviet guns fell silent as the three-hour lull set in. Konev and Petrov waited at their command post near Dresden. Their troops had stopped and waited too. The answer never came. German POWs later testified that commanding officers of Schörner's Army Group had concealed the surrender from their troops, urging them to fight on and to shoot deserters.

The Soviet forces resumed their offensive. On the night of May 9 the 3rd and 4th Tank Armies of the 1st Ukrainian Front made an 80-kilometre thrust towards Prague and their vanguard units burst into the city at dawn. By 1000 hours Prague had been fully cleared of the last resisting German troops. At 1300 hours the troops of the 1st and 2nd Ukrainian Fronts linked up at a point 35 kilometres south east of Prague and in the evening a motorized group of the 4th Ukrainian Front entered the city.

That, however, was not yet the end of the fighting. The remnants of Schörner's Army Group—half a million officers and men—had been encircled but refused to surrender. Though demoralized and disorganized and lacking general direction, they were embittered and desperate. The Soviet troops were wiping out the last pockets of resistance one after another.

The day of Prague's liberation by the Red Army was a memorable one for Petrov and his staff for one more reason. Despite the high efficiency of communications and the success of Soviet troops, the staff was unable to transmit reliable information on the location and actions of individual units. The Front Commander and General Headquarters were expecting reports but Petrov was in a quandary: no reports were coming in from the Soviet units in Prague. That was a full-scale emergency and a breach of discipline.

Marshal Konev recalled that day:

—It was clear that Prague had been freed, but none of the Army Commanders had yet sent us a coherent message. As we learned later, the reason for that was the jubilation of the people of Prague which had made a mockery of the rules of subordination. All the streets were thronged by demonstrators. Any Soviet officer appearing in town was immediately surrounded by a happy crowd, hugged and kissed and showered with flowers. All my communications officers became captives of their new friends and could not go about their duties. . . .

—Ignoring their high ranks, jubilant crowds barred the way for the vehicles of Soviet generals—Lelyushenko, Rybalko and Gordov, so none of them could get out of Prague and come back to their command posts and communication centres to report the situation.—

The General Staff was in the meantime demanding impatiently:

—Report the latest developments. The Victory Salute will be fired today.

What is happening at your end? The general surrender has long been signed, but there is no news from you yet. We expect your answer immediately.—

Finally, all the details were cleared up, finalized and reported to Moscow. Stalin addressed his new order of the day to Marshal Konev and General of the Army Petrov:

—The troops of the 1st Ukrainian Front, following a swift all-night manoeuvre of armoured and infantry formations, have broken German resistance and at 0400 hours today, on May 9, 1945, have liberated from the German invaders the capital of our ally Czechoslovakia—the city of Prague. . . .—

Later in the day the Supreme Commander issued another order, which we trench fighters had been looking forward to during the four long years of the war, straining every nerve to win it, shedding our blood, defying suffering and death. Therefore, it is presented below in full.

The Order of the Supreme Commander to the Red Army, Navy and Air Force

—On May 8, 1945, the Act of Unconditional Surrender of the German Armed Forces was signed by representatives of the German High Command in Berlin.

—The Great Patriotic War the Soviet people have waged against the German Fascist invaders has culminated in victory. Germany has been completely routed.

—Comrades, Red Army and Navy men, sergeants and officers of the Army, Navy and Air Force, Generals, Admirals and Marshals, I congratulate you on the victorious completion of the Great Patriotic War.

—To mark the complete victory over Germany, today on May 9, on Victory Day, at 22 hours, the capital city of Moscow shall salute the valiant officers and men of the Red Army, Navy and Air Force, who have achieved this brilliant victory, with 30 artillery salvoes from 1,000 guns.

—May the glory of the heroes who fell in the battles for the freedom and independence of this country live forever!

—Long live the victorious Red Army, Navy and Air Force!

Supreme Commander, Marshal
of the Soviet Union Joseph Stalin.
—9 May, 1945, No. 369.—

The country was jubilant. The peoples of Europe, including the German people, could finally heave a sigh of relief. Moscow was saluting the victors. The troops were also saluting victory, firing into the air. Whoever had a gun was firing and shouting with joy, at the time of the victory salute. That was the general ecstasy of victory.

*   *   *

General Petrov was involved in the capture of the former White Guard Generals Krasnov and Shkuro, and General Vlasov, who had betrayed their native country and collaborated with the Nazis as their servile yes-men. Colonel Dotsenko and General Maleyev of the Don Cossack Cavalry Corps had seen Krasnov and Shkuro in Soviet captivity. Dotsenko gave this story:

—The room we had entered looked like a factory shop. There were benches and striped mats spread out on a large platform. A dozen old men in military uniform rose lazily from their seats as we approached them. A tall old man with inflamed eyelids stepped forward followed by a paunchy squab of a man with the red face of a drinker. Both wore silver-threaded shoulder straps of Generals.

—Major General Pavlov, Commander of the Soviet garrison of Judenburg, addressed them: "Your names, gentlemen."

—"General Krasnov," the tall old man uttered drily.

—"General Shkuro," mumbled his companion.

—Maleyev was silently watching the prisoners.

—"I beg your pardon, General," Krasnov ventured a question. "Do you know why Boris Mikhailovich Shaposhnikov has died?"

—"Marshal Shaposhnikov was very sick," Maleyev said.

—"Are Budenny and Voroshilov in good health?" Shkuro inquired.

—"They are, if it matters to you."

—"It does very much. We had met on many occasions. On the battlefield, of course. You were too young to fight in those days. . . ."

—"You are wrong there. I was a cavalryman in Budenny's Corps."

—Shkuro made a grimace of contempt: "The rank-and-file did not know much."

—Maleyev kept his temper and said: "We knew enough to thrash your cavalry at Voronezh, Kastornaya, and the Northern Donets and put you to flight in your foreign car."

—"Well, we also chased your cavalry. . .," Shkuro retorted and stopped short under Krasnov's disapproving gaze.

—"Shall I be allowed to write my memoirs?" Krasnov asked.

—"I don't know. The government will decide it. The people's will shall be respected," Maleyev answered.

—"I have always stood for the Russian people. . . ."

—"It's a lie", Maleyev interrupted him. "You have always betrayed them. You tried to strangle their revolution in its cradle. Don't you remember the fight at Pulkovo. You, however, got what you deserved."

—Krasnov made a wry face and looked away.

—"Listen carefully, General," Shkuro hissed sarcastically. There was a chuckle behind his back.

—Krasnov protested excitedly: "All these years I was saving Russia, upon my honour!"

—Maleyev raised his voice: "Your honour is not worth a damn. You doublecrossed Lenin. You pledged your honour, you wouldn't fight us. But you sold yourself to the Kaiser and fought us in the Civil War. You served Hitler as a loyal subject, too. Even your shoulder straps are like a Nazi general's."

—"We couldn't find anything else," Shkuro said apologetically.

—General Pavlov looked at his watch. We understood it was time to leave.—

In January 1947, the Supreme Court of the USSR sentenced Krasnov and Shkuro along with a group of other war criminals to capital punishment.

There are different stories of the traitor Vlasov's capture, so it seems relevant to quote the official report of General Fominykh of the 25th Tank Corps:

—At 16:00 on May 12, 1945, Colonel Mishchenko, Commander of the 162nd Tank Brigade, instructed Captain Yakushev to move his battalion to the assembly area of the 1st Division of the ROA (Russian Liberation Army) and arrest Vlasov with his staff and the divisional commander Bunyachenko.

—At a point 2 kilometres south of Breszi, Captain Yakushev met Captain Kuchinsky, a battalion commander of the 1st ROA Division, who informed him that Vlasov was riding in a car with a convoy of divisional staff vehicles on the road ahead.

—Captain Yakushev passed the convoy and brought his vehicle to a halt, blocking the road. Vlasov was absent in the first car he checked but one of the officers pointed at a car standing behind. Captain Yakushev inspected it and discovered Vlasov in the back seat hiding under a blanket and a carpet behind his interpreter and a woman passenger.

—Captain Yakushev ordered Vlasov to follow him to the headquarters of the 162nd Tank Brigade. Vlasov refused to comply, arguing that he was going to American Army headquarters. Captain Yakushev threatened to shoot him on the spot and forced him into his vehicle at gunpoint. On their way back Vlasov attempted to jump out but was overpowered.

—After two days, on May 15, 1945, the Commander of the 1st ROA Division Bunyachenko, his Chief of Staff Nikolayev, aide-de-camp Olkhovik and Vlasov's personal interpreter Ressler were also detained.—

Vlasov was taken to the Front Headquarters on the outskirts of Dresden. He stood silently, his eyes down cast, in front of the Soviet generals, and Petrov watched him with mixed feelings of curiosity and disgust. General Krainyukov asked Vlasov in a tone of contempt: "Well, Mr. Judas, how does it feel to be a turncoat?"

Vlasov was flown to Moscow under guard. The Military Collegium of the Supreme Court sentenced him to death for high treason and war crimes, and he was hanged.

The fighting in Czechoslovakia had lasted until May 12. The report on the completion of Operation Prague submitted on May 12, 1945 said: 258,661 German officers and men were taken prisoner, 649 tanks and self-propelled guns, 3,069 pieces of artillery, 793 aircraft, 41,131 motor vehicles and large quantities of other war trophies were captured.

The last war communiqué issued by the Soviet Information Bureau on May 15, 1945 was the shortest one in the history of the war:

—The surrender of German troops on all fronts has been completed.—

It was only in the woods and mountains in the area of the 1st Ukrainian Front that Soviet troops continued mopping up scattered groups of SS men and others who could not expect a pardon for their atrocities.

The Rescue of the Dresden Art Gallery

Before telling the readers about the retrieval of Dresden's art treasures, I wish to remind them of the city's tragic lot in the closing months of the war.

As is known, Dresden was one of the most beautiful cities of Europe. It had been dubbed the German Florence and Germany's Museum for its numerous masterpieces of architecture and the fine arts. Before the war Dresden had a population of 630,000 but in the war years the exodus of refugees from all over Germany swelled it to 1,500,000.

The war was drawing to a close. It was clear that Dresden would soon be taken by Soviet troops, and under the decisions of the Yalta Conference of the Big Three the city was to become part of the Soviet zone. In February 1945 Dresden was still in the deep rear of the German forces. It had no war industries that could make fat targets for air attacks.

On the night of February 13, 1945, however, an Allied force of 1,400 bombers made a devastating air raid over Dresden, dropping a total of 3,749 tons of explosives, of which 75 per cent were incendiary bombs. The whole city was ablaze. Within three hours of the first raid when townspeople were rescuing survivors trapped under the ruins and fighting fires there was another raid of equal ferocity. After another eight hours a third air attack razed the city to the ground. That was not the end. Hundreds of fighter planes of the bomber force escort chased people fleeing along the blazing streets, cutting them down with machine-gun fire in tree-top flying, to complete the massacre.

More than 135,000 civilians were killed and many thousands suffered burns and injuries. The fires lasted for almost a week, and their glow was seen dozens of miles away. It was part of the Thunderclap plan of shattering German civilian morale, as well as a demonstration of the Allied military might to the Red Army.

But what happened to the world-famous Dresden Art Gallery? As far back as 1943 the paintings and other art treasures had been hidden in abandoned stone mines hastily converted to shelters which were poorly heated and ventilated. The canvases were gradually deteriorating.

227

As the Red Army was advancing into the German heartland the paintings were taken to various other shelters lest they fall into Soviet hands, ignoring the danger of irreparable damage to them. The German art scholars Ruth and Max Seidewitz testify:

—In the Pockau-Lengefeld mine shelter the damp air was not the only hazard to the art collections stowed away there. The mine was also used as a storage place of ammunition and explosives. Crates with art treasures were handled roughly, because the workers did not know what they contained.—

All the art shelters were mined and were to be blown up in the event of their capture by Soviet troops.

When Soviet troops entered the city, the scene of its devastation stunned even the most battle-hardened soldiers. Whoever knew of the famous Dresden Art Gallery immediately went to see what remained of the Zwinger Museum. They found nothing but ruins on the site of what had been one of Dresden's most beautiful palaces. Local residents knew nothing of the fate of its collections.

Junior Lieutenant Rabinovich of the 164th battalion of the 5th Guards Army, who had been an artist before the war, was familiar with the Dresden collections as a professional and initiated a search for the missing treasures. A fluent speaker of German, he found a few former members of the museum personnel and little by little collected information that put him on the right trail.

The loss of the collections was immediately reported to General Petrov and he detailed a special team of engineers and mine defusion experts to aid the men of the 164th battalion in their search. General Krainyukov recalls:

—A large body of men joined in the search for the missing masterpieces of art: intelligence officers of the Front Headquarters, the Front Political Department, counterintelligence services and military commandants, German officials of the city and district magistrates of Dresden.—

The first shelter was discovered in a mine near the village of Gross Kott. Soviet sappers defused the explosives planted at the entrance to the tunnel and found a railway car hidden inside a shed of wooden boards. The car was loaded with paintings. They were in a sorry state but the rescue team had been warned not to move them until art experts arrived.

Another shelter was found in the Pockau-Lengefeld mine. The Soviet rescue team had to fight off an SS unit whose men were laying explosives to blow up the shelter. The collections were saved and placed under guard.

Finally, many other art shelters were tracked down in various places. The Military Council of the 1st Ukrainian Front sent a message about the finds to the Committee for the Fine Arts in Moscow. Within a few days a team of experts and restorers was formed and flown out to Dresden.

The city had no building where the retrieved paintings could be stored, so the Front Command supplied the team with vehicles specially adapted for carrying them to the summer palace of the Saxon Kings at Pilnitz some 8 kilometres away. The crate with Raphael's Sistine Madonna was opened on May 26, 1945. When its cover had been removed and the Virgin Mary holding the baby Jesus in her arms became visible, all took off their hats in reverential admiration. Somebody remarked that a list of eyewitnesses of that historic event should be drawn up and preserved for posterity. The Moscow art scholar Sokolova, who represented the Committee for the Fine Arts, compiled such a list. It contains among others the names of Marshal Konev and General Petrov, which was a pleasant surprise to the present writer.

Many paintings found in secret shelters were covered with mould, and the layer of paint had peeled off in many places. They could not be touched without causing damage to them, because the paint was sticking to the fingers. The team of experts led by Rototayev consisted of the art scholar Grigorov, the artists Churakov, Volodin and Ponomarev. Their skilful hands worked wonders, applying plasters to damaged canvases and making all sorts of guarding devices to protect them in transit. They were as careful as mine experts, because any mistake might result in the loss of priceless masterpieces. All windows and doors in the palace were securely shut to prevent draughts and let the canvases dry in still air. After a month some windows were opened to let in fresh air. The paintings were now in better shape, and mould was removed from them with great caution.

The collections were taken to Moscow on a heavily guarded special train with a heavy duty locomotive running some distance ahead of it to check the state of the tracks. The state security agencies had taken steps to frustrate attempts to derail the train on its way to Moscow. The train arrived safely on August 10, 1945.

The paintings were placed in the repositories of the Pushkin Fine Arts Museum, one of the best of its kind in the USSR. Restoration work was started immediately under the guidance of the renowned Soviet artist Korin, and went on for a full ten years. Now the conditions of storage were ideal, and all efforts to restore the canvases to their original beauty were made on scientific lines. The results were brilliant and surpassed all expectations.

In 1955 the Soviet Government by a special decision restored all the treasures of the Dresden Art Gallery to the German Democratic Republic. A farewell exhibition was held in Moscow before the collections were taken to their home at the Zwinger Museum completely rebuilt by skilful German architects, artists and workers.

The Homecoming

On May 29, 1945 General Petrov was awarded the Gold Star of Hero of the Soviet Union. Either the joy of victory had softened the Supreme Commander or he had realized that it would be too unfair to deny the veteran soldier what he had deserved by his splendid record in the war, but justice triumphed after all. I associate that award with Stalin's decision, because high-ranking generals were nominated for that supreme distinction on his personal instructions or with his consent.

In accordance with an agreement between the Allies a few army groups were formed to assure compliance with the provisions of the Act of Surrender of the Armed Forces of Nazi Germany. The Central Group formed from troops of the 1st Ukrainian Front on June 10, 1945, was deployed in Austria and Hungary and had its headquarters in Vienna. Marshal Konev was appointed commander of the Central Group with General Petrov as his deputy. Apart from their official duties of control, their troops helped local authorities and the population to repair the ravages of the war and organize the work of industries and transport services.

In September Petrov received a phone call from Moscow; he was offered command of the Turkestan Military District. He could not wish for a better assignment and accepted at once. He was happy: he would soon see his mother and surround her with care and attention in her old age, his sister and his numerous friends of prewar years. The order for his transfer came promptly. He was given a cordial send-off by Marshal Konev and his colleagues and left for Moscow to proceed to his new quarters in Tashkent.

In the meantime, his son Yuri and I enrolled at the Frunze Military Academy in Moscow. Both of us had been discharged from an army hospital where we had been recuperating from our war wounds. Yuri soon got married and became a father. His first born Vladimir is a grown-up man today. His second son was christened Ivan after his grandfather. The old general lavished his affections on the youngsters and they stayed with him in Tashkent longer than with their parents in Moscow.

Petrov wanted his grandsons to become professional soldiers and sent them to the Suvorov officer school. But then disaster struck. Ivan developed an incurable case of cancer. Today two Ivan Petrovs—a General of the Army and a young cadet—rest in peace in the same grave at the Novodevichy cemetery in Moscow

...On his arrival in the Turkestan Military District Petrov visited all the republics of Central Asia and places he remembered from his youth. He met many old comrades and veterans of the Civil War and they exchanged endless stories of their experiences. Some of them had just come back from the war, others, local residents who had fought the *Basmach* gangs side by side with him, were venerable old men with large families. He was a welcome guest in any home and was invited to see the collective farms. He had much in common with these kind and hard-working people and much to remember together.

In those days he made friends with Usman Yusupov, First Secretary of the Communist Party of Uzbekistan. A simple drayman in his youth, Yusupov had risen through the party ranks to a position of leadership. He was a typical self-made man and a favourite of the people who owed his success to his competence and hard work. He had done very much for the Soviet war effort.

Many industrial plants had been evacuated to Uzbekistan in wartime. The war demanded enormous quantities of equipment, weapons and ammunition. Under his vigorous guidance the plants moved to Uzbekistan resumed production in a record time. Here is one example. It takes years to build an industrial plant, but the embattled Red Army could not wait. Yusupov ordered machine-tools brought from Russia to be set up on concrete foundations laid in the open air. They were linked to power lines and went into operation at once. The walls and roofs were built later. A large plant worked at full capacity in two or three months.

... In 1947 Yuri Petrov and I graduated from the Academy and our paths diverged. He was made commander of a motorcyclists' battalion, and I was directed to the Higher Academic Course under the General Staff for further training.

In October of the same year General Petrov paid his last respects to his mother Evdokiya Onufriyevna. A hard-working woman of peasant parentage, she had lived to the age of 85. Petrov remembered her wish for a funeral with martial music and fulfilled it. A military band escorted her coffin to her last resting place. Petrov with his friend Usman Yusupov by his side headed the long funeral procession. His mother had believed in God, and he had never argued with her in matters of faith. As she had asked him before she died, a funeral service was performed for her at the Church of Alexander Nevsky, and she was buried at the Russian cemetery on the outskirts of Tashkent.

... After completing my term on the Higher Academic Course I was assigned to a job at the General Staff, while Yuri Petrov continued his service in the Turkestan Military District. Every year I came to Tashkent and stayed with my parents during my leave of absence, and I often visited the Petrovs. Strange as it may seem, we almost never talked about the war. The memories of the war dead and the suffering of the people were fresh and we were afraid to stir them. Our hearts were still bleeding.

Now that the four hard years of the war had receded into the past the Petrovs were enjoying the peace and quiet of family life. It seemed nothing would disturb it any more. Fate, however, had always been cruel to General Petrov, and it was not long before it dealt him another terrible blow.

The Ashkhabad Earthquake

Late at night on October 5, 1948, violent earth tremors shook the city of Ashkhabad, the capital of Turkmenia, and destroyed it completely. Petrov was alerted by a phone call and flew to the disaster area immediately. His son Yuri accompanied him on the plane.

The Central Committee of the Communist Party of Turkmenia formed a special commission to deal with the emergency. The Military District Commander was among its members. Petrov promptly moved army units into the city to help its people.

Thousands of residents were trapped under the ruins. The quake had taken sleeping people by surprise, and very many had remained under the ruins of collapsed buildings. Survivors were digging in the debris, hoping to rescue their relatives and neighbours.

Petrov acted swiftly and with his habitual precision. First of all, it was necessary to clear the roads for motor vehicles to evacuate the wounded and remove numerous dead bodies which were beginning to decompose under the hot southern sun. The next step was to organize emergency medical aid and food supplies, because all stocks of medicines and provisions had perished. Most of those who had narrowly escaped death in their sleep were in their underwear and had to be supplied with clothes.

As often happens in time of disaster, criminal elements took advantage of the general confusion to break into ruined shops and homes and steal whatever valuables they could find. On Petrov's orders armed patrols were posted throughout the city to maintain law and order and arrest marauders.

Now I come to the tragic story of Yuri Petrov's death. It happened on the outskirts of Ashkhabad, not far from the airport, on October 7. Riding in an army vehicle, Yuri caught sight of a man carrying a heavy bag. He was in police uniform but without a cap on his head and a belt on his tunic. The man was obviously drunk.

Yuri asked the driver to wait and stopped the stranger:

"What do you have in that bag?"

"None of your damned business! Get out of my way!"

235

Yuri ordered the driver to bring along an army patrol and stayed to guard the marauder.

What happened next is described in the file of the case of the murder of Lieutenant Colonel Yuri I. Petrov. This file contains an eyewitness account by Antonina Varlacheva, who identified the killer.

I found her in Novosibirsk in Siberia and though she is 90 she remembers that tragic event as clearly as if it were yesterday. This is part of her story:

—. . . The officer ordered the marauder to sit down and sent the driver to find a patrol. The marauder was shouting abuse at the officer who had turned his back on him and was looking down the road, waiting for a patrol. All of a sudden, the marauder drew a pistol and shot the officer in the back of his head, and then broke into a run.

—I rushed to the officer lying on the ground. The bullet made a hole in his face but he was still alive. I stopped a passing lorry and he was taken to the airport medical unit.

—. . . At first, the search for the killer gave no results. I was taken around town in a police car several times as I tried to identify him, all to no avail. After some time, however, a marauder was detained who was carrying a gun with one cartridge missing. I was immediately called for. As soon as I saw him, I recognized the murderer.—

. . . Yuri died on the plane taking him to a hospital in Tashkent. His father had sent a note to his wife with the doctor who accompanied his son: "Mother, you need all your courage now. Your son's life is in danger."

General Petrov had only a few hours to come to Tashkent for his son's funeral. He walked behind the coffin to the cemetery and then immediately flew back to Ashkhabad where he was needed desperately.

The Epilogue

The war years were accurately described by a phrase "the roaring forties", an allusion to the stormy oceanic latitudes and the storms of war that had swept the planet in the forties. Unfortunately, the storms had not subsided with the ending of the Second World War. Those years were stormy not only for my country but for the whole world as well, because they saw the advent of the terrible nuclear weapons which have placed the human race in jeopardy and are threatening all life on earth with total extinction.

What had ushered in those "roaring forties" and who was the first to suspend the sword of Damocles over the world is well known to the readers. Atomic weapons, as no other weapons in the past, are the subject of much writing and discussion and the cause of great alarm today.

At the end of the war, on the eve of Nazi Germany's total defeat, President Truman, who had just entered office, delivered an emotional speech in which he said that no nation or group of nations should be allowed to settle disputes with bombs and bayonets again and that mankind should learn to live in peace unless it wanted to perish in war. And on the very same day he received the leaders of the Manhattan Project with a report on the making of the atomic bomb which was ready for use.

... It is known to many from numerous reminiscences and other sources that at the Potsdam Conference Truman attempted to intimidate the Soviet delegation by announcing a new weapon of "unusual destructive power" and that later, motivated by a desire to give a practical demonstration of America's new overkill weapon to the USSR and the rest of the world, Truman ordered atom bombs to be dropped on Hiroshima and Nagasaki.

The after-effects of these bombings are widely known, so I will omit their terrifying details. I shall only mention what I saw with my own eyes in Hiroshima and Nagasaki in 1982. I visited the memorial museum, saw photographs, films and genuine material evidence of the atomic strikes and visited a hospital. At the time of my visit it was still full of patients afflicted with radiation sickness. I walked from one ward to another, talked with these people and listened to the doctors' explanations. The following casualties of the atomic bombing are often cited: more than 240,000 people were killed instantly, and another 160,000 suffered radiation exposure. These, however, are but the initial figures. Ever since the atomic explosions in Japan people have been dying in slow agony, and the final death toll will be much larger

I also happened to visit the United States. There I saw many fascinating, exciting and horrifying scenes, but I will not record them here. Most of all I was amazed by the fact that, every year, on the days when the first atom bombs were dropped, in the early days of August, the veterans of the first atomic air raid have a get-together in New York's most luxurious restaurant. They have a merry time drinking champagne and celebrating their cannibalistic victory. A thought crossed my mind: would they choke on their gorgeous meals if they saw what I had seen in the Hiroshima hospital wards? But then I remembered that they had certainly seen photographs of the explosions, the scenes of devastation, the victims burned to death or maimed by radiation lesions; all of them had watched these horrors in films.

The news of a new terrible weapon developed in the United States was not a surprise to the Soviet Government. Nuclear research had also been going on for some time in the USSR. It was directed by academician Kurchatev, and its results are known to all today.

Once these weapons of Armageddon had come on the scene, they inevitably entailed, as it had often happened in history, a revision of military doctrine, strategy and tactics, and the art of warfare in general.

The Soviet Government was well aware of what the U.S. strategists were up to and took vigorous steps to strengthen the country's security by stimulating scientific research on the technical aspects and capabilities of nuclear weapons and the development of new operational art, tactics and strategy.

I will not venture to discuss this research, but I know much about General Petrov's involvement in that work of crucial importance for national defence. In fact, General Petrov was one of the Soviet military leaders who laid the groundwork for the modern strategy and tactics of defensive nuclear warfare.

As far back as 1951, when Petrov was still in command of the Turkestan Military District, he was instructed by the General Staff to draw up a plan of military exercises with the intent of working out the ways of survival and the methods of effective combat in conditions of nuclear attack. The exercises were to be carried out in the area of his Military District with the participation of his troops and the use of simulated nuclear weapons.

The District Staff compiled the plan under Petrov's guidance. The General Staff, however, objected to some of its elements failing to meet the objectives of modern defence pursued by that supreme body of theoretical and practical direction of armed forces development. A list of critical remarks, suggestions and amendments was forwarded to Tashkent for General Petrov's observation. The General Staff explained that his work was appreciated but the exigencies of recent advances in the military field demanded further efforts to bring the plan up to date. It was a new age of rapid change, indeed Petrov requested some time and aid from experts familiar with the specific effects of nuclear weapons to set the guidelines for troops on the simulated battlefield.

His own expertise needed a fresh approach and a reappraisal.

His opinion was respected. The General Staff formed a team of experts to assist the headquarters of the Turkestan Military District. The team consisted of six General Staff officers headed by Lieutenant General Gryzlov. I was one of them. An air force plane promptly took us to Tashkent.

At Petrov's headquarters we lined up in front of the General and Gryzlov introduced us one by one. When it was my turn to shake the General's hand, he watched my face, smiling amiably:

"Now you have come to teach new tricks to an old dog. It's never too late to learn, however."

Petrov came to our offices every day to consult us or give us advice, listening carefully to junior officers. It was part of his nature to heed the opinion of younger personnel, and he could not care less for ranks when the essence of the matter needed analysis.

We worked in the Military District headquarters for a week jointly with its staff officers and finally came up with a plan that satisfied the General Staff and was approved by the Minister of Defence. The theoretical stage of the exercises was followed by their practical stage, i.e. the operations of troops on open terrain exposed to simulated nuclear attack and residual radiation. I acted as an arbiter attached to a large formation.

The details of these exercises were summed up and analyzed to provide Soviet tacticians with data indispensable for working out new methods of combat.

The USSR is compelled to reckon with the U.S. military doctrine of pre-emptive attack. The United States has turned down the Soviet Union's repeated proposals to renounce the use of nuclear weapons and under cover of verbiage about its commitment to peace is building up its nuclear arsenal, developing new, ever more powerful, nuclear arms and steadily increasing their numbers. The U.S. military strategists contemplate various types of offensive nuclear war, such as an all-out global attack by delivering strikes with all types of nuclear weapons from all bases, surface ships, submarines, from all continents and oceans and a theatre attack with nuclear weapons in Europe or another region.

This scheme is based on simple arithmetic: a missile fired from Western Europe will reach Soviet territory in 5 to 6 minutes, whereas a missile fired from the USSR will reach U.S. territory in 30 minutes. The U.S. military strategists hope, therefore, that the USSR will be knocked out before it can retaliate, while the United States will remain unscathed.

The U.S. military often refer to the terrifying destructive power of their nuclear weapons and are refraining from discussions of a possible retaliatory strike. They inure the people to the idea that it may never take place and if it does, it will not be catastrophic.

My experience of participation in military exercises under Petrov's direction and what I learned in the period of my service at the General Staff entitle me to say that a nuclear war, should it be unleashed by an overconfident aggressor, will not follow only an American scenario.

It is claimed, as the press has repeatedly made known to the public, that the U.S. stocks of nuclear explosives are sufficient to devastate Soviet territory many times over. The Soviet appeals to the U.S. Administration for a freeze on the existing parity of their nuclear weapons mean that the Soviet nuclear arsenal is sufficient for a retaliation that will devastate U.S. territory many times over, too. Mind-numbing arithmetic, is it not?

Imagine two opponents pointing their guns at each other's hearts, their triggers connected by a string, so that neither of them can fire his gun without killing himself.

. . . But now I get back to my story. The next year following the exercises in the Turkestan Military District General Petrov was transferred to a position at the Ministry of Defence in Moscow. Along with routine work, such as inspection of troops, verifying the progress of combat training, direction of military exercises, field trials of new military equipment and many other affairs of national defence, new methods of combat in modern warfare were being formulated on a practical as well as theoretical plane.

It became known to Soviet defence planners that large-scale military exercises involving large troop formations fighting a realistic nuclear battle against a potential enemy on a battlefield where a rear nuclear device was exploded had been carried out beyond the Atlantic. That was a full-scale peacetime emergency dictating the need for similar exercises to be carried out by the Soviet Army which was yet to go through realistic training for effective defence in the event of nuclear war. The Soviet High Command was in need of concrete facts and figures to draw the right conclusions for further practical steps to make all Soviet troops fully capable of dealing with a nuclear surprise attack.

Marshal Zhukov in his capacity of First Deputy Minister of Defence assumed general direction of the forthcoming all-important exercises. The very fact of his appointment to command of the troops that were to fight a realistic miniwar with real nuclear weapons evidence the critical significance attached to that new development.

Marshal Zhukov clearly realized that competence and presence of mind mattered most in handling the operations he was to organize and direct under a flawless plan and hence regarded the choice of his second-in-command and closest aid as a matter of first priority.

It may be relevant to recall that he had a brilliant constellation of names to choose from. All the Front Commanders of the Great Patriotic War—the celebrated Marshals who had proved their superior skill in the biggest battles of the Second World War—were still alive.

Zhukov decided upon General Petrov. The Marshal knew of his brilliance and tremendous work powers. He had seen them in Petrov's splendid achievements in defensive and offensive battles in the Northern Caucasus, on the 4th Ukrainian Front, and in the Battle of Berlin and heard a lot about his good fame as a man of integrity and honour. And, what mattered most, Zhukov, who was known for his intolerance of any negligence or incompetence, highly regarded General Petrov as a model officer utterly devoted to duty.

Petrov got down to work on his new assignment with his customary precision and energy. The enormity of the problems facing troops exposed to a nuclear attack was a new challenge, as well as a personal test for fitness to fight a battle he had never fought before.

For several months Petrov was busy with co-ordinating the work of equipment in the battle exercise area with objects of different strength and shape at different distances from the focus of the planned nuclear explosion. Defence fortifications of different types were erected, ranging from conventional infantry trenches to heavily fortified, deeply echeloned defences with a network of communications and a system of ferroconcrete pillboxes and shelters. Every detail of the battlefield was carefully planned with an eye to a nuclear strike to be followed by inspection of the degrees of destruction and practical conclusions for future defence work.

The personnel of the units which were to take part in these experimental battles of the nuclear age were thoroughly trained and instructed in the details of survival tactics. Political and commanding officers were preparing for realistic combat: young soldiers of a new generation who had no experience even in conventional warfare let alone such a gruelling test the like of which had not been seen even by battle-wise veterans.

The wartime generation of trench fighters had long been demobbed or discharged from active service on completion of their term. Only a limited number of frontline officers were still doing their stint in the army but they were gradually being replaced by postwar graduates of officer schools and military academies.

Petrov stayed with the troops in the field, working almost around the clock, explaining, instructing, briefing officers and analyzing reports. He knew that again human lives depended on his efficiency as much as in the battles of the last war. He did not feel his age despite the great strain of his duties. He was tired but satisfied.

For understandable reasons I cannot go into the details of those realistic exercises and shall only say that they went without a hitch. All their objectives were attained without loss of life. The nuclear attack was delivered at chosen targets with pinpoint accuracy and caused the exact extent of destruction as had been predicted in the battle plan. The troops fearlessly moved into the area of devastation, crossed its centre and radiation zones and overran the simulated enemy positions.

Needless to say, all officers and men were dressed in radiation-proof protective masks and clothes and radiation safety precautions had been taken in advance to stave off whatever health hazards might be caused by the explosion. All events in the process of that sham battle were recorded on film and photographed and described in the minutest detail in the accompanying reports. This material was analyzed by experts from all arms and services, and their conclusions provided the basis for updating revisions in Soviet defence tactics.

General Petrov was made responsible for the direction of all combat training of the Soviet Army. He taught troops to fight a modern war, relying on the experience of defeats and victories in the last great war fought with conventional weapons and on the newly-gained knowledge of the formidable power of nuclear arms.

General Petrov never retired and served his country to his last day. He died in 1958 at the age of 62.

Now the life of Ivan Efimovich Petrov is known to the reader, in rough outline, of course. It was the life of a soldier. I have avoided description of his private life, because it would have involved a different set of events. He certainly had wide interests outside military service, many friends and relatives and relations of various complexity with them.

In my story Petrov is at war, on the fields of battle, large or small, in the process of advancement from an ensign in the Russian Imperial Army to a top-ranking Soviet general.

I add no high-flown epithets to his leadership. Perhaps it would be too much to describe the victories won by the troops he led as brilliant, but they were without question hard-won victories. Just recall the year 1941, the early months of the war, the communiqués of the Soviet Information Bureau about abandoned Soviet cities. The invaders took them after a few days of fighting, or after a few hours, or even on the run, as was the case sometimes.

· In the defence of Odessa, however, the Soviet troops led by Petrov fought back for 73 days, and in the Battle of Sevastopol the Soviet defenders under his command, with their backs to the sea and cut off from the rest of the country, held their ground for 250 days. It is true the Soviet High Command gave them whatever help it could provide in that disastrous period of the war, but they were still fighting against overwhelming odds. Small wonder, therefore, that the Supreme Commander Stalin praised their tenacious defence in these words:

—The selfless struggle of the Sevastopol defenders is a model of heroism to the Red Army and the Soviet people.—

Later Petrov's armies had to fight their way across formidable mountain ranges, sea straits, coastal lakes, wide rivers and treacherous swamps.

In all these theatres of war they were opposed by well-trained and well-armed enemy divisions provided with whatever fortifications they needed for defensive warfare.

Indeed, fortune never favoured the brave as far as Petrov and his troops were concerned. Suffice it to recall their ordeal in battling an entrenched enemy as they pushed forward across the Carpathians with only two armies of tired infantry troops under his command.

I can see in my mind's eye Petrov's soldiers and officers in their heavy boots and clothes soaked with sweat, rain and snow labouring under a load of arms as they climb precipitous rocks, charge and drive the enemy off the mountain tops and then, after a brief rest, go into attack against the next stronghold on the next mountain range soaring beyond; and the next and the next. . . . That seems endless, because mountain ranges follow in waves for hundreds of kilometres.

What was Petrov's role in these battles? He was not, of course, climbing steep rocks or fighting by the side of his soldiers under a rain of bullets. But his heart and mind were with them. And, most important, he was straining every nerve to help them. They knew it. They were defending their country, their near and dear ones. And one of these people dear to them was Ivan Petrov. Their affection, trust and respect for him gave them added strength to conquer the enemy and the mountains. These words are not mine. They were said by a veteran soldier who had served under his command.

Many people remember General Petrov, his victories over the ferocious enemy, his good deeds in war and peacetime. Human memory, however, is not eternal, because human beings are mortal. It is sad to know that people who knew General Petrov also die. Only what is written on paper remains for posterity. Paradoxically, for all its flimsiness paper is the most durable material on which history is settled and preserved.

Of course, I do not mean to pronounce judgement on history. I only want our children and grandchildren, who are still feeling the ravages of the most terrible of wars, to remember thankfully those who sacrificed themselves to protect their lives and freedom. General Petrov was one of these people, who are the pride of Soviet history.

I am happy to have been closely linked with this remarkable man. And I am glad to have been able to bring my narrative to completion.

I wonder what Ivan Petrov himself would say if he had read this story. He would have certainly berated me for so many compliments paid to him, because he was a modest man. But I hope my readers will be lenient with me, if I have carried it too far. My affection and respect for General Petrov are so great that they must excuse me. Indeed, can a man be reproached for sincere love.

And so I end my narrative with the Latin saying I quoted at the beginning of it:

"I have done my best, and let others do better."